Winning Chess
Strategies

Proven principles
from one of the
U.S.A.'s top
chess players

From the bestselling author of
Play Winning Chess and
Winning Chess Tactics

Yasser Seirawan

INTERNATIONAL GRAND MASTER
with Jeremy Silman

Microsoft
PRESS

PUBLISHED BY
Microsoft Press
A Division of Microsoft Corporation
One Microsoft Way
Redmond, Washington 98052-6399

Library of Congress Cataloging-in-Publication Data
Seirawan, Yasser, 1960-
    Winning Chess Strategies / Yasser Seirawan with Jeremy Silman.
       p. cm.
    Includes index.
    ISBN 1-55615-663-4
    ISBN 0-7356-0604-8 (Reissue)
    1. Chess. I. Silman, Jeremy. II. Title.
    GV1449.5.S455 1994
    794.1'2--dc20   94-32285
                                          CIP

Printed and bound in the United States of America.

1 2 3 4 5 6 7 8 9 MLML   3 2 1 0 9 8

Distributed in Canada by ITP Nelson, a division of Thomson Canada Limited.

A CIP catalogue record for this book is available from the British Library.

Microsoft Press books are available through booksellers and distributors worldwide. For further information about international editions, contact your local Microsoft Corporation office or contact Microsoft Press International directly at fax (425) 936-7329. Visit our Web site at mspress.microsoft.com.

Tempus and the Tempus Books logo are registered trademarks of Microsoft Corporation. Tempus Books is an imprint of Microsoft Press.

The photographs in Chapter 11 of Wilhelm Steinitz, Aaron Nimzovich, José Raúl Capablanca, and Akiba Rubinstein are from *A Picture History of Chess,* by Fred Wilson, courtesy of Dover Publications, Inc. The photographs in Chapter 11 of Tigran Petrosian and Anatoly Karpov are courtesy of International Chess Enterprises, Inc., and the Russian Chess Federation.

Acquisitions Editors: Casey D. Doyle, Kim Fryer
Project Editors: Kerry A. Lehto, Saul Candib
Editing and Production: Online Press Inc.

Contents

Acknowledgments   v

Introduction   vii

CHAPTER ONE   The Importance of Strategy   1

CHAPTER TWO   Making the Most of a Material Advantage   7

CHAPTER THREE   Stopping Enemy Counterplay   25

CHAPTER FOUR   Understanding Where the Pieces Go   37

CHAPTER FIVE   Superior Minor Pieces   79

CHAPTER SIX   How to Use Pawns   99

CHAPTER SEVEN   The Creation of Targets   127

CHAPTER EIGHT   Territorial Domination   149

CHAPTER NINE   Attacking the King   167

CHAPTER TEN   Faulty Strategies   185

CHAPTER ELEVEN   The Great Masters of Strategy   199

CHAPTER TWELVE   Solutions to Problems   227

Glossary   237

Index   251

Acknowledgments

As usual, what starts off as an individual effort quickly evolves into a team one. This work wouldn't have been possible without the support of a lot of people. Hearty thanks to Jeremy Silman and Yvette Nagel from the "chess side" of things. Thanks also to Larry Powelson of Microsoft Corporation. To the folks at Microsoft Press, especially Kerry Lehto and Wallis Bolz, a warning: By carefully finding my mistakes, you're falling into my trap, and pretty soon you'll all become chess players! To Joyce Cox at Online Press: Joyce, this was our third book together, and each one gets more fun. You were all great. Thanks.

Introduction

I have now written three books about "winning chess." All the rules and basic information were covered in my first book, *Play Winning Chess*; tactical themes were explored in my second book, *Winning Chess Tactics*; and now, in *Winning Chess Strategies*, I take you on a journey to a whole different level of chess understanding. On this level, you no longer spend entire games reacting to your opponent; instead, you are proactive. You think through a position, set a goal, and methodically find ways to reach it.

Hundreds of thousands of books have been written about chess. What can you hope to learn from this one? With all modesty, a lot. The aim of this book is simple: to make you think about chess in a different way. In my two previous books, I showed you chess as an *art* and a *sport*. In this book, I show you chess as a *science*. My goal in this book is to make you realize that behind the pushing of little wooden men around a checkered board lies a lot of thought. Some of the ideas that make up the science of chess have been used for centuries—millennia, in fact. They have been researched, recreated, and refined to suit our purposes and are used by today's Grandmasters to reach the perennial goal: to win that next game of chess.

To be able to understand the techniques I teach in the next eleven chapters, you should already know the following:

- You must know the rules of the game—how the pieces move, how to castle, what en-passant is, and so on. (You'll find all these rules explained in *Play Winning Chess*.)
- You must know the relative values of the pieces.

- You should be familiar with basic chess terminology. For those of you who don't know *luft* from a *fork* and *counterplay* from a *blockade*, I have added a glossary at the end of this book. If you come across a word or phrase you don't know, look it up in the glossary before continuing on; otherwise, you might miss a crucial bit of information in the explanation of a strategy or description of a game.

- You must be able to read algebraic chess notation. If you can't, the sample games will appear to be nothing but gibberish! (Algebraic chess notation is explained briefly in the glossary and more completely in *Play Winning Chess*.)

- Though not absolutely necessary, you will find it useful to know the four elements of chess—force (material), time, space, and pawn structure—and their associated principles, as described in *Play Winning Chess*.

With these humble building blocks, I will teach you how to understand what is happening in any given chess position and how to formulate a plan for success based on the clues you can find in the position. By focusing on the positional features rather than the tactical features of the game, you will learn to build your strategy slowly and confidently, secure in the knowledge that the fundamental principles you are following can't lead you astray.

But isn't positional chess boring? Isn't it more exciting to sacrifice a few pieces and hack your enemy's King to death? Yes, a sacrificial attack is enormous fun, but just as a skilled counter-punching boxer can eventually knock out a pure slugger, a skilled positional chess player can usually take the force out of an attack and grind his opponent into the dust. You will learn that haymaker blows must come from positionally superior situations, which means that even the finest attackers in history have had to master planning and strategy. Few amateur players work at developing their strategic skills, so the fact that you are reading this book should give you an enormous advantage over your competition. Imagine your opponents' positions falling apart again and again, and imagine their frustration when they can't figure out why they keep losing to you! As a player who earns his living on the strength of his strategic skills, I can attest to the fact that it's no fun being squeezed to death by a positionally savvy opponent. But it's oh-so satisfying to be the one who is doing the squeezing!

As in my previous books, I refer to all chess players as *he*. Boys and men continue to make up the vast majority of the chess playing public, though there are some encouraging indications that girls are becoming more interested in the sport. (For instance, a few girls now enroll in my chess camp for children in Wisconsin each summer.) Hopefully, some of them will read this book, and some of them will go on to tournament competition armed with the strategic skills they will learn here. Watch out men! They will be formidable opponents!

Yasser Seirawan
Seattle, Washington

The Importance of Strategy

From the beginnings of human history, people have played games. And of all the games in the world, chess is aptly known as the *Royal Game* or the *King of Games*. Heady praise indeed! The unique beauty of chess has attracted some of the greatest minds of human history. Why? What makes chess so fascinating? Critics of the game see only grown men brooding endless hours away, sporadically pushing a few wooden pieces around a checkered board. In this critical light, why would anyone want to play chess? There must be something that makes this game so fascinating. Otherwise, how could it have survived for these many millennia?

Obviously, if the critics were right, chess would not exist. Yet chess has not only survived but is doing very well. The FIDE—the Fédération International des Échecs—is the third-largest sporting body in the world, representing over one hundred and sixty nations. (The largest sporting body is the IOC—the International Olympic Committee—and the second-largest is the FIFA—the Fédération International Football Association, which governs the world's most popular sport, soccer.) Why has chess survived?

Things survive the test of time because they are needed. Stop and think for a moment. What is there in your life that has survived for thousands of years? Tools like the spoon have survived. They have evolved to perfectly fit a need. If there were no need for them, such tools would not exist.

Games—and there are thousands, perhaps millions, of them—have been used by societies for eons as tools for physical, emotional, and mental growth. Of all these games, chess is the perfect tool for developing the mind. As Goethe said, "The game of chess is the touchstone of the intellect." At the root of chess is a battle of minds. Chess is a reflection of life, requiring a determination to compete and a desire to win. To succeed, you must become clever. Will power alone is not enough. You have to use your brain. You must think. And you must train yourself to think in different ways.

When I teach young people the game of chess, I inform them and their parents that chess will teach them the five *R*'s. I then go on to explain:

- *R* number 1: To play chess competitively according to the international rules of FIDE, a player must *(w)rite* down his moves.

- *R* number 2: As a player continues to compete, he will experience many losses. Dissatisfied, the player will seek to sharpen his skill and stop repeating the mistakes of the past by *reading* books on chess.

- *R* number 3: To get better at chess, a player must be able to keep score. He starts the game with eight pawns. As the game progresses, pieces get swapped, and pawns get pushed forward and lost. He now has two Rooks and four pawns left for a point count of 14 (5+5+4), and his opponent has a Rook, a Bishop, a Knight, and five pawns for a point count of 16 (5+3+3+5). The opponent therefore has a material advantage of two. Simple. He has just used *(a)rithmetic*.

- *R* number 4: The player undertakes these first three *R*'s because it is his *responsibility*. No one else's. When playing chess, the player has no excuses for his blunders. A teammate didn't drop a perfect pass or miss a shot. He and only he is responsible.

- *R* number 5: The last *R* is also the most important. Suppose the player's Queen is attacked. If he doesn't move it, the Queen will be captured. If he pulls it back in retreat, it will be safe. If he moves it forward, the Queen can capture a pawn and still be safe. He decides to go for the pawn, and in making his decision, he exercises his powers of *reasoning*.

These five *R*'s combine to produce that which all education is about: critical thinking. When you get right down to it, education has two elements: information and information processing. Information by itself is worthless. It is the critical thinking that allows us to process the information that gives the information its value.

Critical thinking occurs in every game of chess, even those played by weak players who have barely learned the moves. Your hand reaches out, your eye gleams, you lift a Knight and pounce on a pawn. You are sneaky, conniving, and ruthless. The pawn is yours! But wait a moment. Your opponent has made a pact with the devil. He takes your valiant Knight. Rats! How did that happen? What should you have done instead? What should you do next? Critical thinking has occurred.

Looking at chess with uninitiated eyes, what does the observer see? Two equal, opposing armies facing each other on a 64-square checkered board. What could possibly be so engrossing? And why can one player consistently beat another? One player is obviously better than the other. Given the same army as his opponent, he is outplaying him. Why? Because he is outthinking his opponent. What's his secret weapon? Strategy.

What Is Strategy?

Many players love quick, slash-and-burn chess games but get restless, impatient, and even frightened when matched with a thoughtful positional player. In their shortsightedness, they either don't understand why their enemy sometimes takes his time in deciding where to move, or they fear that the mental ability of this type of opponent will overwhelm them. The real problem is that they simply know nothing about chess strategy.

In the following pages, I will teach you what strategy is and how to create and harness specific strategies for your own use. Once you realize how easy it is to plan and execute a strategy, you'll begin to wonder what all the fuss was about. And your chess-playing friends will come to think of you as an intellectual giant.

First we need a definition. What exactly is chess strategy? Is it setting a trap, crossing our fingers, and hoping the opponent falls into it? Sorry, not even close. Is it the same as calculating all the move variations implicit in a position? Wrong again.

The fact that strategy has little in common with calculation is surprising, until you consider some of the definitions of strategy that have been offered. My colleague Grandmaster Larry Evans calls strategy "...a long-range master plan," while Hooper and Whyld, in the *Oxford Companion to Chess*, say that strategy is "...the planning and conduct of the long-term objectives in a game." Calculation, on the other hand, is a computer-like crunching of moves with no clear objective in sight.

Phrases such as "long-range" and "long-term" imply in-depth analysis, but in fact, Evans, Hooper, and Whyld are alluding to positional play—the slow, systematic building up of small advantages. Perhaps the late World Champion Max Euwe put it best when he said, "Strategy requires thought; tactics requires observation." He meant that a strategic plan is created by combining positional features involving material, space, piece mobility, and pawn structure over a long span of moves, whereas a tactic is not so much a creation as an observation that can be implemented to take advantage of a short-term opportunity.

An example of strategic thinking goes as follows: You realize that you can give your opponent a set of doubled pawns by trading your Bishop for his Knight. You decide that your long-term goal will be to attack and eventually win one of these newly created doubled pawns, thereby gaining a material advantage. This plan governs your following moves, because everything you do is now motivated by your intention of capturing one or both of these doubled pawns.

Strategy, then, is the purposeful pursuit of a simple goal: to gain an advantage of some sort over your opponent. With some idea of the intellectual meaning of strategy, we can begin to see its usefulness. No more aimlessly charging from move to meaningless move. And no more blank staring at a board that makes no sense to us at all. Far from complicating our games, strategy actually simplifies them!

The promise of simplicity has begun to call us, but how do we actually use this wonderful new tool? In the chapters that follow, I'll define and illustrate the most admired and time-tested strategic concepts—in other words, those that work! You'll see how to recognize when a particular strategy is ideal and how to implement it with a minimum of effort. All you have to do is sit at your chess board, follow along, and immerse yourself in the rewarding world of positional chess—a world where ten-move plans can be created quickly and easily when you recognize and understand the basic strategies of the game.

What Is a Chess Advantage?

The goal of a strategy is to gain a chess advantage. Being the proud owner of a chess advantage simply means that your position has certain positive features that your opponent's is lacking. There are two types of advantages: static and dynamic. A *static advantage* is a long-term one—permanent. A *dynamic advantage* is like a tactic—temporary. You may have a dynamic advantage because your King is safe, whereas your opponent hasn't yet castled. When your opponent castles and brings his King to safety, your dynamic advantage disappears. For this reason, it is important to take every opportunity to create static advantages. Put your faith in only those features that will be part of your position for a long time.

The role of strategy is to create one or more of the following static advantages:

- More material (force)
- Superior piece mobility
- Superior pawn structure
- More territory (space)
- Safe King position (usually when castled)

It's up to you to recognize the possibility of an advantage in a position and then come up with a plan that enables you to overcome the opposition by dint of the power the advantage gives you.

Will knowledge of how to create static advantages turn you into a good player? It certainly helps, but obviously your opponent will be (or should be!) creating his own advantages. Real skill in chess comes when you can determine whose advantages are more real—which positive features will eventually rise up in triumph. For example, you may have a material advantage (say, an extra pawn), but if your opponent has superior pawn structure, extra space, and more active pieces, you will probably wish you could start the game all over again. Or you may create a material advantage by winning a piece but, in the process, weaken your King's defenses. What good is holding an extra piece if all you can do is stand by and watch yourself getting checkmated? You have misjudged the advantage of winning a piece, and in a nutshell, you've been outplayed.

It is this kind of complex, intricate battle between players who are constantly trading their existing advantages for new ones that makes chess such a rewarding sport. After you read through this book, you will be able to take part in those battles armed with new knowledge and insights into chess that can help you build a reputation as a consistent winner.

CHAPTER TWO

Making the Most of a Material Advantage

O f all the advantages you can possess, a material advantage is by far the most powerful and the easiest to understand. A material surplus gives you options that don't normally exist, whereas a material deficit usually provokes something akin to panic. Why panic? Suppose you lose a piece right from the opening and can capture absolutely nothing in return. Can you look forward to a quiet positional middlegame? No. A material deficit in the middlegame is bad news. Even worse is a material deficit in the endgame. Any normal extension of such a game should lead to your defeat, simply because your opponent's army is bigger than yours!

Eating your opponent's pieces has the obvious effect of opening up the board, and it also affects the psychological state of both you and your opponent. Small wonder that masters always prefer to play for a material advantage rather than engage in exciting but uncertain skirmishes, such as the kingside attack.

In this chapter, we will explore the two most common methods of capitalizing on a material advantage:

- Using your superior forces to overwhelm your opponent
- Trading pieces with the express purpose of going into a winning endgame

In the following discussion, I assume that you are familiar with the numeric values assigned to the pieces—pawn: 1 point; Knight: 2 points; Bishop: 3 points; Rook: 5 points; and Queen: 9 points—and that you can figure out whether you are ahead or behind at any time in the game by adding up the values of your pieces and comparing your total point count with that of your opponent. I also assume that you are familiar with the concept of development—the process of moving your pieces from their starting posts to new and more effective positions. If you need to refresh your memory about ways of winning material or ways of developing your pieces, you might want to read Chapters Two and Three of *Play Winning Chess*, where I expound on the principles of force (material) and time (development), two of the four principles of the Seirawan method of playing chess.

Overwhelming Your Opponent

It stands to reason that a group of ten well-trained warriors will defeat an equally skilled group of nine. This fact is so obvious that I have to wonder why more players don't make better use of their material. Instead, less-experienced players often win a piece during the opening and then attack madly with only two or three men, leaving the rest of their army to meditate on its fate back at home. The usual result of such folly? In a high-level tournament, any player who charged ahead in this way would be eaten alive! How can you expect to succeed by crossing the center of the board into enemy territory and attacking a force of seven or eight pieces and countless pawns with only three pieces?

If you follow this simple strategy, you will find that most material advantages will resolve themselves in your favor:

After winning material, don't immediately attack your opponent. Instead, quietly consolidate your position by developing all your forces and getting your King to safety. Only when everything is protected and your army is fully mobilized should you start marching up the board.

At that point, you can afford to trade pieces because if you go into an endgame with extra wood, you will usually win. And if your opponent doesn't want to trade, your superior forces will wipe him out in different ways. In summary:

Be patient and get your stuff out!

Let's take a look at an example of this strategy in action. Diagram 1 shows the board after 13 moves in my 1982 game against World Champion Anatoly Karpov. I am White, and I am behind in development. However, I have a chance to win a piece. After a thorough examination of the possibilities for both sides, I decide that I can take the piece and eventually get the rest of my pieces into play. I am well aware that this is the game's critical moment. If I can grab the piece *and* catch up in development, I will

DIAGRAM 1. White to play.
Seirawan–Karpov
London, 1982

win this game. Study the following moves to see what I did.

14.Re3!

This move takes the pressure off the e-file and attacks the Black Queen. Note that I can counter a retreat likc 14...Qd8 with 15.Rxe8+ because the White Queen on a4 is also eyeing the e8-square. Black has only one way to defend against this threat.

14...Be6

Now Black's Knight on a6 is left undefended and ready to pluck.

15.Qxa6

So I now have a material advantage. The question is, "Can I get my other pieces out and shuffle my King to safety?"

15...cxd4

Black picks up a pawn, attacks my Rook, and opens up the c-file for his Rooks. The World Champion must play with energy, or else I'll succeed in consolidating my position.

16.Rb3!

I didn't fall for 16.Nxd4?? Qb4+, which loses my d4-Knight.

16...Bf5

17.Bg2

The tempting 17.Nxd4?? is still a loser because after 17...Qc5, there is no defense against the dual threats of ...Qc1 checkmate and ...Qxd4, which wins back the piece.

17...Bc2   **18.Nxd4 Bxb3**

19.Nxb3

By giving back a bit of material, I reduce Karpov's attacking force and make my defense easier. The material advantage of my two pieces vs. Black's Rook is still sufficient for victory if I can get my King out of the center. One of the strengths of a material advantage is that it gives you great defensive diversity; you can sacrifice some wood defensively and still come out ahead in the end. Remember this:

A material advantage is a bit like ballast in a hot air balloon. If you start sinking, you can throw some of it over the side to stop your descent.

19...Rac8

20.Bf3

I defend my e2-pawn and create a hiding place for my King in the event of 20...Qb4+ 21.Kf1 followed by Kg2, which has White burrowing in on the Kingside. Notice how I avoid the time-wasting 20.Bxd5? even though it grabs a pawn? I don't intend to capture anything else until I get my King to a safe place! Once that is done, I'll give my greed full rein.

20...Rc2

21.0-0

My King's safety is finally taken care of! With his majesty tucked away, it's time to launch my own threats.

21...Rxb2

22.Rd1

Stage one was winning material, and stage two was consolidation and King security. With this move, I begin stage three: attack and destroy Black's weak spots, the first of which is his d5-pawn.

22...Rd8

23.Nd4!

I centralize my Knight and threaten 24.Nc6 with a juicy fork. Note that 23...Qd7 stops Kd4-c6 but fails to 24.Qa3, when Black's b2-Rook is ensnared!

23...Rd7   24.Nc6 Qe8

25.Nxa7

My material advantage once again becomes pronounced. This meal was quite satisfying at the time, because there is nothing I like more than devouring my opponent's pieces and pawns.

25...Rc7

26.a4

After eating one of my opponent's pawns, my Knight found itself out of play on the side of the board. With this move, I am protecting the b5-square and preparing for the Knight's return to the center. In so doing, I am once again sticking to the plan: Take material and then consolidate the position.

26...Qa8

Black pins my Knight, but I have prepared a trick of my own.

27.Rxd5!

Now 27...Rxa7 28.Qd3 leaves Black without an answer to 29.Rd8+, which captures the Black Queen.

27...Qxa7   28.Rd8+ Kh7

29.Qd3+ f5

A sad neccessity. If Black plays 29...g6, then 30.Qd4 carries the double threat of Qd4xb2, which wins the Rook, and Qd4-h8 checkmate. Black would be forced to give up his f-pawn by playing 30...Rb1+, which leads to 31.Kg2 f6 32.Qxf6 and a fate similar to the one that occurred in the actual game.

30.Qxf5+ g6

31.Qe6, 1-0

Black gives up because he sees that 31...h5 32.Qg8+ Kh6 33.Qh8+ creates a double attack on his King and Rook on b2, with the inevitable loss of the Rook. Note that 31...Rg7 32.Qe8 renews my threats against his King.

Beating a World Champion is always exhilirating. This win was possible only because I remembered that a material surplus is one of the most important advantages you can possess and because I followed these rules:

1. After you gain material, immediately consolidate your position by developing all your pieces and ensuring your King's safety.

2. Once you have consolidated your position, seek out new goodies to devour.

3. If you have a large material advantage, don't hesitate to give up some of your gains if doing so will stop enemy threats while allowing you to remain equal or ahead in material.

For our next example, imagine that you have the upper hand in the very one-sided position in Diagram 2. Though victory is much more likely in this game, you could still falter without a strategy to guide you. In this case, the strategy is:

Try to find a target and then build a plan around it. The target will show you where to concentrate your energies, while the plan will tell you what to do.

In Diagram 2, White has an enormous material advantage. Black could

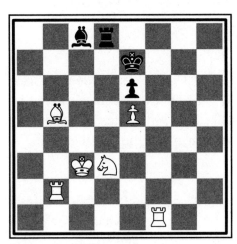

DIAGRAM 2. White to play.

quietly resign this position but nobody ever won a game by giving up, so he decides to hang on for dear life. How should White finish off his opponent? Actually, anything White does short of handing material back to Black wins. But let's put ourselves in White's shoes and attempt to beat Black in an orderly fashion. We need a target and a plan of attack. The target will show us where to concentrate our energies, and the plan will tell us what to do.

In this case, we will choose the Black pawn on e6 as our target. Why this pawn? Because it cannot move. It stands to reason that it is easier to attack something if we can train our sights on it. We don't want a moving target, so the e6-pawn is an ideal candidate.

One sensible first move would be **1.Bc4**, which opens the b-file for White's b2-Rook and brings the Bishop's powers to bear against the e6-pawn. Black is completely helpless, so nothing he does will have much consequence. He plays **1...Rh8**. Now White continues his e6-pawn assault with **2.Rf6**, and Black once again moves his Rook with **2...Rd8**. Notice how every White move is dictated by our chosen course of action. The goal is to win the e6-pawn, and the plan of action is to bring White's pieces to positions where they can attack this target.

From the position in Diagram 2, we have seen the moves 1.Bc4 Rh8 2.Rf6 Rd8. Now how should White continue? So far, he has attacked with two pieces (the Bishop and Rook), but the enemy defenses are easily holding against this small raiding party. The key to winning this position and most others is to involve the entire White army in the assault. Suppose you are the employer of four workers, two of whom never make any effort to do their jobs. Would you tolerate this situation? No! So why would you allow any of your pieces to act in the same manner? Make them earn their keep!

Applying this philosophy to our present game, White forces the lazy b2-Rook to join in the attack on the e6-pawn with **3.Rb6**. Now the e6-pawn is attacked three times and defended only twice, meaning that White will win it. Note that if Black could somehow defend his pawn a third time, White would make use of his Knight (a fourth attacker!) by playing it to c5 or f4.

This example shows how important it is to use your whole army instead of just part of it. As a game of warfare, chess is a group activity, and each member of the group—pawns and pieces alike—must make a contribution.

Throwing Away a Material Advantage

Sometimes a material advantage carries with it an aura of invisibility. Lulled by a sense of secure victory, a player with a material surplus will forget the other components of the strategy that turn a material advantage into a win. Here are a couple of examples of this kind of forgetfulness.

Did you notice that White's Queen is missing in Diagram 3? What's going on? The game we are about to look at was played "at odds." Today, such games are rare. They are designed to give a weak player a chance to beat someone much stronger. How do you play an odds game? You simply set up the pieces in the normal way and then take off whatever piece or pawn the stronger player (the odds-giver) offers you. In this case, the stronger player offered his Queen, and the game is said to be "at Queen odds."

I can already hear you asking, "How can White hope to win without his Queen?" Against an opponent of equal ability, White would really have no hope at all. However, in this case White is William Norwood Potter, an experienced player, and he knows that his opponent, a beginner, will make mistakes. The question is: Will these mistakes be big enough to allow the Queenless Potter a chance at victory? First, I'll give you the game's moves without notes. Play through the game on your own board, and see if you can spot the mistakes for yourself.

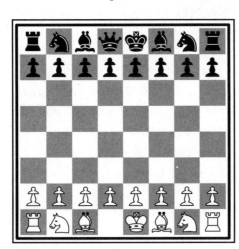

DIAGRAM 3.
Potter–Amateur
London, 1870
Queen Odds

1.e4 e5	2.Nf3 Nc6
3.Bc4 Nf6	4.Nc3 Na5
5.Nxe5 Nxe4	6.d3 Nc5
7.Bxf7+ Ke7	8.Bg5+ Kd6
9.Nb5+ Kxe5	10.f4+ Kf5
11.Nd4+ Kg4	12.h3+ Kg3
13.Ne2+ Kxg2	14.Bd5+ Ne4
15.Bxe4 checkmate	

It doesn't take a master to see that Black dies a horrible death. Why?

Did you figure out his fundamental errors? Aside from the fact that he is unable to see basic threats, the main reason for his demise is that he does not develop his pieces. Let's look at the game again, this time with notes that explain the mistakes.

1.e4

White intends to develop his pieces as quickly as possible so that he can whack Black off the board before the lack of a Queen drags him into the abyss of defeat.

1...e5   2.Nf3 Nc6

3.Bc4 Nf6   4.Nc3 Na5?

So far Black has played well. He has gained some central space (with 1...e5) and developed his two Knights. But now he suddenly stops bringing pieces out and instead begins to play with only his two horses. If he had mobilized his whole army with 4...Bc5 followed by 5.0-0 (which also moves the King to safety) and 6...d6, White would not have been able to stave off an eventual loss, and Black would have won.

5.Nxe5 Nxe4?

Black loses a pawn, but, with the advantage afforded by his Queen, this loss really doesn't mean anything at all. If he had now traded off White's attacking forces with 5...Nxc4, the game might still have been his.

6.d3

White has lost all respect for his opponent and dares Black to make a good move. The immediate 6.Bxf7+ would have been better, because now Black can still pull out White's fangs with 6...Nxc4, which ends the attack by trading off the pieces that could have done Black harm. However, Black blunders.

6...Nc5??

Black has moved his two Knights over and over again while the rest of his army is still sitting at home. You won't win games if you play like this!

7.Bxf7+

Black failed to notice that this point was attacked twice. Now Black's King is forced into the center, where it perishes under a brutal assault.

7...Ke7

8.Bg5+

White might have been tempted to continue his attack with 8.Nd5+ using only his three developed pieces. Instead, he wisely brings a new piece into the fray. He knows Black has made a mistake in not mobilizing his pieces, and he has no intention of repeating his opponent's errors.

8...Kd6

9.Nb5+

White's plan is to force Black to capture the Knight on e5. He reasons that since he is already a Queen down, the loss of an additional piece won't make much difference to the result. The important thing is to draw the enemy King so far forward that it drowns in deep waters.

9...Kxe5 **10.f4+ Kf5**

11.Nd4+

Of course, White could compensate for giving Queen odds by capturing Black's Queen, but at the moment he is hunting a larger trophy.

11...Kg4 **12.h3+ Kg3**

13.Ne2+ Kxg2 **14.Bd5+ Ne4**

15.Bxe4 checkmate

Black got what he deserved. If you don't develop your pieces, you'll find yourself in hot water again and again.

As you have seen, a lead in development can make up for a material deficit. However, if the less-developed army is able to catch up and match the opponent's development, then the material advantage will begin to assert itself. If you are ahead in material, don't simply feed on your enemy's men and forget about your own mobilization.

I'll demonstrate this concept further by using another odds game. As Diagram 4 shows, White has less confidence this time (or is more in touch with reality) and gives odds of his Queen-Knight. With the Knight removed from b1, play begins.

1.e4 e5

2.f4

White immediately shows his willingness to give up more material to open lines for his pieces.

2...exf4

3.Nf3 f5?

A very poor move. Black weakens the pawn protection around his King and fails to develop a piece. Something like 2...d5 (which frees his c8-Bishop) or 2...d6 (which stops White from attacking the Knight with e4-e5) followed by 3...Nf6 would be better.

4.Bc4!

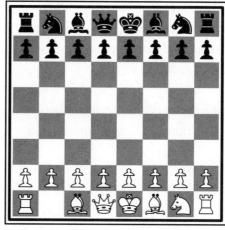

DIAGRAM 4.
Ward–Browne
Nottingham, 1874
Queen–Knight Odds

White rushes to get all his pieces out so that he can start an attack against the Black King. Further loss of material doesn't worry him because he is already so far down in force that a quiet game would only lead to his doom.

4...fxe4

5.0-0!

White begs Black to capture the Knight and at the same time develops even more of his forces.

5...exf3?

Look at the Black position. Has he developed any of his pieces? Before playing 5...exf3, he enjoyed a material advantage of a Knight and two pawns. He didn't need to take anything else! Instead of capturing his opponent's pieces, he should be getting his own pieces out and keeping the files and diagonals closed so that his King will be able to get to safety. A much saner move would be 5...d5 (which closes down the a2-g8 diagonal and frees his own light-squared Bishop) or 5...Nf6 followed by 6...d5. In either case, Black's huge material advantage would eventually triumph.

6.Qxf3 Bc5+?

A better move for Black is 6...Nf6, which develops a piece. As things stand, White is able to give up one more pawn in order to get every piece he owns into the fight.

7.d4!

Very nice. White throws this pawn away but frees his c1-Bishop with tempo. Development is now more important than simple material considerations.

7...Bxd4+

8.Kh1 d6

Black finally gets around to moving his pieces. But because he previously ignored his development, this effort comes too late.

9.Bxf4 Nf6

10.Rae1+

Black thinks that he is two pieces and a pawn ahead. However, look at Diagram 5. Notice the guys sitting on a8, b8, c8, d8, and h8. What are they doing? Nothing at all! Now look at the White army. Everybody is hard at work! As a result, White has a much larger force at his disposal than Black. (In a strange way, this position actually puts White ahead in material!) Of course, if Black can get his pieces out, he will win, so White is forced to play for a quick knockout before the reinforcements arrive.

10...Kf8

11.Qd5!

White threatens checkmate on f7 and hopes that Black will fall for 11...Nxd5 12.Bxd6++ Kg8 13.Bxd5+ Be6 14.Bxe6 checkmate. This kind of tactic may seem shocking to the amateur player, but White knows that shocking moves are the equivalent to swinging fists, and he must land a haymaker.

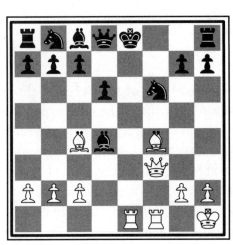

DIAGRAM 5.

11...Qd7

12.Qxd4 Nc6

White gets one of his pieces back, but Black manages to develop a piece. Has White's attack fizzled out?

13.Qxf6+!!

Black's King loses its protective cover.

13...gxf6   **14.Bh6+ Qg7**

15.Rxf6 checkmate

With the exception of the King, every White piece participated in this checkmate.

Does the fact that superior development can make up for a material deficit mean that a material advantage is not really so important? Not at all! Black would have won this game if he had been less greedy and more attentive to his development. Here's the strategy once again:

When you are already way behind in material, you can happily give away more. You are already down, so you have nothing to lose! When you are ahead, though, you should refuse new gifts until your entire army is developed and your King is safe. Once you have accomplished these goals, you are free to take everything in sight.

PROBLEM 1. Black is a Queen up in material, but now his Queen is under attack. It's his move. How should he deal with this problem?

Tarrasch–Schroeder
Nuremberg, 1890

Trading Pieces for a Winning Endgame

From the previous examples, you've probably realized that when you have less material than your opponent and no compensation for this deficit, you are often reduced to playing for a lucky shot—a move that depends more on your opponent making a mistake than on any brilliance of your own. In chess parlance, this situation is known as *playing for a cheap shot* or *cheapo* for short. On the other hand, if you have a material advantage, you want to eliminate as many of the potential tricks in a position as possible. Trading pieces when you are ahead in material is a wonderful way to avoid being the target of a cheapo. Here's the strategy:

When you are materially ahead, trade, trade, trade!

The concept of trading pieces is particularly useful if you can wind up in the endgame with an advantage of a pawn or more. Then your poor opponent, down to his last piece or two, will face a miserable defense with no chances to attack whatsoever. A couple of examples will demonstrate the efficacy of this strategy.

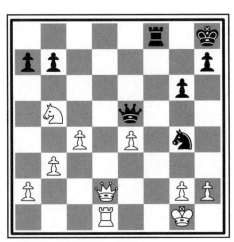

DIAGRAM 6. White to play.

White is two pawns ahead in Diagram 6, but Black, with threats of 1...Qxh2+ and 1...Rf2, is trying to make things difficult. Is it time for White to panic, or is there an easy way out? If White employs the trading strategy, then all his problems will disappear after **1.Qd4** (1.Qc3 is also fine). When the Queens leave the board, Black's threats cease to exist, and White can try for victory in a nice, safe, two-pawn-up endgame.

We see the same idea in Diagram 7, though in this case, the solution is a bit more imaginative. White has a fat four-pawn advantage, but Black threatens 1...Nxh2 and 1...Nf2 checkmate. If White plays 1.Qd6, then Black saves himself with 1...Nf2+ 2.Kh2 Ng4+, and White must accept the draw by perpetual check. If White can only trade Queens, all his problems will be over, but such a trade appears to be impossible. Or is it? It turns out that White can win

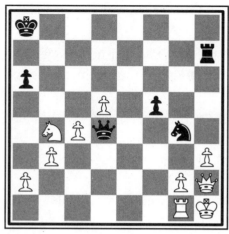

DIAGRAM 7. **White to play.**

with the tricky **1.Qb8+! Kxb8 2.Nc6+**, forking the King and Queen and leading to a winning endgame. After **2...Kb7 3.Nxd4 Nf2+ 4.Kh2 Ng4+ 5.Kg3**, Black can do nothing better than give up.

Obviously, trading can be a very important defensive strategy. Sometimes it may not be easy to find a way to accomplish the desired exchange, but the end result is usually well worth the effort.

Our next example shows White sacrificing a pawn so that he can quickly mobilize his army. In Diagram 8, White has just castled and dares Black, who is already behind in development, to take the b2-pawn bait. Before capturing this pawn, Black must ask himself the two questions on the next page.

DIAGRAM 8. **Black to play.**
Gormon–Silman
Ervin Memorial, 1987

1.

1. After capturing the b2-pawn, can I eventually catch up in development?

2. Can White take advantage of the open lines my capture will create and get to me in a hurry?

Foremost in Black's mind is a simple fact: If he can survive White's attack, the extra material will give him an excellent chance to win. He decides to go for it!

1...Qxb2

2.Qd2 h6

A sharp move, even though it doesn't immediately develop a piece. Its deeper purpose is to gain time by attacking the Bishop and prepare the way for placing the f8-Bishop on the h8-a1 diagonal. Black has faith in his position because his pawn structure acts like a thick leather hide, keeping out any annoying flies that might wish to bite him. Note how the pawns on c6 and d6 defend the important b5, c5, d5, and e5 squares, making them uninhabitable for the enemy pieces.

3.Bh4?

Having already sacrificed a pawn, White should have kept his nerve and played 3.Rab1 Qa3 4.Rb3. Then Rf1-b1 would have allowed him to use the b-file to advantage. Instead, White's move falls in line with Black's plan of development.

3...g5!

Normally these kinds of flank weaknesses aren't recommended. In this setting, however, Black must develop his army as quickly as possible. Coming as it does with tempo, this is Black's best move.

4.Rab1 Qa3

5.Rb3

White's Rook has taken control of the b-file with gain of tempo, but he is still unable to inflict any damage on the Black position.

5...Qa5

6.Bg3 Bg7

Now the Bishop on g7 is very strong, and Black is ready with 7...0-0 to get his King to safety. White tries to tear down the Black kingside pawn structure, but in doing so, he allows Black to initiate a series of moves that ultimately lead to a trade of Queens.

7.h4?! gxh4

8.Bxh4 Bxd4!

Black would not normally trade his fine Bishop for the d4-Knight, but in this case, the move represents more than a simple exchange of pieces.

9.Qxd4 Qe5

Now Black threatens both 10...Qxd4 and 10...Qh2 checkmate. White must trade Queens and accept an inferior, pawn-down endgame.

10.Qxe5 Nxe5

11.Rb7 f6

White's control of the b-file allows him to apply some pressure, but not enough to compensate for an unhealthy pawn deficit. With 11...f6, Black continues to consolidate his position by creating a safe haven on f7 for his King.

12.f3 Bc8

Black forces the Rook to get off the dangerous 7th rank. Note that Black doesn't hurry to swing out and attack. He just slowly improves his position. When you are ahead in material and have a safe position, you can afford to take your time and torture your opponent. This cat-and-mouse theme is a favorite strategy of the masters.

13.Rb4 Rg8   14.Kh1 Kf7

15.Rfb1 Rd8!

A subtle move. This Rook will eventually reach the b-file by ...Rd7-b7.

16.Bg3 c5

17.Rb8 Rxb8

Black is quite happy to trade pieces because he can feel victory drawing a little closer with every exchange.

18.Rxb8 Nc6

The Black Knight chases the White Rook to a less-active square.

19.Rb2 Rd7   20.Bf4 h5

21.Nd5 Rb7

This move signals the end of White's domination of the b-file and forces another exchange.

22.Bc1 Rxb2

23.Bxb2 Be6

Black has achieved a winning position, and White knows it. As you have seen, the important theme to keep in mind is this:

One of the clearest advantages you can have in chess is to win the opponent's pawns or pieces. But there is a risk! As you're grabbing material, you're not developing your army. Winning material is fine, if you can catch up to your opponent's level of mobilization.

Silman–Malachi
Lloyds Bank Masters, 1978

PROBLEM 2. Black has sacrificed two pawns for what appears to be a strong attack. It's White's move. How should he cope with his kingside problems?

24

Stopping Enemy Counterplay

A t some time or other, we all find ourselves with an advantage in position—be it large or small. It's part of the natural ebb and flow of the game. Whether we can parlay that advantage into a win is a completely different matter. Rarely will your opponent be so depressed over his positional shortcomings that he will lay back and allow you to wreak havoc upon him. More than likely, the guy sitting across from you will begin his own aggressive action, fighting for some sort of counterplay. In these cases, you must stay calm, refuse to overreact, and implement this strategy:

Try to find the perfect balance between defense and a continuation that furthers your own plans.

Let's look at an example. The position in Diagram 9 is very favorable for White. With his extra pawn and powerful centralized Bishop, he is clearly winning the game. However, Black has a trump of his own: his aggressively placed Rook on the 7th rank. The power of this piece enables him to threaten 1...Qg5. If White allows this move, Black will win the game because checkmate on g2 can be avoided only by 2.Qf2 (which loses the Queen to 2...Rxf2)

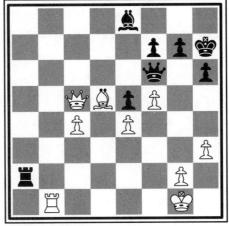

DIAGRAM 9. **White to play.**
Botvinnik–Kan
Leningrad, 1939

or 2.g4 (which allows 2...Qd2 with a quick checkmate to follow).

How should White react? Threats to one's King often breed mindless terror. Many players would panic and try something like 1.Qb4?? Qg5 2.Rb2. The idea is good—trading would indeed take the sting out of Black's attack. However, Black would then play 2...Qc1+, picking up the White Rook and turning a lost position into an easy win.

Having seen the Black threat, if all White thinks about is defense, he will lose the game. Instead, after noting the threat, he should look at his own advantages and try to combine an aggressive plan of action that makes use of his pluses with a defensive scheme. This is how it is done.

White is a pawn ahead. Because it is a passed pawn, he would love to push it down the board and create a new Queen. What's preventing the promotion? The White Queen is in the way of its own pawn. He must move the Queen if he wants to make immediate use of the extra pawn on c4. Now comes the critical decision: Where can he move the White Queen that also prevents the Black threat of ...Qg5? Because White has a material advantage, he would love to trade Queens, and the answer 1.Qe3! is best. This move both stops the enemy attack in its tracks and furthers White's own goals.

In the sections that follow, we will examine two methods of dealing with enemy counterplay. The first is to constantly be on the alert for your opponent's tactical threats. The second is to keep your opponent as helpless as possible.

Spotting Tactical Threats

Often when you are winning a chess game, there comes a moment when you want to get things over with. As soon as your opponent moves, you rush in with your own response. This lack of care has led many potential victors down the road to oblivion. It takes only one moment of inattention to fall for some hidden tactical trick.

As I explain in *Winning Chess Tactics*, tactics are maneuvers that take advantage of short-term opportunities with the goal of supporting your own strategy or destroying your opponent's strategy. For more information about specific tactics, I will refer you to *Winning Chess Tactics*. Here, we will look at a couple of examples of what can happen if you underestimate your opponent's tactical possibilities.

In Diagram 10, Black is about to lose his Queen and will soon be a piece down. However, his passed pawns on the queenside are so strong that one of them will be promoted very soon, and Black will win the game. Confident that victory will soon be his, Black could easily throw out 1...b3?? as his move. Imagine his

DIAGRAM 10. Black to play.
Makogonov–Botvinnik
U.S.S.R., 1943

horror when he realizes that 2.Rxe7+ Kxe7 3.Bc5+ followed by Bxa3 does lead to a win, but for the other side!

Alert to this possibility, Black plays the simple **1...Qxf7+!** instead. After **2.Kxf7 b3,** White is helpless before the threat of 3...b2 followed by 4...b1=Q and gives up.

One of the worst (and most costly) examples of inattention that I've ever seen occurred in a Junior World Championship event. Both players were nine-year old girls who had long ago lost interest in the game. White, behind by three pawns, had already resigned herself to defeat and was playing only through inertia. Black, who had decided that the game was as good as over, was not even looking at the board. Instead, she was literally dancing for joy, because with this victory came the title of World Champion for girls under ten! Black's coaches and parents were frantic. They wanted her to sit down and take the game seriously; there would be plenty of time for celebration after the competition. But because nobody is allowed to offer advice while a contest is in progress, they were forced to watch in horror as the drama unfolded.

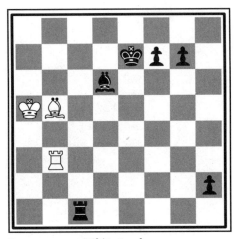

DIAGRAM 11. White to play.

From the position in Diagram 11, White decided to throw in a couple of spite checks before giving up, and played **1.Re3+**. Now 1...Kd8 2.Re8+ Kc7 would end the game, as would 1...Kf6 2.Rf3+ Kg6. However, Black was in a world of her own. Without so much as a glance at the board, she grabbed her King and played **1...Kf8??**. The reply **2.Re8 checkmate** brought poor Black crashing back to reality, but by then it was too late. The World Champion title was gone, and euphoria was replaced by hysteria. The moral of this story?

"It's not over till it's over" may be trite, but it's true—for all sports.

Avoid overconfidence and never play quick moves.

Remember: The game is not over until your opponent either resigns or achieves a checkmate!

DIAGRAM 12. Black to play.
Reshevsky–Fischer
U.S. Championship, 1963–64

At times you may think you have a clear advantage, and then the sudden appearance of a tactic will force you to reassess the situation. When these nasty situations arise, you must keep your head clear and go into damage-control mode, just as Bobby Fischer did when faced with the situation in Diagram 12. Here, Black is a pawn up. He would like to defend his pawn on b6, which is being attacked by the White pieces on b2 and b4. The obvious defense is 1...Rb8, a move that most people would play without too much hesitation. However, this defense would be squashed by 2.Bf1 Bxf1 3.Rxb6!!, and White would win immediately because of the weakness of Black's back rank (3...Rxb6 4.Ra8+ leads to checkmate).

In the actual game, Fischer saw his predicament, kept calm in the face of the attack, and accepted that his b6-pawn was a goner. He played to extract White's newly found fangs. After **1...b5 2.Bxb5 Nxb5 3.Rxb5 Rxb5 4.Qxb5 Qe5**, White emerged with a small advantage, but the trades had depleted most of White's aggressive potential, and Black was able to save the game.

PROBLEM 3. It's Black's turn to play. He is obviously winning, and he can choose from among many tempting ideas, such as 1...h3 and 1...Kc3. Is there anything wrong with 1...Kc3?

Keeping Your Opponent Helpless

Chess can be played on several levels. On the one hand, you can play to create a work of art—a brilliant game that other players will study and admire. On the other hand, you can play chess as a sport, in which case you want to achieve victory in the safest, most economical manner. For most people, creating a work of art is not easy, especially when an opponent is determined to get in the way. However, while you are striving to attain the immortality that accompanies the creation of a masterpiece, you can increase your chances of winning games by honing your ability to limit your opponent's chances, which is something that you have more control over.

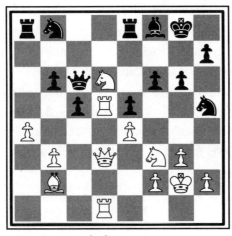

DIAGRAM 13. Black to move.
Keene–Hartston
England, 1968

No matter how clearly defined your static advantage might be, you should first curtail all of your opponent's chances and only then proceed with your plans. This means that if you are lucky enough to get your opponent in a passive position, you should make every effort to keep him in that state. For example, the situation in Diagram 13 is a dream for White. His pieces are pouring into the Black position, and Black has no way to create threats of his own. To win, all White has to do is keep Black's pieces bottled up and slowly ooze down the board, claiming one square after another in a safe but dominant fashion.

1...Re6

Black hopes to trade his inactive pieces for White's active ones.

2.Qc4

White doesn't allow Black to carry out his plan. Now Black needs to address the threats along the a2-g8 diagonal and avoid moves like 2...Bxd6?? 3.Rxd6, which lead to heavy material losses.

2...Ng7

Black defends e6. Notice that he can't do anything but hold on for dear life.

3.Nb5

The White Knight steps back, opening the d-file for the doubled White Rooks.

3...Na6

Black hopes to trade off the strong White Knight with ...Nc7.

4.Rd7

In taking control of the squares along the 7th rank and preventing ...Nc7, White is not playing with any great imagination. He is simply making sure that Black remains trapped in his current position.

4...Kh8

5.Na7

The double threat of 6.Qxa6 and 6.Nxc6 forces Black to part with material.

5...Rxa7

6.Rxa7

White, with seemingly no effort at all, won the Exchange and eventually the game. The moral here is:

Don't try to make it exciting! Try to make it safe and easy!

Here's another example of "better safe than sorry" play. The position in Diagram 14 is completely one-sided. Moves like 1.Ka5, 1.b5, or 1.c6 are all easy wins. However, you never know what mistakes you might make later, and the Black Rook is a strong piece. Wouldn't it make sense to trade it if you got the chance? Then Black would have nothing left that was capable of damaging you. Playing 1.Rf4+ forces the exchange of Rooks and leaves Black with no hope at all.

The move 1.Rf4+ is hardly necessary, but it does illustrate an important state of mind:

When victory is in your grasp, always keep things simple and safe. If possible, take your opponent's weapons away from him, so that he can't shoot you in the back.

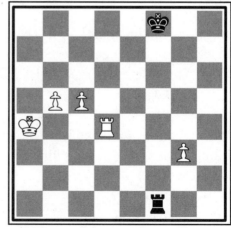

A master of this kind of "kill the counterplay before starting the execution" style of play was World Champion Tigran Petrosian. In the next example, we see him performing a no-counterplay clinic on another World Champion, Boris Spassky.

DIAGRAM 14. **White to play.**

DIAGRAM 15. Black to play.
Spassky–Petrosian
World Championship Match, 1966

As you can see in Diagram 15, Black is a pawn ahead, but central to this position is the fact that both players have castled on opposite sides of the board. Black intends to place his Rooks on the g-file and go for checkmate. He knows that White intends to play a4-a5 and then try to kill off the Black King, and he quite rightly wonders why he should give his opponent any chance to succeed. Why not close off the queenside and proceed to checkmate White at his leisure? Follow the moves below to see how Petrosian stumped Spassky in this game. The key is to stop Spassky's counterplay.

1...c4!

This fine move gives White control of the d4-square but, more importantly, prepares to close down all play on the queenside. The d4-square is a small price to pay for the Black King's safety.

2.Be2 a6!

Black makes his point. Now 3.b5 a5 or 3.a5 b5 both lead to a complete blockade on the queenside. Stripped of all moves against the Black King, White finds himself completely lacking in opportunities for counterplay.

3.Kh1 Rdg8

4.Rg1 Rg4

With all lines of attack closed down on the queenside, Black can safely devote all his energy to his kingside aspirations.

5.Qd2 Rhg8

6.a5 b5

White, who has no play at all, eventually lost this game.

Diagram 16 is another example of the superior side treading carefully to avoid giving the opponent any counterplay. White suffers from a terrible Bishop on g2, a Knight that doesn't appear to be going anywhere, and pawns that are in need of constant defense on c2 and e4. Black's backward d-pawn, on the other hand, is well defended by the Black Queen and King. Black's natural plan is to double his Rooks on the c-file and add to the pressure against c2. Unfortunately, 1...Rc4, which attacks e4 and prepares for

DIAGRAM 16. Black to play.
Matulović–Fischer
Vinkovci, 1968

this doubling, would give White some counterplay chances with 2.g4, because 2...Nxe4 3.Bxe4 Rxe4 4.Ng3 followed by Nf5+ is not what Black wants. The advantages of the position are not going away, so Black decides to kill his enemy's counterplay chances first. Then he will be free to pursue his queenside dreams. Here's how Fischer neutralized Matulović.

1...h5!
Black stops g3-g4 in its tracks.

2.b3
This move keeps the Rook out of c4 but weakens the c3-square.

2...Bxe2!
Why give up this nice Bishop for the lame Knight? Because only the Knight was keeping Black out of c3.

3.Qxe2 Rc3
With White's counterplay crippled, Black can proceed with the occupation of the c-file.

4.Rd3 Rhc8   5.Rxc3 Rxc3
6.Kh2 Qc5

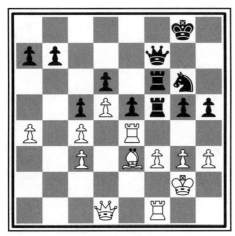

DIAGRAM 17. Black to play.
S. Gligorić–Seirawan
Baden, 1982

White, who is bound hand and foot to the weakling on c2, eventually lost the game. Black, on the other hand, triumphantly demonstrated the wisdom of this principle:

If you have a permanent advantage, take the time to stop any potential enemy counterplay.

Here's another example of this principle at work. Diagram 17 shows a position from my game with S. Gligorić. The center is locked so that all the play is occuring on the wings. My superior pawn structure gives me better long-term chances, and I have a clear advantage on the kingside because of my pressure on the f-file. My only worry is potential play by White on the queenside, the only place left for White to seek counterplay.

My advantages are not going away, so I decide to pause in my kingside assault and walk my King over to the queenside. (Why not put the old guy to work?) With my King defending that side of the board, the rest of my army would be free to take a whack at the White monarch.

1...Kf8!	**2.Rf2 Ke8**
3.Rf1	

White is obviously having trouble coming up with anything constructive.

3...Kd7	**4.Rf2 Kc8**
5.Rf1 Qh7	**6.Bd2**

White doesn't fall for 6.Qd2? Nh4!+ 7.gxh4 Rxf3 8.Rxf3 Qxe4, followed by ...g5-g4.

6...Rf8	
7.Qc1 Qf7	

If White takes the g-pawn, I will be able to break through on the kingside with ...Rxf3.

8.Qd1 Kc7	**9.Be3 Qg7**
10.Kh2 Qh7	**11.Kg2 Rg8**
12.Bd2 Nf8!	

White is helpless, but he is still holding on. Seeing that I can't crack his kingside, I turn my attention to the other advantage in my position: the weak pawns on c4 and a4. Notice how, once you render your opponent helpless, you can take all the time you want to set up different winning attempts.

13.Qb1 Nd7

14.Ree1 Nb6!

White's position is finally starting to fall apart. Here are the concluding moves: **15.Qe4 Nxa4 16.Ra1 Nb6 17.Rxa7 Rf7**. (His Queen is the only thing defending the weak pawn on c4, so I am happy to trade it off.) **18.Re1 Qxe4 19.Rxe4 Rgf8** (I switch my attention back to f3. Now I can win with 20.Bxg5 Rxf3 21.Be3 Nxc4 22.Rxc4 Rxe3.) **20.f4 gxf4 21.gxf4 Nd7 22.Kg3 Rg8+ 23.Kf2 Rfg7** (Notice how the White Rook on a7 is completely out of play.) **24.Ke2 Rg2+ 25.Kd1 Rh2 26.Re2 Rg1+ 27.Be1 Rhh1 28.Kd2 exf4 29.Bh4**. White resigns without waiting for a reply. The finish would have been something like 29...Ne5 30.Bf6 Rd1+ 31.Kc2 Rc1+ 32.Kb3 Rb1+ 33.Kc2 Rhc1+ 34.Kd2 f3 35.Rf2 Rb2+ 36.Kxc1 Nd3+ 37.Kd1 Nxf2+ 38.Kc1 Nd3+ 39.Kd1 f2, and Black goes on to win.

PROBLEM 4. It's Black's move. He is a pawn down, but his Bishop is superior to the White Knight; the pawns on a2, c4, e4, and h5 are all weak; the Black King is well placed; and the Rook on b2 is also very strong. Is 1...Rxa2 a good move?

**Gligorić-Fischer
Siegen, 1970**

Understanding Where the Pieces Go

Where do the pieces go? Seems like a strange question, doesn't it? After all, everyone reading this book knows how to move the pieces, and the majority of readers are also aware that most pieces are stronger if they are placed in the center of the board. However, knowing *how to move the pieces* has nothing to do with knowing *where to put them*. Only when you examine the specific needs of each of the pieces and learn the laws that govern them do you start to understand where the pieces go. In fact, this chapter may be the most important one in the book, because the subtle things you'll learn here will have a practical application in almost all your games. As a result, mastering this information will put you far ahead of most of your competition. We'll look at each piece in turn, starting with the Knight.

The Knight

The Knight, which is represented as a horse in most chess sets, is the only piece that can jump over other pieces and pawns. It has moved in the same way since the game began, and you might think that centuries of familiarity would have deprived it of its mystique. However, the opposite is true! A favorite of some Grandmasters (like Petrosian and myself) and given second billing behind Bishops by others (the great Fischer loves Bishops), this poor jumper is looked down on by many amateurs and secretly feared by others. This love-hate relationship is easy to explain. The fact that a Bishop can actually get an edge over a Knight in the majority of situations breeds disdain for the horse, which appears to be a weakling; but a Knight can wipe a Bishop off the face of the board if the correct environment appears. And so we have the rumblings of a love affair.

Amateurs tend to distrust Knights because:

- Their pieces and pawns are always being forked by the horrible beasts.
- They don't know how to use them properly.

This section is devoted to ending this distrust. It's time to learn how to make the humble Knight rule the board!

Creating Support Points

Unlike the long-range Bishop, the Knight is a short-range piece. This means that it needs to advance up the board to be strong. However, an advanced piece can easily be attacked by enemy pieces and pawns, so the Knight needs a support point, a quiet square where it can safely rest while simultaneously casting a menacing shadow over the board. This desirable square can be considered a support point only if it cannot be attacked by an enemy pawn, or if attacking with the pawn would severely weaken the enemy's position. So we have our first rule concerning knights:

Knights need advanced support points to be effective.

At times, a support point will just magically appear (which means it was created by an enemy blunder). If you notice one, rush your Knight over and gleefully attach it to its post. Usually, however, your opponents won't be so generous, and you will have to find a way to create a support point. Whole strategies are often built around the creation of support points, and for good reason! An advanced Knight sitting on a juicy support point can be the first major step toward a resounding victory. The next discussion explains why.

The 1st and 2nd Ranks

Knights on the 1st and 2nd ranks are purely defensive. If they can't make their way up the board, they will never be effective attackers. Let's look at a couple of examples:

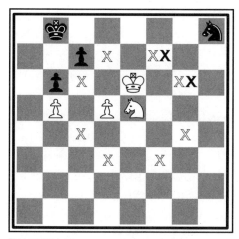

DIAGRAM 18.

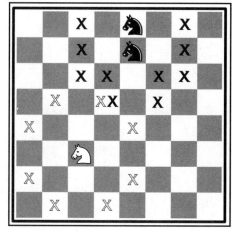

DIAGRAM 19.

The position in Diagram 18 is equal materially but is nonetheless very bad for Black. Aside from White's superior King position, White's Knight is strongly posted on the 5th rank where it controls no less than eight squares, whereas its Black counterpart is on the horrible h8-square where it controls a pathetic two squares. White wins by either 1.d6 cxd6 2.Kxd6 Kb7 3.Kd7 Kb8 4.Kc6 Ka7 5.Kc7 Ka8 6.Kxb6, or by 1.Kf6 followed by 2.Kg7 and 3.Kxh8.

An extreme example is shown in Diagram 19, demonstrating that a Knight on the 1st or 2nd rank is not particularly useful no matter how you look at it. The Knight on the 1st rank controls four squares while its more advanced brother lays claim to six. The combined power of these two pieces is only ten squares, just two more than that of the lonely White Knight on c3. Kind of pathetic, don't you agree? Also note that these Black Knights would need several moves to get down the board and into a position where they could launch an attack into enemy territory. The rule:

Your Knights will not be world-beaters if you allow them to lounge around on the 1st and 2nd ranks!

DIAGRAM 20. White to play.

The 3rd Rank

A Knight on the 3rd rank is useful for defense, but it can also take a more aggressive stance by jumping to the 5th rank in just one move. For example, from the position in Diagram 20, White tries **1.Ng5**, intending to kill Black with 2.Qxh7+. How should Black deal with this transparent but bothersome threat? The best answer would be **1...Nf6**, bringing the Black Knight from the horrible e8-square to the much superior f6 post. From f6, it defends h7 and can aspire to even greener pastures on d5, e4, or g4. Note that g5 is not a support point for the White Knight because Black can gain control of that square easily with ...h7-h6.

The 4th Rank

A Knight on the 4th rank is generally as good as a Bishop and is well poised for both attack and defense. In Diagram 21, for example, the Knight enjoys

DIAGRAM 21.

a firm support point on d5 because it is well defended by the pawn on e6 and can't be chased away by an enemy pawn. Note the Knight's range: It defends the pawn on b6, attacks the pawn on b4, can pounce on c3, e3, or f4 at any time, and can also jump back to c7, e7, or f6 if needed. Compare this Knight with those lurking on the lower ranks in previous diagrams, and you will see a big difference in their punching power and flexibility.

The 5th Rank

A Knight on a support point on the 5th rank is superior to a Bishop. It eyes many points deep in the enemy camp, threatens the enemy pawns, and helps the rest of its own army in forming an attack.

The position in Diagram 22 favors the Black Knight, with both e4 and g4 as fine support points. If it goes to e4, it can join with the Queen and Rook in forming an attack on c3, and if it leaps to g4, it can work with

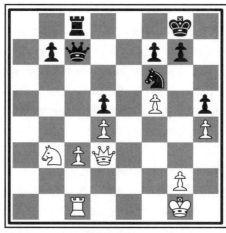

DIAGRAM 22. **Black to play.**

the Queen in creating threats against h2 via ...Qh2+. The White Knight, on the other hand, has no real support point. It can go to c5, but Black's b-pawn would advance to b6 and chase it away.

The 6th Rank

A Knight on the 6th rank acts just like a bone lodged in someone's throat. It sits deep in enemy territory, attacks pieces and pawns, and controls critical squares right in the enemy camp.

In Diagram 23, the Knight on e3 is a virtual parasite. It eyes the pawns on g2 and c4 and prevents the White Rooks from going to f1, d1, or c2. (The c1-Rook would love to move to c2 and defend a2, but the horrible Knight makes that a suicidal choice.)

DIAGRAM 23. **White to play.**

Working in Closed Positions

Knights show a good deal of strength in positions with locked pawns, called *closed positions*. Whereas the other pieces are blocked by the pawns, Knights simply jump over these obstacles—the pawns don't interfere with their activity at all! Let's look at a few examples of why Knights thrive in closed positions while other pieces flounder.

In Diagram 24, the center and the kingside are locked up with pawns. The White Bishop is clearly suffering because of the clogged diagonals. The Black Knight, however, jumps over anything in its path as it makes its way with **1...Nf8** followed by **2...Ng6** and **3...Nf4** to the support point on f4.

On the more esoteric side, Knights prosper when they are placed in front of an enemy passed pawn. This type of guard duty limits most of the other pieces, but Knights are known as the very finest blockers (called *blockaders*) of passed pawns. Take a look at Diagram 25. Some players might think that this position is good for White. He has a Bishop vs. a Black Knight that doesn't seem to be doing much on f6; he has control of more space in the center; and he has a powerful passed pawn on d5. However, the position is actually better for Black. Why? Because White's Bishop is inactive, and the Black Knight is destined for great things after **1...Ne8** followed by **2...Nd6**. On d6, this horse takes on several new dimensions: It attacks both

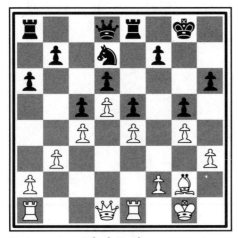

DIAGRAM 24. Black to play.

DIAGRAM 25. Black to play.

c4 and e4, forcing White to always delegate a piece or two to the defense of these pawns; it keeps White's pieces off b5; it eyes other squares like b7, c8, e8, and f7; and it stops the mighty White passed pawn dead in its tracks. Quite an accomplishment for just one piece!

Why does the Knight have more power on d6 (in front of that passed pawn) than a Bishop, Queen, or Rook would have? The answer lies in the Knight's ability to jump over other men. Let's look at Diagram 25 again, this time with a Black Bishop on d6 instead of a Black Knight. This poor, newborn Bishop looks more like a tall pawn than a high-ranking piece because the Black pawns on e5 and c5 are blocking its activity. A Rook on d6 is also terrible, because it needs to roam on open files. As for the Black Queen, such a strong piece is too important to play nursemaid to a mere pawn! A Knight, on the other hand, is happy on d6 in front of the White passed pawn because it can perform an offensive role and a defensive role at the same time—something that other pieces simply can't do.

The following game illustrates some of the points made so far in this section.

Petrosian–Bondarevsky
Moscow, 1950

In this game, we see Black willingly weaken an important square, hoping that White will not be able to make much use of it. Instead, the handler of the White pieces clamps down on this weak point in masterful fashion.

1.Nf3 e6

2.g3 f5

This opening is called the *Dutch Defense*.

3.Bg2 Nf6	**4.0-0 Be7**
5.d4 0-0	**6.c4 c6**
7.Qc2 Qe8	**8.Nbd2 d5**

Black grabs some space and clamps down on the e4-square. A price has been paid though; a hole now exists on e5. Moreover, Black's control of e4 is much more tenuous than White's control of e5. A Black pawn will never

DIAGRAM 26.

be able to chase the White pieces away from e5, but with the simple f2-f3, White can make e4 uninhabitable for Black.

9.Ne5 Nbd7

Black offers an exchange of Knights and dares White to make real use of e5. From the position shown in Diagram 26, can White make any kind of impression on that square?

10.Nd3!

A fine move that adds to his control of e5 and avoids trades that might help Black get a bit more breathing room. "How does this retreat increase White's control of e5?" you ask. With the Knight sitting on e5, only the White pawn on d4 attacked that square. (A piece does not control the square that it is sitting on.) Now, after 10.Nd3, White is attacking the square twice.

10...Ne4

11.Nf3

Another piece wends its way to the e5 promised land.

11...Nd6

12.b3 b5?

This move is a mistake, which allows White to gain a significant amount of space on the queenside. The best move was 12...d6, which restrains White's next move.

13.c5 Nf7

Black is trying hard to keep White out of e5. Having tied Black down to this defensive chore, White now breaks open a queenside file for his Rooks. Though the goal of the battle for e5 is to create a nice home for his Knights, White doesn't ignore his other men. Never forget that chess is a team game. Your whole army has to participate!

14.a4 bxa4

15.Rxa4

Now the pawn on a7 is a target that White will try to win at his leisure.

15...Bf6

Black brings another piece to bear on e5.

16.Bb2

This move counters Black's pressure on e5 and allows the Rook on f1 access to a1.

16...a6	**17.Nfe5 Nfxe5**
18.dxe5	

DIAGRAM 27.

As you can see in Diagram 27, White occupies the e5-square with a pawn.

Why would White allow this? White was willing to part with this support point for two reasons:

- ■ The newly created e5-pawn adds to White's advantage in space.

- ■ The White pawn has moved from d4, opening up the d4-square for occupation by a piece.

18...Be7	**19.f4 Rb8**
20.Rfa1 Rb5	**21.b4**

Black is helpless, so White goes about defending all his pawns. First, he takes time out to play f2-f4 and permanently guard e5. Then he plays b3-b4 and grips c5.

21...h5

22.Bc3

A very flexible move that gives the b4-pawn another defender while simultaneously allowing the Bishop access to the kingside via Bc3-e1.

22...h4

23.e3

Another useful move. White gives the f4-square more support, adds to his control of the d4-square, and clears the f1-a6 diagonal for his light-squared

Bishop. Eventually, he will play this Bishop to f1 so that it can join in the attack against a6.

23...Nb8

24.Ne1

White, by playing Nf3, Nd4, and Bf1, manages to overrun the Black position. Before you leave this game, place the Knight on d4 and look at it for awhile. Notice how it virtually sweeps the board. Important squares like b5 and f5 are touched; the pawns on c6 and e6 are pressured; and other points like b3, c2, e2, and f3 are kept within reach. Clearly, central support points like d4 are extremely important for Knights!

Let's look are another example. In Diagram 28, White enjoys a host of advantages: better King position, control of the open d-file, and a superior Knight on the superb f5 support point. What makes the position particularly pleasing is the fact that Black's Knight can't find the same kind of homebase because the White pawn on e3 covers both d4 and f4. The following moves revolve around White's efforts to penetrate down the d-file with his Rook.

DIAGRAM 28. White to play.
Petrosian–Bannik
U.S.S.R., 1958

1.Nh6!

White prepares to move to g8 and attack the f-pawn.

1...Ne6

2.Ng8 Nf8

Black defends f6 with the Rook. Playing 2...Kf7 fails because with 3.Rd7+ Kxg8 4.Kd5, White gets back his piece and achieves deep penetration at the same time.

3.Rd2 Kf7	4.Nh6+ Ke8
5.Nf5 Ne6	6.Rd6 Rxd6
7.Nxd6+ Kd7	8.Nb5

White allowed the trade of Rooks, but the advantages of his position still remain: superior Knight (which has found another fine post on b5) and dominant King (which is ready to jump into d5 or f5).

8...Ng7

9.h6

The poor Black Knight is getting kicked around like a dog.

9...Ne8

10.Kd5

Suddenly, the game is over! Any pawn moves by Black lose material; Knight moves are also disastrous (10...Nc7+ 11.Nxc7 Kxc7 12.Ke6, and the King feasts on all of Black's kingside pawns); and 10...Ke7 allows 11.Kc6, after which the queenside pawns all fall.

10...f5   **11.Kxe5 fxg4**

12.Nc3

A super Knight. Now it can jump to b5, d5, or e4—truly an endless array of support points.

12...Ke7

13.Ne4

Black resigns because both of his g-pawns will soon fall by the wayside.

PROBLEM 5. It's Black's turn to play. What squares can he claim as support points, and how can his Knight get to them?

The Bishop

Introduced in the 15th century, these relatively new pieces are long-range and streamlined. They work best in pairs because each Bishop is doomed to stay on squares of one color for the length of the game. Two Bishops, though, control squares of both colors and compliment each other in fine fashion.

Diagram 29 shows a dreaded wrong-colored Rook-pawn draw. White is a full Bishop and pawn ahead but can't win because his Bishop, stuck forever on the light squares, can't get the Black King out of the corner. (Only a Rook-pawn produces a draw. Any other pawn would lead to an easy win for White.)

Now take a look at Diagram 30. The addition of an extra Bishop for each side changes the situation entirely. White's material advantage isn't any bigger, but now the win is simplicity itself. Why? Because White's new Bishop gives him control of the dark squares as well as the light squares. After **1.Be5+ Kg8 2.h7+** followed by **3.h8=Q**, Black would be well advised to resign and catch a good movie.

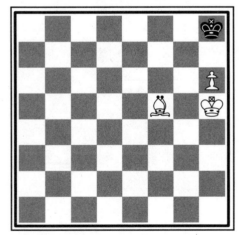

DIAGRAM 29. White to play.

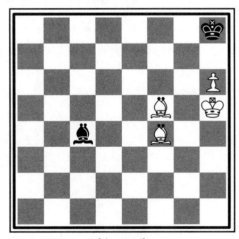

DIAGRAM 30. White to play.

If you are still not convinced that the Bishop's restriction to squares of one color is a real problem that deserves close scrutiny, take a look at the outrageous position in Diagram 31; it's sure to make you a believer! White has a pawn and eight Bishops vs. Black's lone King, but he can't win the game! If you're skeptical, I encourage you to play around with this position for a while and try to prove me wrong. If any one of White's men could change into virtu-

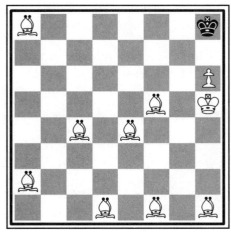

DIAGRAM 31.

ally any other piece, White would score an easy victory because every other piece has the ability to control squares of both colors. Bishops are the only exception, and it is not something that they are proud of.

Bishops are interesting creatures. On the one hand, they are wonderful long-range pieces that can sit in a corner and threaten pieces that live at the other end of the board. On the other hand, they are easily blocked by pawns and are forever stuck in a one-colored dimension. Neither of these attributes makes Bishops particularly strong or weak. The fact that it's up to the player to turn his Bishops into something special is what makes chess such an interesting game.

There are three types of Bishops: good, bad, and active. It's very important to understand these classifications for the compelling reason that if you don't, you won't have any control over how your Bishops turn out.

Good Bishops

A Bishop is considered good when its central pawns are not on its color and thus are not obstructing its activity. For example, White's light-squared

49

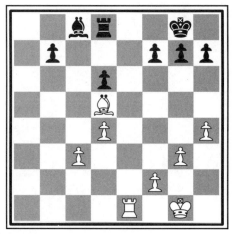

DIAGRAM 32. White to play.

Bishop in Diagram 32 is eyeing two wonderful diagonals: h1-a8 and a2-g8. It is a very strong piece because no White pawns are blocking its path. In this case, the Bishop can work with another piece: the Rook. After **1.Re7**, the double attack on f7 and b7 will lead to the win of material. The strategy here is:

Place a bishop on an unobstructed diagonal; the rewards will pour in immediately.

Bad Bishops

A Bishop is considered bad when its central pawns are on its color and thus block its activity. For example, White is a whole Bishop up in Diagram 33, but this Bishop is so bad that it is virtually useless. Because the lone Bishop can't do anything (*lone* means that there are no other pieces for it to work with) and the White King can't break into the Black position, the game will end in a draw. The moral:

If your Bishop is on the same color as your pawns, you will severely limit its activity.

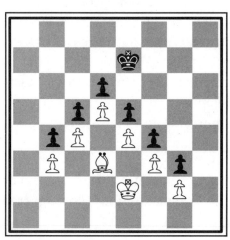

DIAGRAM 33. White to play.

It's interesting to note that if the position in Diagram 33 had an additional White Bishop on h3, White would still be unable to win because all of Black's pawns are on dark squares. The Bishops, because of their one-color limitation, would be nothing more than ghosts, floating around the board but unable to touch anything.

Active Bishops

An active bishop can be either good or bad; it's called *active* simply because it serves an active function. Take a look at the Bishops in Diagram 34, which are easy to label: Black's Bishop is good by definition (his center pawns all rest on dark squares), whereas White's is bad (his center pawns rest on light squares). This bit of name calling would lead us to believe that Black's Bishop is superior. However, nothing

DIAGRAM 34. White to play.

could be further from the truth! White's Bishop, though technically bad, is active because it is resting outside the pawn chain and is therefore not blocked. Black's Bishop, though technically good, has hardly any squares to go to. White has a couple ways to win material in this position; the simplest being **1.Ra8 Rf8 2.Ra7** followed by **3.Bxb7**. The thing to remember about bad bishops is this:

A bad bishop can be a strong piece—if you can get it to an active post.

So if you have a bad Bishop, don't panic! Just implement one of the following strategies and everything should turn out fine.

Freeing the Bishop's Diagonals

If you have a bad Bishop, try to move your pawns to another color and free the Bishop's diagonals. Diagram 35 shows a position for which this strategy is appropriate. A glance should tell you that White's Bishop is bad because two of his center pawns (on

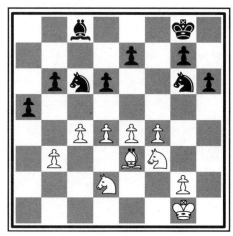

DIAGRAM 35. White to play.

51

d4 and f4) are blocking the Bishop on dark squares. The Bishop's badness is an illusion, though, because White can easily move these pawns and free the Bishop's diagonals. Here's how: **1.f5** (freeing the c1-h6 diagonal) **1...Nf8 2.d5** (freeing the g1-a7 diagonal) **2...Ne5 3.Nxe5 dxe5 4.Bxb6** (4.Bxh6 is a possibility, but the capture on b6 also picks up the pawn on a5). White will then win the game.

Getting the Bishop Outside the Pawn Chain

If you have a bad bishop, activate it by getting it outside the pawn chain. The position in Diagram 36 is not from an actual game, of course, since neither side has a King. However, it provides a good illustration of this principle. White's Bishop is clearly bad; it is also inactive as long as it sits on d2. Does it have to stay there? Of course not! White can turn the Bishop into an active participant in the game by playing Bc1 and then Ba3 (when it comes to life on the a3-f8 diagonal) or by playing Be1 and then Bh4 (when its potency increases because of its control of the h4-d8 diagonal).

Because Bishops can't jump over other pieces, they need unobstructed diagonals if they are going to be effective. If you have Bishops, you must always be trying to rip open the center. A closed, locked pawn formation is nothing but a hindrance in their battle for activity.

DIAGRAM 36.

Bishops are strongest in wide-open positions. A bad Bishop can only become active if you get it outside the pawn chain.

For example, after playing **1.e4 e5 2.d4 exd4 3.c3 dxc3 4.Bc4 cxb2 5.Bxb2**, we reach a position where Bishops rule the board. Knights simply can't compete with them in this kind of wide-open situation. (Of course, this opening, while offering White wonderful diagonals for his

Bishops and a big lead in development, is risky because he has given up two whole pawns.) Compare this position with that reached by **1.d4 Nf6 2.c4 c5 3.d5 e5 4.Nc3 d6 5.e4**. Now White's Bishops are not so valuable because the center is completely locked up with pawns.

With this discussion behind us, you are better able to understand the position in Diagram 37. What should Black do? The first thing to address is the fact that Black has a dark-

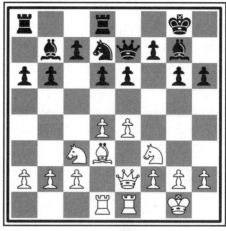

DIAGRAM 37. Black to play.

squared Bishop and White does not. Is this important? Only if you want it to be! If you have such a piece, you must find a way to make it a force in the game. Because White's center pawns are blocking the Bishop, Black should play **1...c5!** and blast open the h8-a1 diagonal. After **2.dxc5 Nxc5**, Black will have the better position because his powerful Bishop, the same piece

that was blocked a moment ago, is now shredding the board.

When All Else Fails, Trade

If you have a bad bishop that you cannot activate in the two ways just discussed, trade it for a piece of equal or greater value. In Diagram 38, White's game is clearly more comfortable than Black's. He has two Bishops, his Knight has access to b5 and d5, and Black's lone Bishop is bad because it is blocked by the pawn on e5. Turn the page to see how Black should proceed.

DIAGRAM 38. Black to play.
Cramling–Yurjola
Gausdal, 1984

1...h5!

A fine move that prepares to swap the poor piece on g7 for the very active Bishop on e3.

2.Nb5 Rc8

3.c3

Good play by White. The pawn on c3 keeps Black out of both d4 and b4. Notice how masters always try to deprive enemy pieces of good squares.

3...Kh7

Now we see the point of 1...h5. Black is finally ready to initiate the trade of dark-squared Bishops with ...Bh6.

4.Na3 Bh6   5.Bxh6 Qxh6

6.Qxh6+ Kxh6

Black has equalized the position and eventually drew the game. The moral here is:

If you don't like the piece you own, improve its position or trade it.

Larsen–Fischer
Candidates Match, 1971

Now let's look at a game where no less an authority than Bobby Fischer uses the laws that we have been discussing.

DIAGRAM 39.

1.c4 g6	2.Nf3 Bg7
3.d4 Nf6	4.Nc3 0-0
5.e4 d6	6.Be2 e5
7.0-0 Nc6	8.d5 Ne7
9.Nd2 c5	10.Rb1 Ne8
11.b4 b6	12.a4 f5
13.a5 Nf6	14.Qa4 Bd7
15.Qa3	

In Diagram 39, the center is closed, so both sides have been busy with their respective pawn breaks on the wings. White has made considerable progress on the queenside, and you might expect Black to be in a big hurry with his own attack on the other side of the board. Fischer, though, has a different idea here: He knows that an eventual ...f5-f4 advance is Black's usual way of gaining more kingside space and pursuing his checkmating aspirations. However, that advance will kill the Black Bishop on g7, which is already looking rather useless because of the closed nature of the position. Never a player to forget about the welfare of his pieces, the great Fischer first brings this piece outside the pawn chain.

15...Bh6!

Suddenly, the pathetic piece on g7 has become active.

16.Bd3

Black was threatening to win the e-pawn by 16...Bxd2 followed by 17...fxe4, so White gives this pawn more support.

16...Qc7	**17.bxc5 bxc5**
18.exf5 gxf5	**19.Bc2**

White now has the option of getting his own bad Bishop outside the pawn chain with Ba4.

19...a6

Black takes away the b5-square from the White Knight.

20.Nde4?

White would like to play 20.Ba4 but would lose a pawn after 20...Qxa5. The move White actually plays is tricky (it uncovers an attack against h6 via the Bishop on c1), but it only leads to exchanges that speed up Black's kingside attack.

20...Bxc1

Black is delighted to trade his bad Bishop for White's good one.

21.Nxf6+ Rxf6	**22.Rfxc1 Raf8**
23.Rb6 Bc8	

Black defends the a-pawn (why give anything away?) and is finally ready to go after the White King.

24.Ne2 f4!

With his dark-squared Bishop gone, Black is happy to push this pawn. Notice how this advance also frees the c8-h3 diagonal for his light-squared Bishop.

25.Be4 Nf5

Having attended to his Bishop problems, Black now brings his Knight into the attack.

26.Rc6 Qg7   27.Rb1 Nh4

28.Qd3 Bf5

Normally, Black would not trade his good Bishop for White's poor one. However, in this case the White Bishop was defending the critical g2-square, so Black removed it.

29.Kh1 f3!

30.Ng3

Forced. White cannot allow 30.gxf3 Qg2 checkmate.

30...fxg2+   31.Kg1 Bxe4

32.Qxe4 Nf3+   33.Kxg2 Nd2

White is doomed. His Queen and Rook are forked, and the pawn on f2 hangs to the battery on the f-file. So Larsen gave up.

PROBLEM 6. Don't look for moves here. Instead, label all the Bishops as either good, bad, active, or inactive.

The Rook

Before the Queen's new way of moving was introduced in the 15th century, the Rook was by far the strongest piece in the game. It was so powerful, in fact, that a player attacking it was expected to call "check-Rook." The Rook's powers have remained the same throughout the history of chess, and though its status has been diminished by the Queen, it is still a piece of extraordinary importance. Funnily enough, this importance is overlooked by most amateurs, who simply don't know how to make use of a Rook's considerable strength. Most beginners ignore their Rooks at the beginning of a game, and even seasoned tournament players of class A or expert strength fail to make the most of these mighty pieces.

Why do players forget about the Rooks? Most likely, because Rooks are situated at the sides of the board and are often the last pieces to be developed. Many players push out a few pawns (the humble foot soldiers), develop the Bishops and Knights (the warriors on horseback), bring up the Queen (the all-powerful general), and then begin a premature attack, forgetting that backup by the Rooks (cannons that blast their way into the enemy position) would do wonders for their chances of victory. Why refuse to use these cannons when you have them at your disposal?

This cannon-like effect is illustrated in Diagram 40. White can blast Black off the board with **1.Qg1,** when there is no answer to the devastating 2.Rg8 checkmate. This rout is made possible because White has followed this strategy:

To be effective, Rooks need to be placed on open files.

This type of penetration in the enemy position was mentioned by the great Nimzovich, who stated, "The aim of all maneuvers on an open file

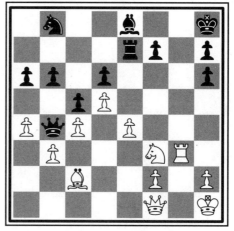

DIAGRAM 40. **White to play.**

57

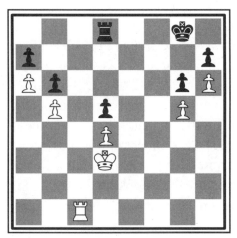

DIAGRAM 41. White to play.

is the ultimate intrusion along this file onto the 7th or 8th rank, i.e., into the enemy position." The 7th rank is important because most enemy pawns reside there, and control of that critical rank also tends to tie down the enemy King.

Diagram 41 clearly illustrates the importance of the 7th rank. Material is even, but White will win easily after **1.Rc7**. His control of the 7th rank leaves Black helpless because the Black King is trapped on the back rank and 2.Rxa7 is threatened. A response of **1...Ra8** is met by **2.Rd7**, picking up the d-pawn.

Let's see how former World Champion Botvinnik made use of this same idea to take down one of the greatest champions in history. White has the better position in Diagram 42 because both his Rooks are already placed on the open c- and e-files.

DIAGRAM 42. White to play.
Botvinnik–Alekhine
A.V.R.O., 1938

1.Qc2

White's first move adds to his control of the c-file by doubling, a process where you attempt to lay claim to a particular file with two Rooks or a Rook and Queen. White's move announces, "The c-file is mine!"

1...Re7

Now Black cannot challenge White's claim to the file with ...Rc7, so he turns his attention to the e-file to make sure that White doesn't get that file, too.

2.Rxe7 Qxe7

3.Qc7!

This trade of Queens allows the White Rook to penetrate into the enemy position and take control of the 7th rank.

3...Qxc7   **4.Rxc7 f6**

5.Kf1

The King prepares to enter the battle. This move also stops future Back Rank Mates and keeps the enemy Rook off the e2-square.

5...Rf7

Black kicks White off the 7th rank.

6.Rc8+ Rf8

7.Rc3!

White's Rook is clearly superior to its Black counterpart, so White wisely avoids further trades. Don't trade any of your good pieces for the enemy's inferior ones!

7...g5   **8.Ne1 h5**

9.h4!

White is trying to get Black to weaken his pawn structure or give up control of some critical squares. Now 9...g4 gives White control of f4 after Nd3 and Nf4, while 9...gxh4 10.Nf3 regains the pawn and leaves Black with a shattered pawn formation.

9...Nd7   **10.Rc7 Rf7**

11.Nf3 g4   **12.Ne1**

White was willing to waste a little time and force Black to create a hole on f4. Now the White Knight hurries to its new home.

12...f5

Not wanting to allow White access to f4, Black tries to plug that square with a pawn.

13.Nd3 f4   **14.f3 gxf3**

15.gxf3 a5   **16.a4**

A good move that fixes the enemy b-pawn on b6.

16...Kf8

17.Rc6

The difference in Rooks is striking. White's Rook is greedily eyeing all the Black pawns, while the ponderous Black Rook is playing a purely defensive role. In the end, White's Rooks will eat most of the Black pawns in this series of moves: **17...Ke7 18.Kf2 Rf5 19.b3 Kd8 20.Ke2 Nb8** (not allowing 21.Rxb6 Kc7 followed by 22...Nc6) **21.Rg6 Kc7 22.Ne5 Na6 23.Rg7+ Kc8 24.Nc6 Rf6 25.Ne7+ Kb8 26.Nxd5 Rd6 27.Rg5 Nb4 28.Nxb4 axb4 29.Rxh5 Rc6 30.Rb5 Kc7 31.Rxb4 Rh6 32.Rb5 Rxh4 33.Kd3**, and White wins.

As strong as doubling on a file can be, tripling is even stronger. In the next example, we see Alekhine's demonstration of how a file should be taken! The only open file on the board in Diagram 43 is the c-file, so Alekhine brings all his big guns to bear on it.

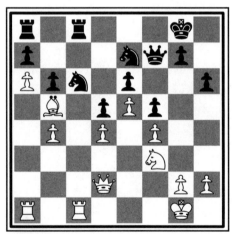

DIAGRAM 43. White to play.
Alekhine–Nimzovich
San Remo, 1930

1.Rc2

White prepares to double.

1...Qe8

Black walks into a series of pins. However, he didn't like the look of 1...Nd8 2.Bd7 Rxc2 3.Qxc2, which gives White control of the c-file.

2.Rac1 Rab8

3.Qe3 Rc7

Black intends to double his own Rooks and challenge White for control of the c-file. White answers by going one better. He will triple!

4.Rc3 Qd7   **5.R1c2 Kf8**

6.Qc1

This formation—a Queen behind doubled Rooks—is known as *Alekhine's Gun* in deference to his play in this game.

6...Rbc8

Black has to defend his Knight on c6.

7.Ba4!

White intends to make use of the pin on the c-file by playing b4-b5, which will win a piece.

7...b5

Black puts off this embarrassment by giving up a pawn.

8.Bxb5 Ke8

9.Ba4 Kd8

The Rook on c7 is well defended, and now 10.b5 can be safely met by 10...Na5. Is Black safe?

10.h4!

The answer is a resounding "No!" It turns out that Black is in a rare zugzwang situation—any move he makes will worsen his position. For example, after 10...h5 11.Kh2 g6 12.Kh1, Black is out of moves. The c6-Knight can't budge because of the pin on the a4-e8 diagonal; 12...g5 just hangs some pawns; 12...Qe8 or 12...Ke8 takes away a defender from c7 and loses a piece after 13.b5; and any move by the Knight on e7 or the Rooks drops the c6-Knight. In despair, Black gives up.

We have seen the carnage a Rook can perpetrate on an enemy position. However, the files necessary for this slaughter do not just magically appear. They have to be created in the opening—tailor-made for your Rooks. Most classic openings take the Rook's future into account. For example, after **1.e4 c5 2.Nf3 Nc6 3.d4** (the Sicilian Defense), Black is quite happy to play **3...cxd4** because he knows he has just created a half-open c-file for his Rooks. He will then play with the goal of getting a Rook on c8 as quickly as possible.

The same reasoning applies to another classic opening, the Queen's Gambit Declined. After **1.d4 d5 2.c4 e6 3.Nc3 Nf6 4.Bg5**, White will eventually place a Rook on c1 and open up the c-file with cxd5.

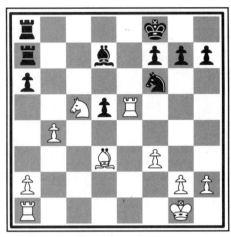

DIAGRAM 44. White to play.
Fischer–Petrosian
Candidates Match, 1971

We even see this strategy at work in the somewhat boring Petroff Defense. Play starts with **1.e4 e5 2.Nf3 Nf6 3.Nxe5 d6 4.Nf3 Nxe4 5.d4 d5 6.Bd3 Be7 7.0-0 0-0.** And with **8.Re1**, the White Rook becomes an instant participant in the battle.

The creation and control of open files is so important that sometimes a player will give up quite a bit for the opportunity to use a file to penetrate into the enemy position. In the following game, Fischer accomplishes this goal in a very surprising way. Take a look at Diagram 44, where White's advantage is clear. He has a good Bishop, whereas Black has a bad one (Black's center pawn is on the same color as his Bishop), and the Black pawns on a6 and d5 are both weak. One of White's most important advantages, however, is his wonderful Knight on c5, a piece that eyes the whole board and joins the Bishop in applying pressure to a6. Because of the power of this Knight, White's next move is quite remarkable.

1.Nxd7!+

He gives up his pride and joy! Why do this when the Knight was perfectly safe and Black had no threats? Because White sees that this exchange will enable him to penetrate into the Black position along the c-file. He trades one advantage (his super Knight) for another (a super Rook).

1...Rxd7

This move is forced, because 1...Nxd7 2.Rxd5 loses the d-pawn.

2.Rc1

White pounces on the tasty file.

2...Rd6

Black stops 3.Rc6 but gives up control of the 7th rank.

3.Rc7 Nd7	4.Re2 g6
5.Kf2 h5	6.f4 h4
7.Kf3 f5	8.Ke3

Having goaded most of the Black pawns onto light squares (where they are vulnerable to attack by the Bishop), White now aims to bring his King to the dominant d4 post. Notice how great players make use of every man they possess.

8...d4+

This move keeps White's King out of d4 but also opens the a2-g8 diagonal for White's Bishop.

9.Kd2 Nb6

10.R2e7

Doubled Rooks on the 7th (colorfully called *Pigs on the 7th*) are extremely strong and, in most cases, constitute a winning advantage.

10...Nd5	11.Rf7+ Ke8
12.Rb7 Nxb4	13.Bc4

Black gives up because 13...Nc6 14.Rh7 Rf6 15.Rh8+ Rf8 16.Bf7+ leads to immediate death.

So we have seen that it is a huge mistake to neglect your Rooks. As you play, keep in mind this strategy:

Whenever possible, get your Rooks to open files that will allow them to move to the 7th or 8th rank. And if you can double your Rooks on the 7th rank, you'll usually have an enormous advantage.

PROBLEM 7. It's White's turn to play. Is 1.d3 a good move, or should White try something else?

PROBLEM 8. White is two pawns behind, and it's his turn to play. Is he in trouble?

The King

The King has always been allowed to move one square in any direction. This movement may seem limited, but the eight squares that a centralized King controls make it quite an imposing piece. Actually, the King is a powerful part of your army. If only its capture didn't lead to loss of the game, you could bring it to the center and make use of it immediately.

Taking the King for a Walk

Though you will usually want to castle quickly to get the King to safety (and

DIAGRAM 45. White to play.
Seirawan–Timman
Wijk aan Zee, 1980

also get the Rook into the center), I must admit that once in awhile I enjoy throwing caution to the wind and making use of my King. When people express wonder at my nerve, I ask, "Why should I have to pamper the lazy thing? If it wants to eat, then let it work like all my other men!" Here are a couple of examples of how I've used the King in my games.

As Diagram 45 shows, in this game I have allowed myself to fall behind in development in order to build a strong pawn center and lay claim to a healthy extra pawn. Unfortunately, Black now threatens to wipe me out with 1...Nc2+. Because 1.Qc3 Qxd4! 2.Qxd4 Nc2+ will result in the destruction of my center and the loss of my pawn, I am forced to pick up my King and make it play an active, defensive role.

1.Kd2!

This move looks crazy, and indeed, it caused quite a commotion at the time in the chess community. But just how silly is my concept? My monarch keeps the enemy Knight out of c2, and if necessary, it can go to c3 where it would guard my important d4-pawn. If I can get my remaining army out before Black somehow punishes me for this violation of an accepted chess dictum, then my King will be safe enough, and my center (not to mention my extra pawn!) will guarantee me a clear advantage. The follow-up proves the soundness of my strategy:

1...a5

2.a3

My first task is to deprive the enemy pieces of advanced squares.

2...Na6

3.Kc2 Qd7

Now I should go on to play 4.b3 b5 5.c5 Be7 6.Bb2. Then everything is in order, I have an obvious edge in space, and I can still boast about my extra pawn.

All right, so in that game I had an extra pawn and was willing to suffer a bit to hold onto it. In the next game, I don't have a material advantage, but I nevertheless move my King when it's the logical way to achieve a desired result. In Diagram 46, you can see that my Bishop on g7 is a monster, and it will take me several

DIAGRAM 46. Black to play.
Kovačević–Seirawan
Wijk aan Zee, 1980

moves to clear away the back rank so that I can castle on the queenside. But what does White have to crow about? All he has is control of the h-file. Can I take it from him? To do so, I need to connect my Queen and Rook so that I can answer a trade after ...Rh8 with ...Qxh8. Following this line of reasoning, I came up with this surprise move:

1...Kd7!

A great move, if I do say so myself. I instantly get the connection I want. Besides, why would my King be in any danger on d7 as soon as it moves to c7?

2.Nbd2 Rh8

That file is *mine*!

3.Rg1 Kc7

4.Rb1 Rh3!

With my King nicely tucked away on c7, it's time for me to penetrate White's position.

5.b3 Qh8

This move doubles on both the h-file and on the h8-a1 diagonal.

6.Nf1 N8d7

Now it's time for more of my pieces to enter the fray. Never get carried away and forget about the rest of your army sitting at home. The Black army dominates this position (and it's White's King that is stuck in the middle of the board, not mine!), so I'll tell you how I won the game without further comment:

7.Bf4 Ne5	**8.Nxe5 Bxe5**
9.Bxe5 Qxe5	**10.f3 Bd7**
11.Qc2 Qd4!	**12.Rg2 Rh1**
13.Rf2 Qh8	**14.f4 Qh4**
15.Rd1 f6	**16.gxf6 exf6**
17.e5 fxe5	**18.fxe5 Rf8**
19.exd6+ Kb7	**20.Bd3 Re8+**

As these two examples illustrate,

Early King walks are OK if they benefit your other pieces in some way.

Now, I want you to understand two things about these games:

■ The center was closed or semi-closed in both games. Never walk your King into a wide-open center!

■ In both games, my King paced across the middle of the board on its way to the other side. In other words, centralizing the King was just a temporary measure. Notice that it was White's King that got killed in the center in my Kovačević game. My King was safely placed on the wing.

So how do you know if it's safe to take your King for a walk? A closed center makes such a stroll a lot safer, but it all really comes down to a question of necessity. Is there a clear purpose to the walk? If it helps other aspects of your game, then by all means move that King. But remember: There is a big difference between bringing the King out on purpose and having it drawn out like a hunted animal! The following well-known game is a fine illustration of a King that is forced to move inevitably toward its own death.

From the position in Diagram 47, White makes the following move:

1.Qxh7+!!

By giving up his Queen, White forces the Black King on a journey from which it will never return. Playing 1.Nxf6+ gxf6 would have allowed the Black Queen to defend h7. Now the Black King is forced into the line of fire of the White Bishop on d3.

1...Kxh7

2.Nxf6++ Kh6

Black hastily avoids 2...Kh8 3.Ng6 checkmate.

DIAGRAM 47. White to play.
E. Lasker–Sir George Thomas
London, 1911

3.Neg4+ Kg5	**4.h4+ Kf4**
5.g3+ Kf3	**6.Be2+ Kg2**
7. Rh2+ Kg1	**8.Kd2 checkmate**

This game hardly teaches any deep chess strategy. It does, however, show what can happen to a King that goes a little too far on the wild side. Remember:

Don't allow your King to be led around the board without your approval.

Putting the King to Work in the Endgame

So far, you have seen that the King can serve a purpose, rather than quivering in fear on the side. You have also seen that it usually can't withstand an attack if several enemy pieces still remain on the board. Once you remove these forces from the board, though, the climate for the King is much more favorable. In general, if both sides have only a couple of pieces left, it's time for you to dust off your King and rush it to the center of the board. There is not enough of the enemy's army left to threaten it (individual checks should not bother you), and you have every right to make use of its considerable strengths. Here's the strategy:

The King is a strong piece and must be used in an endgame. When most of the pieces have been traded, rush your King into the center for some action.

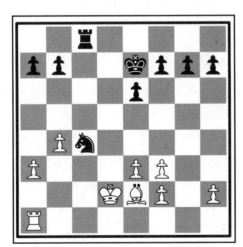

DIAGRAM 48. White to play.
Cohn–Rubinstein
St. Petersburg, 1909

The next game, which makes a strange comparison with the wipeout witnessed in the previous section, illustrates this point. Both Kings make it to the 6th rank, but one gets butchered by the other.

In Diagram 48, both Kings have come to the center to help their dwindling forces. Black's superior pawn structure gives him the better game, but this doesn't mean that White can do nothing but lose. Unfortunately, though, White decides that a mass exchange will help his cause, when all it really does is allow the opposing King to take up a dominating position.

1.Bxc4 Rxc4

2.Rc1?

White was in check by a strong enemy Knight, so an exchange made sense. However, this trade loses the game. Blocking off the Rook's access to the 4th rank with 2.f4 would have been much better.

2...Rxc1

3.Kxc1 Kf6

Black's King makes a beeline to the isolated pawn on h2.

4.Kd2 Kg5	**5.Ke2 Kh4**
6.Kf1 Kh3	**7.Kg1 e5**

Just look at the difference in the Kings' positions. White's King is pushed as far back as it can go, while Black's has trotted up the board with amazing speed. Because White has his hands full defending his h-pawn, Black takes the time to gain extra space with his pawns. Playing 7...e5 prevents White from advancing his f-pawn with 8.f4 because 8...exf4 9.exf4 Kg4 wins a pawn.

8.Kh1 b5

Black immobilizes both of White's queenside pawns with one move.

9.Kg1 f5	**10.Kh1 g5**
11.Kg1 h5	**12.Kh1 g4**

Removing some pawns gives the Black King a clear walkway along the 6th rank. Then he will be able to pick up White's immobile e-pawn with ease.

13.e4 fxe4	**14.fxe4 h4**
15.Kg1 g3	**16.hxg3 hxg3**

White gives up in the face of possibilities like 17.f4 exf4 18.e5 g2 19.e6 Kg3 20.e7 f3 21.e8=Q f2 checkmate or 17.fxg3 Kxg3 18.Kf1 Kf3, which enables Black to pick up the e-pawn because of his dominating King position.

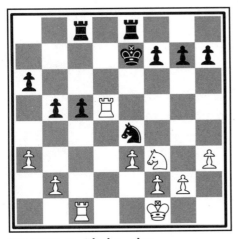

DIAGRAM 49. Black to play.
Larsen–Spassky
Lugano, 1968

This game of Rubinstein's was impressive, but it was a case of King vs. King with no other pieces. How effective is the King if other pieces remain on the board? In Diagram 49, the game is pretty even and has all the makings of a boring draw. Spassky starts by offering a trade.

1...Rcd8

2.Rh5?

Larsen, who is always trying for the win, comes up with a highly imaginative concept. However, his strategy contains a fatal flaw: It's usually not a good idea to give up a file like this. Best was 2.Rcd1, which keeps the d-file.

2...h6   3.b4 c4

4.a4?

The great Dane's idea here is to give Black a passed c-pawn but try to undermine it by attacking b5. Also notice that the White Knight has gained control of the d4-square.

4...Kf6

5.axb5 g6!

Very nice. Black will sacrifice a pawn but succeed in drawing the White Rook completely out of play.

6.Rxh6 axb5   7.Nd4 Nd2+

8.Kg1

White cannot play 8.Ke2 because of 8...Rxd4.

8...Nb3

9.Nxb3 cxb3

The obstruction on the d-file has been cleared away, and the powerful passed pawn on b3 is going to be the death of White.

10.Rb1 Re4

This move threatens the b-pawn, but it also has a meaner intent: The Rook on h6 is about to be surrounded with ...Kg7.

11.g3 Rxb4   12.Rh4 Rxh4

13.gxh4 Rd3   14.Kg2 Ke5

Black wins after his King, which constantly hounded the White Rook, marches to the queenside and assists the b-pawn in queening. Black wins because his King plays a part in the battle and White's does not, putting Black effectively ahead in material.

PROBLEM 9. It's Black's move. Which King is better placed?

PROBLEM 10. It's Black's turn to play. What is his best move?

The Queen

The Queen was the weakest piece on the board (except for the pawns) until new rules were introduced in 1475. Before this change, the Queen was limited to any diagonally adjacent square. Considered to be an advisor to the King, it was given royal status only when it obtained the combined powers of a Rook and Bishop. In Italy, the Queen's new range made such an impression that it was called *rabioso*, which means *furious*. Furious indeed! Almost all kingside attacks are led by this amazon, and though professional players enjoy trading it and playing a quiet game, amateurs are usually quite loath to part with this piece. The urge to use her power in an effort to smash the opposition is just too great!

Protecting the Queen

Funnily enough, the Queen's strength is also a weakness: On the one hand, the Queen loves to be centrally located, which gives it more squares to control; but on the other hand, the Queen can be vulnerable to harassment if it comes out too early. Bearing this in mind, you might want to follow this strategy:

> *Don't place your Queen in a vulnerable position. In general, it should*
> *be one of the last pieces you bring out.*

For example, the following situation often arises in games between beginners. They open like this:

1.e4 e5   **2.Bc4 Bc5**
3.Qh5

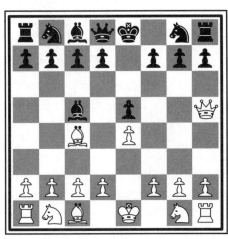

DIAGRAM 50.

The position is shown in Diagram 50. Quite logically, White wants to make use of his Queen as soon as possible. He reasons that creating a double threat of 4.Qxe5+ and 4.Qxf7 checkmate can't be bad, forgetting that his Queen will then be vulnerable to attack. After **3...Qe7**, which defends against both threats, Black will gain tempo by following up with ...Nf6, developing a Knight to a good square, and simultaneously attacking the Queen.

An even more striking example of the Queen's vulnerablity can be seen after **1.e4 d5 2.exd5 Qxd5** (which brings Black's Queen out a little fast; White will be able to gain time by attacking it) **3.Nc3** (tempo number one—the Queen is so much stronger than the Knight that it is forced to run from it in abject terror) **3...Qe5+?** (the correct move here is 3...Qa5, which gets the Queen out of harm's way; a commonly seen blunder is 3...Qc6?? 4.Bb5, when the poor lady makes a quick exit from the game) **4.Be2 Bg4 5.d4** (tempo number two—now the beleaguered Queen must hide from the pawn) **5...Bxe2 6.Ngxe2 Qd6?** (a terrible move that allows White to gain even more time) **7.Bf4** (tempo number three) **7...Qd8**. Disgusted, Black brings his roaming Queen back home. White has developed his whole army while Black played around with just one piece.

Of course, if your Queen can remain on a central square, then don't hesitate to place it there! After **1.e4 e5 2.Nf3 Nc6 3.d4 exd4 4.Nxd4** (the Scotch Opening), Black might be tempted to draw the enemy Queen out with **4...Nxd4 5.Qxd4**. However, Black would be playing to White's advantage because White's Queen could then eye the whole board from its central square.

Why is the Queen safe in this example but poorly placed in the previous example? Because Black can't bring pieces out and attack it with gain of time. Of course, Black could attack it with 5...c5, but after the Queen moves (6.Qa4, for example), what has Black really achieved? Is his pawn happy on c5? No! It blocks his Bishop and has left a big hole on d5. White will follow up with Nc3 and Bc4, when Black's "gain of time" turns out to be nothing more than a suicidal lunge!

The safest way to use a Queen is to first develop your minor pieces, tuck the Queen away on a safe but useful square deep inside your own territory (moving the Queen connects the Rooks), and then bring your Rooks to any open files that may exist.

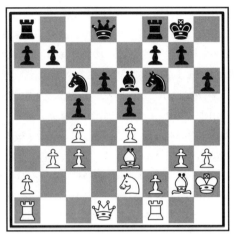

DIAGRAM 51. White to play.

The position in Diagram 51 is a simple illustration of this strategy. The White Queen cannot safely go to any advanced square at the moment, so White will do best to move it to d2 (to put pressure on d6) or to c2 (to give the e-pawn extra support):

1.Qc2 Qe7

Black was in the same situation. He finally decided to put his Queen on e7, a safe square where it supports the backward d6-pawn.

2.Rad1 Rad8

White brings a Rook to the half-open file, and Black responds by giving his only weakness added support.

3.Rd2

White prepares to double on the d-file, and the game goes on and on.

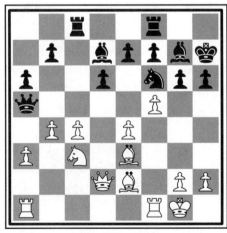

DIAGRAM 52. Black to play.
Larsen–Fischer
Candidates Match, 1971

Risking the Queen

Sometimes you will desperately want to bring your Queen out to an active but somewhat vulnerable position. In these cases, you must carefully weigh the rewards against the risks, and this type of decision can be difficult even for the greatest players. For example, in Diagram 52, White has just played **1.b4**, a move that gains space and threatens the advanced Black Queen. Most people would bring the Black Queen back to a safe square such as d8, but Fischer finds a more active possibility, which though risky, will put the pampered woman to work.

1...Qe5!

The Queen is very strong here; it can work with the g7-Bishop to control the h8-a1 diagonal and can put immediate pressure on the e4-pawn. However, it is also easy to attack and has nowhere to hide!

2.Rae1

The tactical point of Black's play would become apparent after 2.Bf4 (or 2.Bd4) 2...Nxe4!, which wins a pawn.

2...Bc6

Black keeps bringing his pieces to bear on e4.

3.Bf4 Nxe4

4.Nxe4 Qxe4

Black has won a pawn and even threatens checkmate on g2.

5.Bd3 Qd4+

Black is well placed and goes on to win.

In this game, the Queen successfully led the charge, but it's more common to see a Queen dive into enemy territory in an attack against the opponent's King. In fact, in attacks of this kind, it's perfectly normal for the Queen to lead the assault. Here's the strategy:

Queens love to lead attacks against the enemy King, but only if the rest of the army can play a part in the assault.

Diagram 53 shows a position from one of my games, which I'll use as an illustration.

1.d5!

Before penetrating Black's kingside with Qh7, I first open up some lines of attack and free my Bishop on b2.

DIAGRAM 53. White to play.
Seirawan–Korchnoi
Wijk aan Zee, 1980

My Queen can't beat Black by itself, so I insist that other members of my army help it. The pawns that I will give up to accomplish my goal are well worth the price.

1...exd5

2.Qh7

I threaten to capture the pawn on g7.

2...f6

3.Kg1!

I get my King off the dangerous a6-f1 diagonal. Note how I continue the attack only after making sure that my own King is safe!

3...Bxc4

4.Rh4!

I want as many pieces as possible to join in this King hunt.

4...Bxb3   **5.axb3 Kf7**

6.Rg4

I renew my earlier threat against g7.

6...Rg8

7.Re1

My inactive Rook on d1 finds new life on the open e-file.

7...d4

8.Rxd4 Be5

My Queen is torturing the Black King, while Black's Queen is sitting off on the sidelines doing nothing.

9.Rd7 Qxe1+!

Black wants to get rid of my attacking forces.

10.Nxe1 Bxb2

Black has given up his Queen (worth 9 points) for a Rook, Bishop, and pawn (also worth 9 points), so he is not doing badly as far as material is concerned. Unfortunately for Black, his King is still vulnerable, and my Queen proves to be a very speedy piece. Now I should play **11.Qc2! 11...Be5 12.Qc4+ Kf8 13.Qe6 Re8 14.Nf3 Bb8 15.Nh4** (every piece must take part!), when the threats of Ng6+ and Nf5 end the game quickly. (In the game, my 11th move was something different, but I won anyway.)

My Queen turned out to be an excellent general. It led my whole army on a King hunt and brought back the Black King's head as a trophy. Of course, the difference between a Queen that has decisively penetrated into the enemy position and a Queen that is trapped or out of play can be very small, as the next example shows.

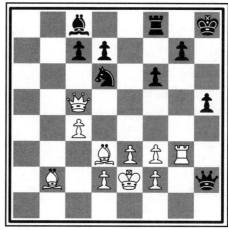

DIAGRAM 54. White to play.
Seirawan–Barbero
Skien, 1979

In Diagram 54, is Black's Queen powerfully posted or out of play? To the untrained eye, Black's Queen may seem to be leading an attack against White's King. But what pieces does it have to help it? None! Such "one-piece attacks" cannot succeed. Now look at White's army. Everything is pointing at Black's kingside. As you'll see if you play through the following game, White has a winning kingside attack. Black's Queen is actually out of play and, as a consequence, will be unable to get back and help defend its King.

1.Rxg7!

This Rook sacrifice draws the Black King into the open and allows the White Queen to join the attack with gain of time.

1...Kxg7

2.Qg5+

White's move is made possible by the pin on the a1-h8 diagonal.

2...Kf7

No better is 2...Kh8, which leads to 3.Qh6+ Kg8 4.Qh7 checkmate.

3.Qxf6+ Ke8   4.Bg6+ Nf7

5.Be5

A nice touch. I gain a critcal tempo by attacking the silly Queen on h2, and Black gives up because 5...Qh3 6.Bxc7 leads to unstoppable checkmate on d8. A true team effort!

PROBLEM 11. This position came about after 1.e4 c5 2.Nf3 d6 3.d4 cxd4 4.Qxd4!?. It's Black's turn to play. Is bringing out the White Queen so early a good move?

Superior Minor Pieces

O ne of the most intense and interesting strategic battles in chess is that which occurs between a Bishop and a Knight. These two pieces are always trying to humiliate each other, and you need to show a lot of ingenuity to prove that your particular piece is boss.

Though many books show some preference for Bishops—a few even say that a Bishop is worth 3½ points compared with 3 for a Knight—in terms of point count, these two pieces are of equal value. Both pieces command a value of 3 points. But of course, you cannot weigh the value of a piece only in terms of point count, and the situation on the board is what delineates the actual worth of a particular piece.

This is where real strategy comes in: If you want to engage in a Bishop-Knight battle, you must know how to create the kind of conditions that suit the piece that you possess. If you own a Knight, you must play for a closed position. If you own a Bishop, you must open the position up. (See Chapter Four, "Understanding Where the Pieces Go," for more details about why these conditions suit each piece.) Do whatever it takes to make your piece dominate the enemy's!

Bishops over Knights

In Chapter Four, you learned that Knights need support points to be effective. It stands to reason, then, that an effective strategy against a Knight is to take away all of its advanced squares so that the poor Knight will never reach its full potential.

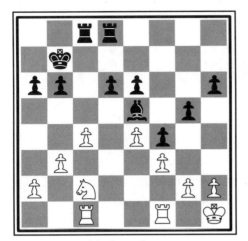

DIAGRAM 55. **Black to play.**

DIAGRAM 56. **White to play.**

In Diagram 55, Black enjoys a clear advantage because his Bishop is situated on the fine h8-a1 diagonal, while the opposing Knight doesn't have access to any advanced squares. This Bishop is therefore superior to the Knight. Compare this position with the one in Diagram 56. White's pieces are all on the same squares as they are in Diagram 55, but I have made two changes in the Black camp: The Black Bishop is now on g7, and the pawn has advanced to e5. These seemingly tiny differences completely reverse the statuses of the Bishop and the Knight! Now the Black Bishop is blocked by its own pawns, and the White Knight has access to the d5-square. White plays **1.Nb4** followed by **2.Nd5**, when his Knight is obviously stronger than the pathetic thing on g7.

So here's the first rule to remember when deciding on Bishop-Knight battle strategies:

A Knight without advanced posts is inferior to an active Bishop. Don't let the enemy Knight find a good square!

And here's the second:

When your Bishop is taking on a Knight, open up the position as much as possible. If your pawns block your Bishop, remove these obstacles and treat that Bishop to some wide-open diagonals!

Let's see how the great Petrosian put
these strategies to work in one of his
games. In Diagram 57, White's dark-
squared Bishop already has a good
diagonal available on the a1-h8 line.
However, his other Bishop is not
doing as well. White knows that he
shouldn't allow it to play dead. He
must find a way to make it a participant in the upcoming battle.

1.g4!

White remembers the excellent
rule: Always attack pawn chains at
their base. He immediately uses his
pawns to blast open the position. By
undermining the f5-pawn, White weakens the Black e4-pawn and simultaneously increases the scope of his Bishop on e2.

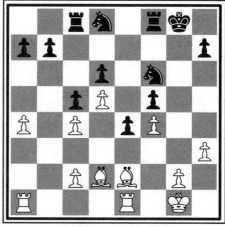

DIAGRAM 57. **White to play.**
Petrosian–Lilienthal
Moscow, 1949

1...fxg4	**2.hxg4 Rc7**	
3.Kf2		

Black threatened ...Rg7, so White gets his King off the dangerous g-file and
brings the handsome monarch a step closer to the center in preparation for
the endgame.

3...h6

4.Rh1

Why not place the Rook on an open file where it attacks a weak pawn?

4...e3+

Black knows that one of his pawns is doomed: White would have surrounded the e-pawn by playing Bc3 and Ke3, and he would have gone after
the h-pawn with Rh4 and Rah1. So Black sells his e-pawn as dearly as
possible: He will force White's Bishop to an inactive square on e3 (away
from the a1-h8 diagonal) and give his Knight a home on e4.

5.Bxe3 Ne4+   6.Kg2 Nf7

7.Bd3

Suddenly, the forgotten Bishop on e2 makes its presence felt. It turns out that the e4-square is not a permanent support point for the Black Knight because Black does not have a pawn that can defend it.

7...Re7

8.Rae1

White prepares to evict the Black Knight from its new home. With the eviction accomplished, the formerly inactive light-squared Bishop will blast a path of fire down the b1-h7 diagonal.

8...Rfe8

Black's pieces may look comfortable, but in reality they are quite unhappy: His Rooks are playing nursemaid to the Knight on e4; the Knight on f7 is serving the same function for the pawn on h6; and, because the White pawn on f4 takes away the e5 and g5 support points, the f7-Knight has no hope of finding an active, advanced square.

9.Bc1 Nc3   10.Rxe7 Rxe7

11.a5 b6   12.axb6 axb6

Black hopes that these exchanges will make his position easier. Unfortunately, he doesn't realize that his Knight is in danger. He has forgotten the important Knights-need-support-points strategy. An advanced Knight without support points is a shaky animal at best.

13.Bd2 Ne2

14.c3!

The poor thing has nowhere to run and will soon be consumed.

14...b5

15.Kf3

And White will win. Notice how contained the Black Knights were throughout this game. While White's Bishops are doing their jobs on d2 and d3, the poor Knight on f7 has no future, and the beast on e2—a piece that dared to try for glory—is not long for the board. Remember:

A Bishop will usually dominate a Knight in an open position. If the position is not open, make every effort to push those pawns out of the way and activate that Bishop!

A Bishop will often beat a Knight in an endgame with passed pawns (or pawn majorities) on both sides of the board because the Bishop's long-range speed allows it to attack enemy pawns from a distance. The position in Diagram 58 shows why a Knight cannot beat a Bishop in situations where the Bishop can use its speed and agility. White threatens to promote his h-pawn to a Queen by h7 and h8. However, though the Black Bishop is far away from the kingside, with **1...Bc2!**, Black can stop White in his tracks. Now it's up to the White Knight to show how it intends to stop the Black passed pawn on a3. As you will soon see, the poor horse is not up to the challenge. White plays **2.Nd1+**, hoping that 2...Bxd1? 3.h7! will allow the White pawn to turn into a Queen after all. But Black responds with **2...Kd2**, and after **3.Nf2 a2**, the game is over. The long-range Bishop did its job, while the short-range Knight could not help White reach his goal.

In Diagram 59, we see Black winning because four small advantages favor his Bishop.

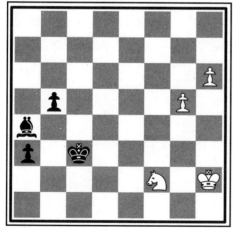

DIAGRAM 58. Black to play.

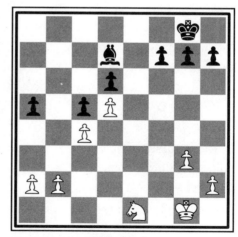

DIAGRAM 59. White to play.
Kalantar–Petrosian
Erevan, 1948

■ White has a majority on the queenside, while Black has a majority on the kingside. Majorities lead to passed pawns, and positions with passed pawns on both sides of the board almost always favor the side with the Bishop.

■ White's queenside pawns are situated on light-colored squares, making these pawns vulnerable to attack by the enemy light-squared Bishop.

■ The position is open, and open positions usually favor Bishops.

■ Black's kingside pawns will take away any potential support points from the Knight, while the White queenside pawns cannot restrict the activity of the enemy Bishop.

Here's how Black takes advantage of this favorable position:

1.Kf2

White correctly brings his King toward the center. Never forget to activate your King in an endgame!

1...f5!

At first glance, Black's move seems illogical because it blocks his Bishop. However, this move fits the needs of the position very well. By pushing his pawn, Black begins to make use of his kingside pawn majority and prepares for the creation of a passed pawn. He will follow up with ...g5, after which the d4, e4, f4, and g4 squares will all be unavailable to the White Knight. If you can, always take away squares from the enemy Knight.

2.Ke3 Kf7

3.Nd3 Bc8

Black intends to attack the c4-pawn and force another White pawn onto a vulnerable light-colored square.

4.b3 g5

Now the White horse can't leap over to f4.

5.Kf3 Kf6

6.Ke3

White cannot do anything active, so he just waits patiently and hopes that Black will not be able to do anything active either.

6...Bd7

The Bishop prepares to swing across the kingside to a point from which it can penetrate into the enemy position.

7.Kf3 Be8	**8.Ke3 h6**
9.Kf3 Bh5+	**10.Ke3 Bd1**
11.Kd2 Bf3	**12.Ke3 Be4**

It's obvious that the Bishop is superior to the Knight.

13.Kd2 Bxd3!

So why does Black trade a superior piece for an inferior one? Because Black's more mobile majority and his more advanced King mean that the resulting King and pawn endgame is winning for Black.

14.Kxd3 Ke5	**15.Ke3 f4+**

16.gxf4+ gxf4+

Black is the first to create a passed pawn.

17.Kf3 Kf5

18.Kf2 Ke4

The Black King's position is now so superior to the White King's that the win becomes easy. Never allow the enemy King to advance this far up the board in an endgame.

19.Ke2 f3+	**20.Kf2 Kf4**
21.h4 h5	**22.a3 Ke4**

White has had enough and resigns because plays like 23.b4 axb4 24.axb4 cxb4 25.c5 Kxd5 or 23.Kf1 Ke3 (23...Kd3 also wins) 24.Ke1 f2+ 25.Kf1 Kf3 26.b4 axb4 27.axb4 cxb4 28.c5 b3 are quite hopeless.

PROBLEM 12. This position is fairly even except that one side owns a Bishop and the other owns a Knight. It's Black's turn to play, and he wants to move his d-pawn. Should he move it to d6 or d5?

The Dominating Knight

As I said in Chapter Four, a Knight can easily beat a Bishop if you can close the position or plant your horse on an advanced support point. How strong is a Knight that is firmly planted on the 5th rank? Let's take a look at Diagram 60 and find out. You can see that I am winning this position against the World Champion because my Knight completely blocks his pawns on c3 and c2, covers several squares deep in the White camp (a3, b2, d2, and e3), and only gives the White King one square (e2) to run to.

How does his Bishop compare with my Knight? It serves a defensive func-

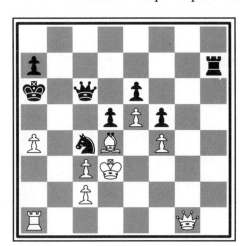

DIAGRAM 60. Black to play.
Karpov–Seirawan
Mar del Plata, 1982

tion on d4 (guarding the c3-pawn) but is blocked by the pawns on c3 and e5. It does have some activity on the g1-a7 diagonal, but nowhere near as much as my accomplished Knight. When you take his endangered King and inferior minor piece into account and then note that his pawns are weak and his Rook is less active than mine, you must agree that I ought to be able to somehow push White over the cliff. Indeed, had I played **1...Qe8!**, which threatens the crushing 2...Rh3+ 3.Ke2 Qh5+, I would have surely been victorious.

Unfortunately, I failed to take this opportunity and ultimately allowed White to escape with a draw. However, my lack of follow through should not detract from your appreciation of the power of my Knight, which is eating White's position alive. A wonderful horse like this will almost always be stronger than any Bishop, and your strategic sense should be alert to any opportunities to create such a beast. Remember:

The prospect of gaining a fine support point for your Knight should excite you. When it can work from a secure base, your horse becomes an extremely powerful piece.

So you have seen that a good support point will make your Knight better than most enemy Bishops. How do closed positions help you? If you don't have any support points in a closed position, your Knight may not be a world beater. However, even an average Knight can beat a hemmed-in Bishop. In closed positions, the locked pawns get in the way of the Bishops and often make them absolutely useless.

Seirawan–Vukic
Nis, 1979

Allow me to demonstrate this closed-position strategy with another of my own games. We'll follow this one through from start to finish.

1.c4 Nf6	2.Nc3 g6
3.g3 Bg7	4.Bg2 0-0
5.e4 c5	6.Nge2

I have chosen the setup known as the *Botvinnik Formation*. I grab firm control of d5, create a space advantage in the center, and dream of pawn advances like b2-b4 (with queenside play) and f2-f4 (with a kingside attack). The price I pay for all these wonderful potential moves is the hole on d4, but I feel that this square can be defended (by the Knight on e2 and the Bishop on e3), and besides, I have always enjoyed playing the White side of this position.

6...Nc6

7.a3 a5

87

This advance, which weakens the b5 square, is unnecessary because I am not threatening to immediately play b2-b4.

8.0-0 d6

9.d3 Ne8

At first glance, this Knight retreat may look strange, but there is actually a lot of logic behind it. Black opens up the a1-h8 diagonal for his Bishop and prepares to swing his Knight over to d4 via c7 and e6. (You didn't think Black was going to leave this Knight on the 1st rank, did you?)

10.Be3 Nd4

11.Bxd4! cxd4

Normally, I would not be in a hurry to give up my fine dark-squared Bishop for a Knight. However, I saw that the resulting position would favor Knights. I can stick one Knight in the hole on b5, while the once-powerful Black Bishop on g7 is now blocked by its own pawn on d4.

12.Nb5 Qb6

13.a4!

As Diagram 61 shows, this move kills Black's chances on the queenside, and if the White Knight on b5 is ever taken, I can play axb5 to give myself a

superior structure (an open a-file for my Rook and more queenside space). Now only I can initiate play on the queenside (via b2-b4). Because the center is closed (meaning that nobody can play there), the kingside is the only area worth fighting over. I must hasten to gain space there and make that side of the board mine.

13...Nc7

14.f4 Na6

Black brings his Knight within sight of the nice support point on c5.

15.h3 e5

DIAGRAM 61.

Black's move gives the d4-pawn support.

16.f5

I now enjoy so much extra space on the kingside that I play for a direct attack against the enemy King.

16...Bh6

This Bishop was dead on g7, so it steps outside the pawn chain and gives itself some scope on the h6-c1 diagonal.

17.h4 Bd7   18.Kh2 Nc5

19.Bh3!

My Bishop on g2 was bad, so I move it to h3 and accomplish two goals: I get it outside the pawn chain and give it a new lease on life on the h3-c8 diagonal; and after I play f5-f6 or fxg6, I will trade light-squared Bishops, swapping my bad Bishop for Black's good one. The exchange leaves Black with just one Bishop—a bad one. The strategy here is to deprive Black of control of both colored squares:

> *If you envision battling your enemy with your Knights, don't allow him*
> *to own two Bishops because they control both colored squares.*

19...g5?

A poor move that weakens the Black King and allows me to play a winning combination. However, Black's choices are limited at this point. The superior 19...f6 would have allowed me to show the superiority of my Knight over his Bishop because after 20.fxg6 hxg6 21.Bxd7 Nxd7 22.h5! gxh5 23.Ng1, Black's Kingside is weak and his light squares are riddled with holes. I could then capture a pawn on h5 (with Qxh5) and then either plug in the hole on f5 with my Rook or bring my Knight there via Nf3, Nh4, and Nf5. My Knights on f5 and b5 would then both be far superior to the enemy Bishop on h6.

20.Nexd4!

This Knight sacrifice allows me to clear the d1-h5 diagonal with no loss of time and bring my Queen to h5 with crushing effect.

20...exd4

21.Qh5 f6

If Black tries to hold on to his Bishop with 21...Bg7, I would destroy him with 22.f6 Bh8 23.Qxg5+, and checkmate follows in one more move.

22.Qxh6 Bxb5

23.axb5 g4

The picture has changed, and I am now the one with the inferior minor piece—Black's nice Knight on c5 is clearly superior to my very bad Bishop on h3. The position is nevertheless good for me because Black's kingside is crumbling. Though the subtle advantages now lie with Black, chess is ultimately about checkmate, and that is what I am playing for! With 23...g4, Black prevents me from exposing his King to more danger with hxg5. He is hoping for 24.Bxg4 Nxd3, after which he will not only have a newly created passed pawn on d4, but his Knight will be able to sink itself into e5 and always be better than my Bishop. I decide to avoid all these positional considerations and go directly for his throat!

24.Rf4!

Does this piece sacrifice demonstrate my bravery? Not at all! I have no choice: If I don't take his King down, my inferior minor piece will cost me the game.

24...gxh3	**25.Rg4+ Kf7**
26.Rg7+ Ke8	**27.Qxh7 Kd8**
28.b4!	

Very strong. Black can't respond with ...axb4 because of the pin on the a-file, but he can't move his Knight (28...Nxd3, for example) because then 29.Rxb7 threatens both his Queen and Qd7 checkmate.

28...Kc8	**29.bxc5 dxc5**
30.h5	

Black gives up when he sees that 30...a4 31.h6 a3 32.Ra2 leaves him with no useful moves and that the subsequent Rg8 turns my h-pawn into a Queen.

Color Control

One of my favorite things about a Knight is that it can jump to any color. Though anything placed on the opposite color of a Bishop is safe from its influence, nothing is safe from the Knight because it can control complexes of different colors at will. The next example illustrates this point nicely.

In Diagram 62, White's Bishop is on an active post, but because all of Black's pawns rest on or can easily move to dark squares, the Bishop is not a major threat. Can the same be said of the Black Knight? Of course not! It can attack anything on the board, and it can also defend any square. Right now, it is keeping the White King at bay by guarding the c4-square.

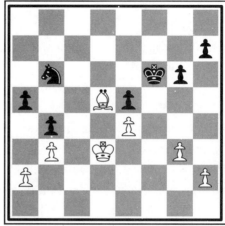

DIAGRAM 62. White to play.
Damjanović–Fischer
Buenos Aires, 1970

Black's first order of business is to bring his King over to c5 so that it can keep a cap on c4. The Knight will then be free to move, and the Black King will constantly be threatening to jump into d4. Because the White Bishop cannot touch anything and because the White King cannot penetrate the Black position, White is unable to create any threats of his own. Black can therefore take all the time he wants to implement his plans.

1.Bc6 Ke7

Black's King takes the first step in the journey to c5.

2.h4 h6

Another pawn finds rest on a safe dark square.

3.Ke3 Nc8

4.Kd3 Nd6

Black secures a more flexible square for the Knight. It still defends c4, but it also eyes e4 and threatens to eventually move to b5 and c3, where it will attack the White pawn on a2.

5.Ke3 Kd8

6.Kd3

Knowing that his opponent can't do anything but go back and forth is a great luxury for Black.

6...Kc7   **7.Ba4 Kb6**

8.Ke3 Kc5

Mission accomplished. The Black King seizes c5.

9.Bd7 Kb6

Black is worried that White will somehow be able to penetrate the Black position via g4, so he decides to go back to the kingside, kill all the play there, and then return to c5. Why shouldn't he take his time? What can White do to punish him?

10.Ba4 Kc7   **11.Kd3 Kd8**

12.Bc6 Ke7   **13.Ke3 Ke6**

14.Kf3 Kf6   **15.g4 g5**

16.h5 Ke7

Now White can no longer penetrate on the kingside, so Black heads back to c5.

17.Ke3 Kd8   **18.Kd3 Kc7**

19.Ba4 Kb6   **20.Bd7 Kc5**

With the King where he wants it, Black can turn his attention to his other pieces.

21.Ba4 Nc8   **22.Be8 Ne7**

23.Ke3 Ng8   **24.Bd7 Nf6**

The Knight attacks both e4 and g4 from f6. Black has all the time in the world, so why not place all his pieces on their best possible squares?

25.Bf5

Notice that the White Bishop is like a ghost. It can't attack any of the Black pieces because they all reside on dark squares.

25...Kb5

26.Kd3 a4

Black threatens to push this pawn to a3, after which White's a2-pawn will be stuck, and a Knight maneuver to c3 will win that pawn and the game.

27.bxa4+

White stops the threat of ...a4-a3, but allows the Black King to get deep into the White position.

27...Kxa4	**28.Kc4 Ka3**
29.Kc5 Kxa2	**30.Kxb4 Kb2**
31.Kc5 Kc3	**32.Kd6 Kd4**
33.Ke6 Nxe4	

The White pawns start to fall, and the end is in sight.

34.Kf7 Nf2	**35.Kg6 e4**
36.Kxh6 e3	**37.Kg7 e2**
38.h6 e1=Q	**39.h7 Qe7+**
40.Kg8 Ne4	

White gives up because 41.h8=Q+ Nf6+ results in the capture of the newly born Queen, while 41.Bxe4 Kxe4 42.h8=Q Qe8+ 43.Kg7 Qxh8+ 44.Kxh8 Kf4 also leads to an easy win for Black. The guiding principle behind Black's relentless attack is:

When your opponent is help-less, take your time and tor-ture him!

You have seen that it is very important always to be on the lookout for ways to make a minor piece superior to its enemy counterpart. In the next example, Black has a chance to saddle White with a very bad Bishop. With the position shown in Diagram 63, Black should initiate a series of trades that leave him with strong Knights vs. bad Bishops.

DIAGRAM 63. **Black to play.**
Botvinnik–Bronstein
World Championship Match, 1951

1...Bxe2 **2.Rxe2 Bxc3**
3.Bxb6

Playing 3.bxc3 Nc4 would leave Black with a powerful horse on c4.

3...axb6

4.bxc3 g5!

With this move, Black fixes the enemy pawns on light squares, where they get in the way of their own Bishop. Black would then follow up with ...Nd7, when his Knight (which can always go to c5 or even make its way to f4) would be much stronger than the sad thing on g2. Unfortunately, Black played this position differently and missed this chance.

Seirawan–Short
London, 1982

I finish this chapter with a game in which I first give my opponent my two Bishops. Then I trade off his light-squared Bishop, leaving him weak on the light squares because his remaining dark-squared Bishop cannot influence that color. Finally, I turn my Knight into a rampaging monster that is far stronger than any mere Bishop.

1.d4 Nf6 **2.c4 e6**
3.Bg5 h6 **4.Bxf6 Qxf6**

Black now has two Bishops to my one, so I play to make the position healthy for Knights.

5.Nc3 b6 **6.Nf3 Bb7**
7.e3 g6 **8.Bd3 Bg7**
9.Be4!

I want to get rid of his light-squared Bishop, even if it means sacrificing my own, so that he can no longer control both colored squares with Bishops.

9...Bxe4 **10.Nxe4 Qe7**
11.Qa4 0-0 **12.0-0 d6**
13.Rad1 Nd7 **14.Qc6!**

The trade of Black's queenside Bishop has left him weak on the light squares.

14...Rfc8

15.Ne1

I know. . . Knights don't belong on the 1st rank. But this horse is just on its way to greener pastures; it's heading for c6 via d3 (or c2) and b4.

15...Nf6	**16.Nxf6+ Bxf6**
17.Nc2 Qe8	**18.Nb4! Qxc6**
19.Nxc6	

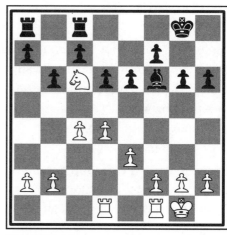

DIAGRAM 64.

Diagram 64 shows that my mighty Knight is paralyzing the Black position, while the enemy Bishop is doing nothing at all.

19...Kf8

20.b4

The b-pawn rushes to give the Knight some support and also gets off the a1-h8 diagonal in case I choose to advance my d-pawn to d5.

20...Ke8	**21.Rd3! Kd7**
22.d5 Bg7	**23.e4 a6**
24.a4	

Black's Bishop controls an open diagonal, but there is nothing on that diagonal to attack!

24...Re8	**25.Rf3! f5**
26.g4	

I am trying to blast open the f-file. Black can't capture either my e- or g-pawn because of the piece-winning Rf7+.

26...Rf8

Playing 26...exd5 27.exd5 is even worse because it leads to ...Re4 28.gxf5 g5 29.Re3!, which wins a pawn.

95

27.gxf5 gxf5

28.exf5 e5?

Better was the obvious 28...exf5, though 29.Re1 would not have given Black any joy. I would then have a far superior position because I would own the e-file, my minor piece would be wonderful, and the Black pawns on f5 and h6 would be weak.

29.Rg3 Bf6   30.f4! exf4

31.Rxf4 Rae8   32.h4!

I want to keep the Bishop out of g5.

32...Re1+   33.Kg2 Ra1

34.Rg6 Ra2+   35.Kh3 h5

36.Re4

I threaten checkmate by 37.Rxf6 and 38.Re7+, utilizing my Knight.

36...Ra3+   37.Kg2 Ra2+

38.Kh3 Ra3+   39.Kg2 Ra2+

40.Kg3 Ra3+   41.Kf2 Bd8

42.Rf4

Now I threaten to push my passed f-pawn to f6.

42...Bf6   43.Re4 Bd8

44.Ke2

Black didn't allow me to push my pawn, so I will have to try another idea.

44...Ra2+   45.Ke3 Rxa4

46.Na7!

By taking the c8-square away from the Black King, I increase the threat of Rg7+ to enormous proportions.

46...Ra3+   47.Ke2 Ra2

48.Kd1 Ra1+   49.Kc2 Bf6

Black is desperately trying to keep me out of g7.

50.Re6 Bh8

51.Rh6

I'm heading for h7. Black can't stop my Rook with 51...Rf7 because that would hang his Bishop.

51...Ra2+   52.Kb3 Rb2+

53.Ka3

Finally, I put a stop to the series of annoying checks.

53...Rg2

Black intends to answer 54.Rh7+ with 54...Rg7. I stop this defense and renew my threat.

54.f6 Rfg8

55.Rh7+

And Black resigns because 55...Kd8 56.Nc6+ Kc8, so 57.Ne7 forks Nc6, which ends in White's King and Rook winning.

PROBLEM 13. It's Black's turn to play. Is 1...Nxc2 a reasonable move?

Sefc–Petrosian
Vienna, 1957

How to Use Pawns

I n 1749, André Philidor announced that pawns were the "soul of chess." Nobody really understood what he was talking about at the time, but 160 years later, Emanuel Lasker explained Philidor's comment this way:

> The pawn, being much more stationary than the pieces, is an element of the structure; the way the array of pawns is placed determines the character of a position and hence also the plan appropriate to it.

Lasker was pointing out something that every master is now well aware of: that the placement of the pawns is one of the most important factors to take into consideration when choosing a strategy. Philidor called pawns the soul of chess because their state determines the plan you will follow. In this chapter, we examine the different types of pawn structures and the strategies that are typically followed because of them.

Using Pawns as Blocking and Restricting Agents

Pawns cannot swoop down the board in a single bound. In fact, they are actually rather ponderous creatures. What they can do, however, is block other pawns and keep the enemy pieces off certain key squares. Diagram 65 shows an example. White is two pawns ahead and threatens to gain more space by playing f4-f5 (which also opens a diagonal for his bad Bishop) or d4-d5 (which turns the blocked c-pawn into a passer).

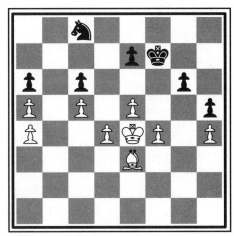

DIAGRAM 65. Black to play.

Black can put an end to White's evil intentions, though, with 1...e6!. This move uses the e-pawn as a blocking unit that immobilizes both the White d- and f-pawns. After 1...e6, Black will play 2...Ne7 and place his Knight on either d5 or f5. Black's beautiful Knight (once it reaches either of these posts) and the fixed nature of the White pawns combine to eradicate any chance White has of winning this game. Black made good use of this strategy:

Whenever you can, use your pawns to fix your opponent's pawns.

Now let's look at Diagram 66. The position is the same as the previous one, with three significant differences: I have moved the White c-pawn back one square from c5 to c4; I have moved the White pawn on h4 back one square to h3; and I have taken the White pawn on a5 and placed it on g3. Now White will win the game because this pawn position ensures that he will be able to play either d4-d5 or f4-f5 at will.

1...e6	2.g4 hxg4
3.hxg4 Ne7	

Black tries to stop White from advancing his pawns.

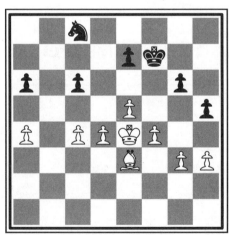

DIAGRAM 66. Black to play.

4.Bf2!

Now with Bh4, White will get his Bishop outside the pawn chain.

4...Ke8

Note how White's pawns on c4 and g4 keep the Knight out of the d5- and f5-squares.

5.Bh4

White threatens to engineer a winning pawn endgame with 6.Bxe7.

5...Ng8

If Black plays 5...Nc8, then White would play 6.a5! to keep the Black Knight out of the b6-square. This is a nice example of using a pawn to restrict the activity of an enemy piece.

6.Bg5!

White dominates the poor Knight. Now it can't go to h6 or f6, and it will be traded if it dares step onto e7.

6...Kd7	**7.f5 gxf5+**
8.gxf5 exf5+	**9.Kxf5 Ke8**
10.d5	

At this point, Black should quietly give up. White has admirably followed this strategy:

Use your pawns to take away squares from the enemy pieces.

Examples from a couple of my own games will further demonstrate this blocking and restricting strategy. In Diagram 67, my opponent's Bishop and e2-Knight are blocked by the pawns on d4 and f4. Naturally, he would like to correct this problem by advancing his f-pawn from f4 to f5. Why should I let him do this? My first move stops his f-pawn in its tracks.

1...g6!

I must admit that this type of move can be dangerous. It does nothing to promote my development, and it weakens the dark squares on the kingside. However, I can disregard both drawbacks because the center is closed, which means that my opponent's pieces can't get to my King, and his Bishop can't jump over his f-pawn to take advantage of the weaknesses I just created.

2.b3 Na6

I don't want him to free his pieces with d4-d5, so I bring my Knight to c7, where it helps control the important d5-square.

DIAGRAM 67. Black to play.
Van der Wiel–Seirawan
Baden, 1980

3.Bb2

White threatens to take advantage of my weakness on the a1-h8 diagonal with 4.d5!, uncovering an attack on my f6-Knight and pinning it to the h8-Rook.

    3...Be7

I defend my f6-Knight. Now I can chop off the White pawn if it dares to advance to d5.

    4.c4 Nc7

    5.Qf3 0-0

White's advances on d5 and f5 have been stopped, so I can now take the time to castle, which I would normally do much earlier.

    6.Nc1 Nce8!

This Knight is heading for g7, where it defends my King and stops f4-f5 once and for all.

    7.Nd3 Ng7   **8.Ne5 Qc7**

    9.h3 Rad8

My well-intentioned move, which puts another defender on d5 and also targets his d-pawn, is slightly inaccurate. The immediate 9...h5! was correct.

    10.Rad1?

White mistakenly gives up on the fight for f5. He should have played 10.Ne2 followed by g4, which keeps my Knights out of both f5 and h5.

    10...h5!

    11.Ne2 h4!

Suddenly, my wishes come true! If my opponent ever plays g2-g4, I will snap off his pawn with ...hxg3, thereby compromising his pawn structure. Now the f5 and h5 squares fall under my complete control because White's g-pawn has been neutralized.

    12.Ng4 Nfh5!   **13.Qc3 Kh7**

    14.Rf3 Nf5   **15.Ne3 Bf6**

The White pawns on d4 and f4 were never allowed to move, and now they turn out to be targets. My pieces on d8, f5, h5, and f6 are all aiming at them!

    16.Ng4 Bh8

    17.Ne5?

This questionable move allows a pretty little combination based on the pin along the d1-d8 file.

17...Nxf4!   **18.Rxf4 Bxe5**

19.Re4 Bf6

White can't play 19.dxe5 because of the unprotected state of the Rook on d1.

20.Rf1 c5!

21.Qd3 cxd4

After I use the pin along the a1-h8 diagonal to pick up his other pawn as well, White resigns. My strategy of restraining his pawns on d4 and f4 proved to be a resounding success!

In the next example, shown in Diagram 68, White has a significant lead in development and will try to defeat me on the kingside with f4, g4, and eventually f5. Because my protected passed pawn is useless at the moment (White will block it by playing Nd3), I must accept that I have no active counterplay opportunities and do something to stop my opponent's plans.

1...h5!

By preventing g2-g4, I stop his kingside pawn-storm and create a useful home on f5 for my Knight. It is very important to get used to this type of restrictive pawn device. Even though I am behind in development, I can live with my pawn move because the center is closed and his pieces can't get to my King. However, if the center were open, I would want to get my King castled fast!

2.Nd3 Nf5

By using my h-pawn to restrict his g-pawn, I have provided the perfect niche on f5 for my Knight.

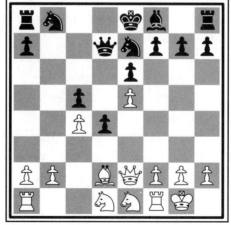

DIAGRAM 68. Black to play.
Timman–Seirawan
Lone Pine, 1978

3.f4?

A poor move that restricts his own pieces! Now the Bishop on d2 and the Knight on d3 are both blocked by the f4-pawn.

3...Qb7	**4.N1f2 Nd7**
5.Qe4 Qxe4	**6.Nxe4 a5!**

I love to use my pawns to shatter my opponent's possibilities. Now b2-b4 is prevented, and if White tries to prepare for b2-b4 with 7.a2-a3, I will play 7...a5-a4! to restrict him further.

7.g3 Be7

8.Kf2 Nh6

I can see that White intends to control the f5-square with h3 and g4, so I will move my pawn to f5 and stop that plan, too!

9.h3 f5	**10.exf6 gxf6**
11.Rae1 Kf7	**12.Ke2 Rhg8!**

Having stopped his g-pawn from advancing, I train my big guns on it and begin to treat it as a weakness.

13.Kd1 Nf5

14.Rg1 Nb6!

Now I take aim at his queenside pawns, too. I won the game after the following skirmish:

15.b3 a4	**16.Ndxc5 axb3**
17.axb3 Nxg3!	**18.Rxg3 Rxg3**
19.Nxg3 Bxc5	**20.f5? exf5**
21.Nxf5 d3	**22.Bc3 Ra3**
23.Kd2 Rxb3	**24.Ra1 Bb4**
25.Ra7+ Kg6	**26.Ne7+ Kg5**
27.Bxb4 Nxc4+	**28.Ke1 Rxb4**
29.Rd7 Rb1+	**30.Kf2 Rb2+**
31.Kg1 d2, 0-1.	

Victory was mine because I used my pawns to fix my enemy's pawns on certain squares, turning them into stationary targets. We all know that it is much easier to hit something that cannot run away!

PROBLEM 14. It's Black's turn to play. He enjoys a superior King and a good Bishop versus White's poor piece on f1. What would you do if you had the Black position?

Advancing Pawns

Pawns love to advance. Sometimes they will happily jump upon the enemy's swords, sacrificing themselves so that other pieces can live better lives. Advancing pawns can push other pawns aside, opening files and diagonals and making previously inactive pieces something to be feared. At other times, they will become runners and try to turn into Queens. In this section, we'll look at examples of strategies involving advancing pawns.

Using Pawns as Sacrificial Lambs

In Diagram 69, White's pawn on d4 appears to be blocking the whole White army. The Bishop on b2 and Queen on a1 are ramming their heads into this pawn; the Rooks are deprived of an open file by its presence; and the Knight on f3 cannot go to d4 because the pawn is already on that square. A good move is 1.Ne3, which prepares to bring the Knight to g4 and also prepares for a d4-d5 advance. However, why not sacrifice the d-pawn? Isn't such a sacrifice worth activating all those pieces?

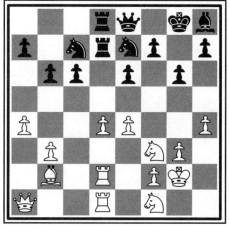

DIAGRAM 69. White to play.

1.d5!

White threatens to capture the Bishop on h8.

1...Bxb2

2.Qxb2

Now the rude d-pawn threatens to advance to d6 and fork the poor Black Knights. Black has no choice; he must take the gift.

2...cxd5

Suddenly, the White pieces are extremely active, and the Black army is held back by its own pawn on d5.

3.Ne5

White brings the Knight into the attack with gain of tempo.

3...Rd6

White threatened to win the Exchange with 4.Nxd7, so Black moves his Rook to safety.

4.Ng4!

Now it's very clear that the weakened dark squares around Black's King will lead to his demise. Threats like 5.Nh6+ Kg8 6.Qh8 check and 5.Nf6+,

DIAGRAM 70. White to play.
Portisch–Pachman
Moscow, 1967

which forks the King and Queen, are unstoppable.

4...e5

Black tries in vain to block the a1-h8 diagonal.

5.Qxe5

And White wins because Black cannot counter the threats mentioned earlier.

In Diagram 70, we see the same ideas as those expressed in the previous example, but not quite so pronounced. The White Bishop on b2 is blocked by its own pawn on d4, while the Bishop on f3 is hitting an unyielding target on c6. By sacrificing his d-pawn, White can blast open files and diagonals and give all his pieces a new lease on life.

1.d5! exd5

2.Bxg7

White, who possesses the two Bishops, would not normally want to allow this kind of exchange. In this instance, however, White sees that the trade of this minor piece will weaken the Black King.

2...Kxg7	**3.cxd5 cxd5**
4.Rdxd5 Qc3	**5.Kg2 b6**
6.Rhf5	

Because of the initial pawn sacrifice, White's pieces are obviously more active than their Black counterparts, and his King is clearly safer than the Black monarch. With 6.Rhf5, White prepares to initiate an attack on the weakened pawns on f7 and h7.

6...Ng6	**7.Rxd7 Rxd7**
8.Bd5	

The Bishop demonstrates its potential for activity and joins in the fight against f7.

8...Re7	**9.Qg4 f6**
10.Rh5	

Though the Bishop's activity has been enhanced, the f7-pawn is no longer weak. So White turns his attention to the target on h7.

10...Qc7	**11.Be4 Qd7**
12.Rxh7+!	

This obvious but pleasing sacrifice crashes through Black's defenses.

12...Kxh7	**13.Qxg6+ Kh8**
14.Qxf6+	

Having captured two pawns and a Bishop and given up a Rook, White does not have a material advantage. It's the attack against the Black King that gives White a winning advantage.

14...Kg8

If Black plays 14...Rg7??, he will face checkmate after 15.Qf8+ Rg8 16.Qh6+.

15.Qg5+ Kf8

16.Bd5

Black resigns because checkmate is threatened on g8, and 16...Rg7 loses the Queen to 17.Qf6+ Ke8 18.Bc6.

We've seen that pawns can run ahead of the pieces and sacrifice themselves to create roads into the enemy camp. Another reason for the marauding pawn to advance to its own death is to vacate a square that would be more suitable for one of its own pieces. For example, in Diagram 71, the Black Knights appear to be playing a purely defensive role. Refusing to accept this fate, Black sacrifices a pawn to create a fine home on the 4th rank for his horses. They can then play a part in the construction of an attack against the White King.

1...f4!

2.gxf4 g4!

Black didn't like 2...gxf4+ because after 3.Kh1, the threat is 4.Rg1.

3.Bg2 Nhf5

DIAGRAM 71. Black to play.
te Kolste–Nimzovich
Baden-Baden, 1925

So Black has lost a pawn, but he has gained a wonderful Knight on f5 and active pawns on the h- and g-files.

4.Qb3

White is in no mood to activate the Black Rooks with 4.Qxb7 Rb8 followed by ...Rxb2.

4...dxc4

Black creates a home on d5 for the other Knight.

5.Qxc4+ Kh8   6.Qc3 h5

7.Rad1 h4

Compare Black's mobile pawns with the blocked, useless thing on f4.

8.Rd3 Nd5	9.Qd2 Rg8
10.Bxd5 cxd5	11.Kh1 g3

Black's strong Knight (courtesy of 1...f4, the vacating pawn advance) and active pawns translate into a powerful Black attack. Note how White's inactive pawns on d4 and f4 are blocking his own pieces on d2, d3, e2, and f1. White would have been well advised to try to implement this strategy:

Make your pawns work for you in an active way. Don't allow them to sit around like lumps, blocking your own pieces.

Grooming Pawns for Promotion

It's clear that pawns can aid the rest of your army. However, their ability to promote to a Queen or a lesser piece if they can reach the last rank makes them a mighty force in their own right. When a pawn's promotion is imminent, the very pieces that once snubbed the lowly pawn will desperately try to block its forward progress with their own bodies. (Knights are particularly good at blocking pawns; see Chapter Four.) If the pawn can manage to get through this blockade, however, it may very well find itself on the way to glory.

If you have a passed pawn, your obvious strategy is to actively work for its promotion. Remember:

Don't allow a passed pawn to get blocked. If your opponent does manage to block it, do everything in your power to remove that blockader.

Once your pawn is free to move forward, it will help you make the enemy army bow before your might.

Let's look at some examples. In Diagram 72, Black has managed to block White's passed pawn with his Knight. Unfortunately for Black,

DIAGRAM 72. White to play.

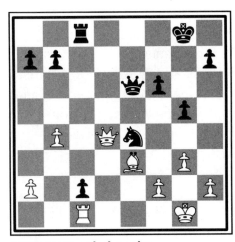

DIAGRAM 73. Black to play.
Korchnoi–Karpov
Moscow, 1971

White can break this blockade with **1.Nb5!**. Black doesn't want to trade Knights because White's c-pawn would queen, so he has to give up the blockade on c7. Then **1...Na8 2.c7 Nb6** (Black is trying to establish a new block on c8) **3.Nd6!** leads to **4.c8=Q Nxc8 5.Nxc8**, and white has won a piece.

In the next example, another passed pawn is driving the opposing forces crazy. In Diagram 73, Black's powerful passed pawn on c2 is dying to turn into a Queen. All Black has to do is break that final block on c1 and push his pawn through the portal of metamorphic change.

1...b6

This simple move restricts the activity of the White Queen and Bishop and also defends against the threat of Qxa7.

2.f3 Nd6

3.Qd3 Rc6!

Black defends the Knight and frees the Queen for active operations. Note that a response of 4.Rxc2?? loses to 4...Rxc2 5.Qxc2 Qxe3+.

4.a4 Qc4

5.Qd2

White decides against the trade and retains the Queens, hoping he can use his Queen to bother the Black King with some checks at a later time.

5...Nf7!

Black's move is both defensive and attacking. On the defensive side, the Knight retreats to a safe place, defends g5 again (preventing any possible Bxg5 sacrifices), and stops any annoying checks on d8. On the attacking side is the potential threat of 6...Ne5, when the duel jumps of 7...Nxf3+ and 7...Nd3 are overwhelming.

6.f4

White keeps the Knight out of e5.

6...g4	**7.b5 Rc8**
8.Qd7 h5	**9.Kf2 Qc3**
10.Qf5 Re8	

White resigns. He has no good way to defend his Bishop, and 11.Qg6+ Kf8 ends the checks, while 11.Re1 Qxe1+ 12.Kxe1 c1=Q+ wins the house.

Diagram 74 shows two opposing pawn majorities. (The concept of majorities is discussed in the next section.) White wants to turn his majority into a powerful passed pawn by playing e5 and d6, so he focuses all his moves on this strategy.

1.Rd1!

White backs up the d-pawn, defends the Queen, and threatens to chop off the Rook on c6.

1...Rc5	**2.e5 e6**
3.d6	

White eventually would have gotten this passed pawn anyway, but Black was hoping to tie White down to the defense of e5.

3...Qd7

This block prevents White from advancing to d7.

4.Qe3 f6	**5.f4 fxe5**
6.fxe5 Rf5	**7.h3 Qa4**
8.Red2! Qd7	

Black cannot allow d6-d7. For example, 8...Rfxe5 9.Qxe5! Rxe5 10.d7 wins immediately.

9.Re1

White has now switched his Rooks around so that both are protected by the Queen. With everything safe,

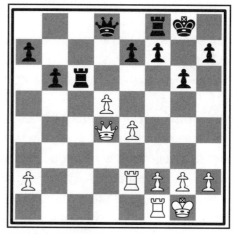

DIAGRAM 74. White to play.
Silman–Grotts
Santa Barbara, 1989

White will trade a pair of Rooks (making it easier to defend the e-pawn) and proceed to break down the blockade on d7.

9...Rf8	10.Rf2 Rxf2
11.Qxf2 Rc8	12.Rf1 Qg7
13.Qf6! Qd7	

Black avoids 13...Qxf6 14.Rxf6 Re8 15.Rxe6! Rxe6 16.d7, which promotes the pawn.

14.h4

Because Black is helpless, White advances his h-pawn and rips open the protective shield of the Black King. Now Black is faced with a horrible choice: checkmate or a Queen trade and a lost Rook endgame.

14...Re8	15.h5 Qg7
16.Qxg7+ Kxg7	17.h6!+

This pawn sacrifice pulls the Black King away from the action and allows the White Rook to penetrate the Black position and ultimately win the e-pawn.

17...Kxh6	18.Rf7 Kg5
19.Re7 Rc8	20.Rxe6 Kf4
21.d7	

Black gives up. Salvation could not be found in either 21...Rc1+ 22.Kh2 Rd1 23.Rd6, or 21...Rd8 22.Re7 Kf5 23.e6 followed by 24.Re8, when the final blockade is shattered and White crowns his new Queen.

Drawbacks to Pawn Advances

We have seen how an advancing pawn can activate pieces and work for its own promotion. However, a pawn's movement up the board can have some negative consequences. The one qualm I have about a pawn advance is that it can easily lead to the weakening of a specific square or a whole complex of squares. I'll show you what I mean.

The rather boring position in Diagram 75 illustrates how pawn advances can create weak squares. White's pawn on c2 controls the b3 and d3 squares. However, it has the potential to control the b4, b5, b6, b7, b8, d4, d5, d6, d7, and d8 squares. That's a lot of potential! Sadly, every time a pawn moves, it loses a bit of that wonderful potential. For example, 1.c3 loses control of d3 and b3, and 1.c4 gives up d3, b3, d4, and b4. It's clear that we pay a heavy price

DIAGRAM 75. White to play.

for every pawn move we make! In the present position, playing **1.c4** is quite good because it blocks Black's c-pawn (which in turn blocks Black's bad Bishop) and gains greater influence over the hole on d5. White does not worry about losing control of d3 or d4 because his other pawn on e2 can control these same squares! White will follow with Nc3 and Nd5, after which his Knight clearly outguns its Black counterpart on f8. Play might continue with **1...Kg7**, and now 2.e4? would be a horrible move because it permanently gives up the d4 square (which Black would make use of by playing ...Ne6-d4). The correct move would be **2.Nc3 Ne6 3.e3!**, when Black's Knight is deprived of that nice central support point.

So while you are seeking out the best strategy to follow from a given position, bear in mind the following:

Aside from running down the board, pawns also keep enemy pieces out of critical squares. Whenever you push a pawn, be sure you are not handing a juicy square to your opponent on a plate!

PROBLEM 15. It's White's turn to play. Is 1.f4 a good move?

PROBLEM 16. Black intends to win White's advanced (but blocked) pawn by ...Ke7, ...f6, ...Kd6-c5, and ...Kxb6. It's White's move. Can he do anything to stop Black?

Working with Pawn Majorities

Possessing a pawn majority means that you have more pawns in a given

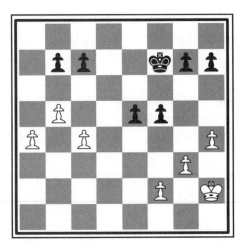

DIAGRAM 76.

area of the board than your opponent does. Pawn majorities are useful in that they usually allow you to create a passed pawn. Many players consider a queenside majority to be stronger than a kingside majority because your opponent's King more often than not castles on his kingside and may be far away from your queenside.

In Diagram 76, we can see two typical pawn majorities. White enjoys a three-to-two majority on the queenside, and Black has a four-to-three majority on the kingside. Whoever has the move obtains the advantage. If White has the first move in this position, he will win with **1.a5** followed by **2.a6** because Black will be unable to stop the pawn from promoting to a Queen. If Black has the first move, he will set up a win by playing **1...b6!**. Black's two pawns will then be stopping White's three, and the immobile, devalued majority becomes nothing more than a target. Play continues with **2.c5** (or 2.Kg2 Ke6 3.Kf3 Kd6 4.Ke3 Kc5 5.Kd3 Kb4, which allows Black to snack on the a-pawn) **2...Ke6!** (and not 2...bxc5?? 3.a5, because then the a-pawn ends up promoting after all) **3.Kg2 Kd5**. Black's King can then eat everything on the queenside.

Of course, you shouldn't place too much emphasis on the value of one majority over another because other factors, such as King position and the quality of the pawns, usually play a part in deciding who will win the game. For example, here is what Alekhine said about the position in Diagram 77: "The ending in this game is noteworthy in the sense that White's celebrated Q-side pawn majority proves to be completely illusory." Regarding this, I must remark that one of the most characteristic prejudices of modern chess theory is the widely held opinion that such a pawn majority is important in itself—without any evaluation of the pawns that constitute this majority, or of the placing of the pieces. In Diagram 77, Black has the following compensation:

1. Great freedom for his King in comparison with the White King.

2. The dominating position of the Rook on the only open file.

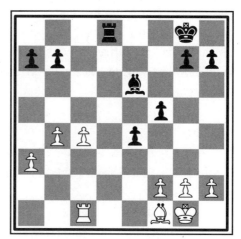

DIAGRAM 77. White to play.
Yates–Alekhine
The Hague, 1921

Used correctly, these two advantages should provide the basis for a win. Let's see how the game was played:

1.g3 Kf7

2.c5 Kf6

Black has a clear advantage because his King will go to e5, where it will eye both sides of the board, and his kingside pawns will roll forward, annexing space and continuing to restrain the White King. In fact, the combined weight of his active Rook, his Bishop, his beautifully centralized King, and his swarming pawns all adds up to a mighty attack against White's King.

3.Bc4 Bc8!

Because Black is playing for an assault against the White King, he correctly reasons that he should keep as many pieces on the board as possible.

4.a4?

The White King should have dashed to e1, from which it can take part in the game.

4...g5

5.b5

White is trying to make use of his majority, but the Black pieces stop his pawns from going anywhere. Don't forget that White is playing a King down—Black has three pieces to use compared with White's two. How can White hope to force his pawns through when he is at such a point-count disadvantage?

5...f4

6.Kf1 Rd2

It's always a good idea to place your Rook on the 7th rank. Here, it traps the White King on the back rank and threatens to go behind the White pawns and attack them.

7.gxf4 gxf4	**8.Ke1 Rb2**
9.Be2 Ke5!	**10.c6 bxc6**
11.Rxc6	

White is trying to get his Rook active. If he plays 11.bxc6, the Bishop on c8 will stop the passed pawn from going anywhere.

11...Be6

12.Bd1 Rb1

Now Black threatens to win a piece with ...Bg4.

13.Rc5+ Kd4

14.Rc2

If Black plays 14...Bg4, White intends to meet it with 15.Rd2+. Black's next move stops this possibility.

14...e3   **15.fxe3+ fxe3**

16.Rc6 Bg4

White's King is pinned to the back rank and surrounded by the Black army. The end is near.

17.Rd6+ Ke5

18.h3 Bh5!

And White resigns. After 19.Rd8 e2, the Black passed pawn will promote no matter what White does.

Pawn Majorities in the Endgame

The fact that a pawn majority often enables you to create a passed pawn proves to be most useful in an endgame. As a result, if you have a healthy majority, you should try to simplify the position so that your majority will have some weight. It does you no good to rave about the wonders of your pawn majority if your opponent can swoop in with his pieces and behead your King! Remember:

The strengths of a pawn majority are best shown in the endgame.

In the following example, Capablanca demonstrates the correct way to use a queenside pawn majority. He trades some pieces, steers the game into a simplified position where kingside attacks and hand-to-hand fighting will simply not take place, and then pushes his pawns for all their worth!

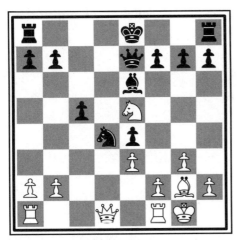

DIAGRAM 78. Black to play.
Marshall–Capablanca
U.S.A., 1909

In Diagram 78, Black possesses a queenside majority, but at the moment this advantage is meaningless because Black's Knight is under attack. If he moves the horse to c6 by 1...Nc6, then 2.Nxc6 bxc6 will turn his once-mighty majority into a weak, doubled mess. A retreat to f5 will also lead to disaster; after 1...Nf5? 2.Qa4+ Bd7 3.Nxd7 Qxd7 4.Qxe4+, the central Black King will feel the heat. Capablanca's answer? His Knight jumps to f3 and forces the exchange of some pieces, which creates a quiet position. Under these less complicated circumstances, Black's queenside majority has a chance to flourish.

1...Nf3+	**2.Nxf3 exf3**
3.Qxf3 0-0	**4.Rfc1?!**

Marshall was a great attacking player, and this series of trades has produced a position that is not to his taste. He understandably did not like 4.Qxb7, which leads to ...Qxb7 5.Bxb7 Rab8 followed by ...Rxb2, but he should have hastened to get his central majority into play by means of 4.e4. White's failure to make use of his own pawn majority allows Black to take control of the game.

4...Rab8	**5.Qe4? Qc7!**
6.Rc3 b5	**7.a3 c4**

It's now clear that Black's queenside pawns are playing an active role in the game while White's central pawns are just sitting around doing nothing.

This difference gives Black a free hand: He doesn't have to deal with the enemy pawns, so he can do whatever he wants.

| 8.Bf3 Rfd8 | 9.Rd1 Rxd1+ |
| 10.Bxd1 Rd8 | 11.Bf3 g6 |

Black takes a moment out to give his King a little breathing room. With no Back Rank Mates to worry about, he can go for the kill without worrying about his own King.

12.Qc6 Qe5	13.Qe4 Qxe4
14.Bxe4 Rd1+!	15.Kg2 a5
16.Rc2 b4	

Everything Black does is designed to make use of the power of his pawn majority.

| 17.axb4 axb4 | 18.Bf3 Rb1 |
| 19.Be2 b3 | 20.Rd2 |

White is trying to hold onto b2. He would lose immediately after 20.Rc3 Rxb2 21.Bxc4 Rc2! 22.Rxc2 bxc2, when the pawn promotes to a Queen.

20...Rc1!

Black threatens to win with 21...Rc2.

| 21.Bd1 c3 | 22.bxc3 b2 |
| 23.Rxb2 Rxd1 | |

Black wins a piece because 23.Bc2 Rxc2 is even worse for White. Black's majority is gone, but he can now lay claim to a material advantage, and he goes on to win in a slow but sure manner. Here are the remaining moves for those who wish to see the great Capablanca's technique:

24.Rc2 Bf5	25.Rb2 Rc1
26.Rb3 Be4+	27.Kh3 Rc2
28.f4 h5	29.g4 hxg4+
30.Kxg4 Rxh2	31.Rb4 f5+
32.Kg3 Re2	33.Rc4 Rxe3+
34.Kh4 Kg7	35.Rc7+ Kf6
36.Rd7 Bg2	37.Rd6+ Kg7

And Black resigns.

Working with Pawn Islands

An isolated group of pawns (or a lone isolated pawn) is known as a *pawn island*. In general, the more pawn islands you have, the weaker your pawns as a whole become. Why? To find an answer, we must look at the old but useful rule:

Always attack a pawn chain at its base.

The base of a pawn chain (a line of connected pawns) is the only place that is not protected by a pawn, making it vulnerable to attack by enemy pieces. So the more pawn islands you have, the more points of attack your opponent has.

I'll illustrate this point with an example. After the well-known opening moves **1.e4 e6 2.d4 d5 3.e5 c5 4.c3 Nc6 5.Nf3**, suppose Black decides to trade by playing **5...cxd4**. (It's a bit early to make this capture because this move frees the c3-square for the White Knight. However, it makes the illustration easier to understand.) White responds with **6.cxd4**, and the position is now as shown in Diagram 79.

Obviously, the e5-pawn is a hard nut to crack. It is well defended by the Knight on f3 and, more impor-

DIAGRAM 79.

tantly, by the pawn on d4. However, the pawns on d4 and e5 are a pawn chain, and Black knows he should always attack a pawn chain at its base. So the pawn on d4 is the one to go after because it is not supported by another pawn. Black should train all his pieces on the d4-pawn and force White to take a defensive stance.

6...Qb6

Now Black has two pieces aiming at d4.

7.Be2 Nge7

8.Na3 Nf5

The Black army is working together rather nicely toward its single-minded goal of attacking the base pawn on d4. Black may not win this pawn, but he is forcing White's pieces to take up passive positions in order to keep it on the board.

How does this example relate to the subject of pawn islands? The more pawn islands you have, the more bases you will have to defend, so the first pawn-island strategy is:

Avoid creating pawn islands, because lots of pawn islands translates to lots of vulnerable pawn bases.

The position in Diagram 80 is a bare-bones example of the disadvantage of multiple pawn islands. Black has one mass of connected pawns (one

pawn island), whereas White has three. The one potential weak point in Black's chain stands on f7. (I talk more about weak squares in Chapter Seven.) White, though, has three vulnerable base points on b2, f4, and h4. If this were a real position with pieces on the board, White could face some hardship simply because he has three points to defend compared with Black's one.

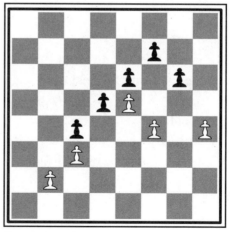

DIAGRAM 80.

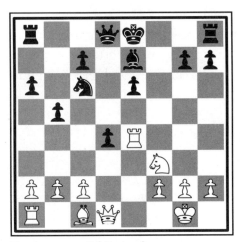

DIAGRAM 81. White to play.
Fischer–Trifunović
Bled, 1961

The flip side of the first pawn island strategy—avoiding the creation of your own pawn islands—is this second strategy:

Whenever you can, create pawn islands in your opponent's camp. Those islands give you extra weaknesses to attack!

The next example shows the importance of this strategy. In Diagram 81, Fischer needs to recapture his pawn, and at the moment he has two options: He can capture on e6 with 1.Rxe6, but this move leaves the pawn island count even at two each. Or he can capture on d4, which leaves Black with three pawn islands—the one on e6 being particularly vulnerable to attack. Fischer chooses the second option.

| 1.Nxd4 0-0 | 2.Qg4 Nxd4 |
| 3.Rxd4 Qc8 | 4.Re4 |

White forces Black to defend his e-pawn.

4...Rf6

5.Be3

Having tied Black down to the defense of the pawn on e6, White takes a moment to bring the rest of his army into play.

5...Qd7	6.Rd1 Qc6
7.Bd4 Rg6	8.Qe2 Rd8
9.g3 Qd5	10.Re1

White has defended himself against Black's cheap tricks and now gangs up on that e-pawn again.

10...c5	11.Bc3 Rd6
12.Be5 Rd8	13.Bf4 c4
14.Rxe6 Rxe6	15.Qxe6+ Qxe6
16.Rxe6	

White makes use of his extra pawn and eventually wins the game.

Fischer isn't the only Grandmaster who recognizes the weakness of multiple pawn islands. I have followed this strategy myself on many occasions, and the next example is from one of my own games. Analysis has shown that, given the position in Diagram 82, my best plan is 19.Nfd4 followed by b4 (gaining lots of queen-

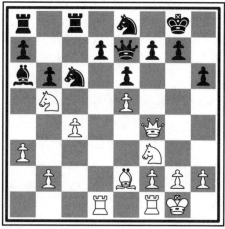

DIAGRAM 82. White to play.
Seirawan–Kveinys
Manila, 1992

side space). I considered this idea, but preferred to generate immediate pressure down the half-open d-file. Though Black could gain a measure of freedom by ...f7-f6, I felt that the pawn islands this move created would ultimately lead to my advantage. Here's how the game went:

1.Rd2 f6	2.exf6 Qxf6
3.Qxf6 gxf6	

I don't mind allowing these exchanges because the weakness of Black's three pawn islands will give me all the winning chances.

4.Rfd1 Bxb5	5.cxb5 Nb8
6.Nd4	

Black is under pressure. He can't play 6...e5 because he then cedes the f5-square to my Knight. Also horrible is 6...d6 or d5 because that move hangs the pawn on e6. It's clear that his central pawn island—and later his pawns on a7 and h6—are going to be real sore spots in his position for the rest of the game.

6...Kf7	7.Bh5+ Ke7
8.Bxe8 Kxe8	9.f4 Rc5
10.Kf2 h5	11.Kg3

Black's game is horrible. His pawns on d7 and h5 are weak, and his Knight is all but useless. Though I ultimately botched this game and let my opponent escape with a draw, you should now be able to see why taking on extra pawn islands is a responsibility that players should not accept lightly.

In my final pawn-island example, Grandmaster Hübner deliberately plays into a position where he has more pawn islands than his opponent in the hope that he can generate active piece play to compensate for the weaknesses that the pawn islands leave in their wake. Alas, poor Hübner finds that these weaknesses are harder to defend than he anticipated.

In Diagram 83, White has the better game because his pawn structure is superior. Black has three pawn islands to two, and his isolated pawn on a7 is a constant source of worry. Also bothersome are his pawns on c6 and c7. Black wants to maintain his pawn on c6 because it keeps the White army out of d5. However, if he plays ...d7-d6, his c6-pawn will be chopped off by the White Bishop on g2. If Black could magically merge his two queenside pawn islands by placing his a-pawn on b7, then his problems would be solved. The d-pawn could then advance to d6 (because the newly created pawn on b7 would defend c6), and the once weak a-pawn would fit snugly with the rest of the pawns. But this magical cure is just fantasy. Black's a-pawn will never get to b7, and he will be forced to worry about it and the doubled c-pawns for the rest of the game.

DIAGRAM 83. White to play.
Larsen–Hübner
Busum, 1969

1.Rb1

White wants to develop his dark-squared Bishop on d2 and move his Queen to a4. This course of action would take away all of the b-pawn's defenders, though, so White gives it extra support and gets his Rook off the vulnerable a1-h8 diagonal.

1...Rd8

2.Rd1

The Rook goes to the half-open d-file, where it can eye the Black d7-pawn.

2...Nh6	**3.h3 Nf5**
4.Bd2 Qe7	**5.Qa4**

Everything is defended, so White is finally ready to go after Black's weak-points.

5...Bb7

6.Qa5

White threatens to eat the c7-pawn. He avoids 6.Qxa7?? because after 6...Ra8! 7.Qxb7 Reb8 8.Qxc7 Be5, the White Queen is trapped.

6....Qe5

7.Ne4

White welcomes ...Qxa5 because Bxa5 would bring the Bishop to a square where it can carry on the attack against c7. In the meantime, White hops his Knight in the direction of the fine c5-square.

7...d5	**8.cxd5 cxd5**
9.Nc5	

Black has undoubled his pawns, but his a- and c-pawns continue to be targets, the c-file has become available for the White Rooks, and the c5-square has turned into a huge hole that screams to be filled by the White Knight.

9...Ba8

10.Bc3

White simultaneously defends his b-pawn and attacks the Black Queen.

10...d4

Tired of being pushed around, Black sacrifices a pawn in a desperate bid to relieve some of the pressure.

11.exd4 Qe7   **12.d5 Bxc3**

13.Qxc3 Nd6

Black is a pawn down and has no compensation at all. He simply can't overcome the weakness of his two queenside pawn islands.

14.a4

White keeps the Black Knight out of b5 and prepares to advance his queenside pawns and gain extra space there.

14...Qe2   **15.b4 a5**

16.b5 Qc4   **17.Rbc1 Qxc3**

18.Rxc3 Ne8   **19.Rcd3 Rb6**

20.Nb3

The imminent loss of Black's a-pawn signals the end of the game, and he resigns.

A. Ivanov–Seirawan
U.S. Championship, 1992

PROBLEM 18. It's White's turn to play. How many pawn islands does each side have, and which side would you prefer to play?

The Creation of Targets

Most people think that chess is all about checkmating the enemy King. Though this is technically true, in the vast majority of master games, an actual checkmate occurs only after the waging of a bitter positional struggle. Usually, the winning player first builds up a series of small advantages that inevitably reveal weaknesses in the enemy camp. By eventually penetrating onto weak squares and making them his own, or by winning weak pawns, the player emerges victorious by virtue of the superior size of his army.

One of the most important chess-playing traits you can develop is a mind-set that I call *target consciousness.* When you have this mind-set, you are always looking for ways to exploit the weaknesses of your opponent. You should become so enamored with this idea that when you play, you become obsessed with creating targets (weak points) in the enemy position. Once the target materializes, you should systematically search for ways to hit it, and you should not rest until every weakness of your opponent has been turned into an advantage of your own! Here is the strategy:

Emulate the great chess masters. They are all mini-Terminators. They scope out targets and hunt them down mercilessly until they can use them to their own advantage!

Weak Pawns

An isolated pawn, a doubled pawn, or a backward pawn is usually thought to be weak. Indeed, most amateurs will do just about anything to avoid these kinds of pawns because they believe the pervasive misinformation that labels such pawns as doomed to eventual destruction. This kind of labeling is actually a form of chess bigotry. Why should the words *isolated, doubled,*

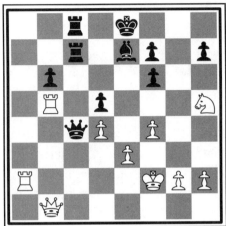

DIAGRAM 84. White to play.
Petrosian–Barcza
Budapest, 1955

or *backward* signify that a pawn is *weak*? In chess, a pawn or a square is only weak if it can be attacked. If an enemy piece cannot get your pawn, then there is no reason to worry about its safety, regardless of whether it is isolated, doubled, or backward.

In Diagram 84, we see a position where the so-called weak pawns actually deserve their name! Black's pawns are all horribly weak. They are so rotten, in fact, that White will just eat one after another. The Black pawn on b6 is isolated and stands on an open file, which makes it easy to attack. The Black d- and h-pawns are also isolated, and the miserable doubled f-pawns speak for themselves. Compare this wreck of a pawn position to White's pawns. All the White pawns, with the exception of the backward pawn on e3, are healthy. They are well protected, can move to safe squares, and should be on the board for a lot longer than the sick Black ones. (Those of you who read Chapter Six will note that Black has four pawn islands to White's one.) Small wonder that Black's pawns will drop like overripe apples.

1.Rxb6

The first victim falls. Now 2.Nxf6+ is threatened.

1...Rc6	**2.Rxc6 Rxc6**
3.Ra8+ Kd7	**4.Ra7+ Rc7**
5.Rxc7+	

White, who is dining on Black pawns and will soon have a significant material advantage, is happy to trade pieces because this thinning of material keeps Black's counterplay to a minimum.

| **5...Kxc7** | **6.Qxh7 Qa2+** |

128

7.Kf3 Qd2

Black threatens 8...Qd1+.

8.Qb1!

White stops the check. When you are ahead in material, your first priority is to stop all enemy counterplay (see Chapter Three). Then if you can restore the positional balance, your material edge will give you a certain victory.

8...f5

9.Ng3

All the White pieces come home to aid their King.

9...Bh4

10.Ne2

White gives Black nothing with this move. Playing either 10.Qxf5 Qd1+ or 10.Nxf5 Qf2+ would make things unnecessarily messy.

10...Be7   **11.h3 Bb4**

12.Ng3

Now the possibility of a check on f2 is gone, so White can eat another meal.

12...Kc6   **13.Nxf5 Kb5**

14.Nd6+ Ka4   **15.Nxf7 Ba3**

16.Ne5

Having devoured everything, the satiated Knight returns home. Because 16...Be1 can now be met by either 17.Ng4 or 17.Qd3, Black gives up. He has endured more than enough punishment!

Now let's compare the doubled pawns in the game we just looked at with the ones in the next example. The position in Diagram 85 came about after these boring but common opening moves: **1.e4 e5 2.Nf3 Nc6 3.Nc3 Nf6 4.Bc4 Bc5 5.0-0 0-0 6.d3 d6**. In this position (typically

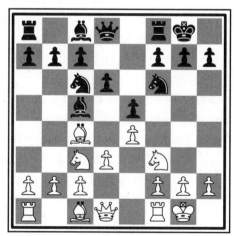

DIAGRAM 85. White to play.

129

seen in children's matches), White can play the excellent **7.Be3!**, after which 7...Bxe3 8.fxe3 gives White doubled e-pawns. Why does White allow this? The doubled pawns are welcomed by White because he sees that, at the moment, the pawn on f2 is doing nothing at all. On e3, though, it becomes a dynamic contributor because the doubled pawns on e3 and e4 defend the critical d4, d5, f4, and f5 central squares. In addition, the f2-pawn's absence from the f-file gives White a half-open file for his Rooks. Finally, White also sees that his doubled pawns will not be weak. Do they appear weak to you? The e4-pawn is well defended, so the only pawn that could by any stretch of the imagination be a target is the guy on e3. How can Black attack this pawn? It doesn't stand on an open file, so the enemy Rooks can't do anything to it. After something like 8...Ng4, White can simply defend himself with 9.Qe2 (or 9.Qe1) and then chase the bothersome horse away with h3. So these doubled e-pawns are not weak at all. On the contrary, they are active participants in the battle for key central squares.

Given all these considerations, Black would be well advised to avoid 7...Bxe3 and instead play either **7...Bb6** (inviting 8.Bxb6? axb6!, which suddenly gives Black an a8-Rook with a half-open file to use and doubled b-pawns that are not weak at all) or **7...Bg4!**. After the latter move, 8.Bxc5 dxc5 would make Black happier than White. Why? Because the c-pawns are quite safe (let White try to attack them after Black plays ...b7-b6!), and the pawn on c5 helps control the important d4-square. To make matters even better for Black, the pawn's removal from d6 gives Black use of the half-open d-file, which benefits both his Queen and Rooks.

Clearly, doubled pawns are not necessarily weak! Attackable weak pawns might result from an enemy error, but you cannot count on any opponent to make this kind of error. It is up to you to find ways to create these weaknesses. That is what this particular strategy is all about. Once you create the target, then you can go all out and attack it. One of the most useful methods of creating weak pawn targets is a strategy known as the *minority attack*, which goes like this:

Employ two pawns to attack a pawn majority of three, with the goal of leaving your enemy with weak squares and pawns.

Diagram 86 illustrates the minority attack strategy quite nicely. White is playing on the queenside because his pawns point in that direction (his pawn chain occupies f2-e3-d4) and give him extra territory there. By advancing his b-pawn, White intends to play b4-b5 followed by bxc6, when Black will be left with a weakness (a pawn that cannot be protected by another pawn) on either d5 or c6. If Black answers this capture with ...bxc6, he will be left with a backward c-pawn on an open file (meaning that it can be easily at-

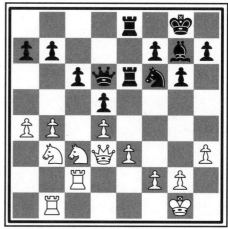

DIAGRAM 86. Black to play.
Reshevsky–Miagmasuren
Sousse, 1967

tacked). Black strives to avoid this fate, but he ends up with a target on d5 instead.

1...b6

Black hopes to answer 2.b5 with 2...c5. A more common and more dangerous plan for Black is to seek counterchances on the kingside, because that is where Black's extra territory exists. For an example of this plan, see the Bobotsov-Petrosian game in Chapter Nine.

2.Nc1!

White is in no hurry to play b4-b5 and instead improves the positioning of his pieces. Bringing this Knight to the center (it's heading for e2) defends c3, d4, and f4 and helps deprive the enemy of counterplay because all of White's key points will soon be well guarded.

2...Bh6   3.N1e2 Nh5
4.b5

Now Black cannot play 4...c5 because of 5.dxc5 and 6.Qxd5, which wins a pawn.

4...Qd7   5.bxc6 Rxc6
6.Qb5

Having deprived the d-pawn of its c6-support, White goes about attacking this newly created target.

6...Rec8

Black avoids the obvious 6...Nf6, which loses to 7.Nxd5! Rxc2 8.Nxf6+.

7.Rbc1 R8c7

Black is hoping that the pin on the c-file will save him. Unfortunately, White's next move leaves Black's position in tatters.

8.g4! a6

Black has no other options because his poor Knight cannot move! Both 8...Nf6 and 8...Ng7 run into 9.Nxd5!, after which a recapture on d5 allows 10.Rxc6, and 9...Rxc2 loses the Queen to 10.Nf6+.

9.Qxa6 Nf6

Black sacrificed a pawn to draw the White Queen away so that it would no longer attack c6. This solution to his problems turns out to be an illusion, though.

10.Nxd5!

Black thought he had prevented this capture! Now what can he do? Playing 10...Rxc2 is still met with 11.Nxf6+.

10...Nxg4

Desperation. Black finally noticed that his intended 10...Nxd5 fails because of 11.Rxc6 Rxc6 12.Qa8+, when White eats a snack on c6 after all.

11.Rxc6 Qxd5

12.Qa8+

Black gives up because he sees that 12...Kg7 13.Rxg6+! leads to the loss of his Queen.

Averbakh–Donner
Beverwijk, 1962

It is amazing how quickly a position can collapse when you actively seek to create targets and attack them. This complete game example shows a more typical minority attack battle.

1.d4 d5	2.c4 e6
3.Nf3 Nf6	4.Nc3 Be7
5.cxd5 exd5	6.Bg5 c6
7.Qc2 g6	8.e3 Bf5
9.Bd3 Bxd3	10.Qxd3 0-0
11.0-0 Re8	

DIAGRAM 87.

The game is quiet, and, as Diagram 87 shows, neither side has any real weaknesses. White decides he has to strike at something, so he starts an immediate minority attack.

12.Bxf6

This move draws the Black Bishop away from its control of b4 and allows White to safely advance his pawn to that square.

12...Bxf6	13.b4 Nd7
14.b5 Nb6	15.bxc6 bxc6

The game now revolves around the newly created weakness on c6.

16.Rac1

White brings his pieces to bear on the c6-target.

16...Be7	17.Rc2 Bd6
18.Nb1 Rc8	19.Rfc1 Qf6

Black indirectly defends the c6-pawn. Now 20.Rxc6?? loses to 20...Rxc6 21.Rxc6 Bxh2+ followed by 22...Qxc6.

20.Nbd2

White brings his Knight back into play. (Never leave a Knight sitting around on the 1st rank.) He also keeps the enemy horse out of c4.

20...Rc7

21.g3

This move restricts the scope of the Black Bishop and gives the King a little room to breathe. Now 22.Rxc6 is a real threat.

21...Rec8

22.Kg2

Black is on the defensive, so White takes a moment off to bring an extra defender to his f3-Knight. The King also keeps enemy pieces out of h3.

22...Qe7

23.e4!

White gains space in the center. He doesn't fear 23...dxe4 because 24.Nxe4 just helps to activate his Knight. True, White would then have an isolated d-pawn, but none of the Black pieces would be in a position to attack it.

23...Bb4   24.h4 Qd8

25.e5

White keeps taking more and more space. Realizing that he is being pushed back on all fronts, Black tries to activate his pieces with ...c6-c5.

25...c5   26.dxc5 Rxc5

27.Rxc5 Rxc5   28.Rxc5 Bxc5

Black managed to get the Rooks off the board (a good trade because the White Rooks were more active than their Black counterparts), but he still has an isolated d-pawn. White hastens to block it with his Knights, fixing the pawn on d5 and also demonstrating that his Knights have found a permanent hole on d4. Remember:

Always strive to dominate the square directly in front of an isolated pawn!

29.Nb3

White attacks the Bishop and brings everything to bear on d4.

29...Be7

30.Nbd4

This Knight is very strong on d4. Now 30...Nc4?? loses to 31.Nc6 Qd7 32.Qxd5! Qxd5 33.Nxe7+, which wins a piece and a pawn.

30...Qc8   31.Qb5 Kf8

32.Nc6

White is eyeing the pawns on a7 and d5.

32...Qb7

33.Nfd4

It's clear that Black's Bishop is inferior to White's Knights.

33...a6	**34.Qa5 Ke8**

35.Nxe7

White would not normally be in a hurry to trade off his wonderful Knight, but the exposed position of the Black King gives White a chance to start a decisive attack.

35...Kxe7	**36.Qc5+ Ke8**
37.e6! Nc8	**38.exf7+ Kxf7**

39.Nc6

White is threatening 40.Qxd5 and 40.Nd8+.

39...Kg7	**40.Qd4+ Kh6**

41.Qf6

Black is helpless against the threat of 42.Ne5 followed by a check on f7 or g4. If he plays 41...d4, White's easiest answer is 42.Kh2, breaking the pin. Black resigns. White's strategy has paid off:

Weak enemy pawns don't just magically appear; you must create them.

PROBLEM 19. It's White's turn to play. My last move was 1...Qc7, attacking White's pawn on f4. After 2.g3, I had achieved an important goal. What was that goal? And how should I continue?

Wood–Seirawan
Seattle, 1994

Weak Squares

Though most players can easily understand the concept of a weak pawn, they sometimes find it much harder to grasp the idea of a weak square, also known as a *hole*. I remember one player arguing with me, "You always say that a pawn is weak only if it can be attacked, so you must hope you'll eventually capture it. But you can't ever capture a square. So how can you call a square weak?" My answer was that you *can* capture a square! Of course, I don't mean you can take it off the board and place it in a box with the other captured pieces. By capturing a square, I mean you can make it serve your army by acting as a home for your pieces.

For example, in Chapter Four, you learned that Knights need advanced support points to reach their full potential. A support point is nothing more than a square that has been swayed to your own cause. It supplies a safe haven for your Knight while the horse makes threats in all directions. You can claim that a square is yours—that you have captured it—when it is safe from attack by enemy pawns and is nailed down by several of your own pieces. Because these captured squares increase the power of your pieces, they are obviously quite valuable. How do you get your hands on these valuable items? Do they just fall into your lap or, as with weak pawns, do you have to fight to create them? In the next example, Karpov shows us how it's done in a game against Browne in San Antonio in 1972.

After **1.c4 c5 2.b3 Nf6 3.Bb2 g6**, a glance at the board shows that no weak squares exist at the moment. Karpov changes this assessment with a surprising capture.

4.Bxf6! exf6

White does not give up his strong fianchettoed Bishop to double Black's pawns because the doubled pawns won't be weak in any way. He gives it up because he sees that when the e-pawn is drawn away from e7, it will not be able to exert any control over d5. In other words, White is playing to create a weak square!

5.Nc3

Having created a weakness on d5, White proceeds to "capture the square" by training the sights of all his pieces in that direction.

5...Bg7

6.g3

With 5.Nc3, White obtained a firm grip on d5, but he is not satisfied with just a little control: He wants total domination of that square! By playing 6.g3, he allows his light-squared Bishop to join in the d5 orgy.

6...Nc6

7.Bg2 f5

Black also has a Knight, a Bishop, and a pawn hitting d4. Does that mean that he can lay claim to that square? No.

8.e3

Now none of the Black pieces can land on d4.

8...0-0

9.Nge2

White intends to add to his control of d5 with an eventual Nf4, and in fact White went on to win this game. The rest of the moves are not important here. What is important is how White went out of his way to create the weak square, and how White rushed all his pieces to it. It's also important to pay attention to why White owned d5, while Black didn't own d4. The d4-square was not Black's because the White e3-pawn defended it.

The creation of weak squares is one of the most important strategies in chess because it affects the strength of your pieces. Every good player is well aware of this fact. Let's see how Bobby Fischer uses weak squares to create homes for his men. The position in Diagram 88 seems solid for both sides. No holes seem to exist, but appearances were never enough for Fischer. Watch how he plays directly for the creation of a weak square.

DIAGRAM 88. White to play.
Fischer–Durao
Havana Olympiad, 1966

1.dxc5 dxc5

White makes this seemingly harmless exchange because he wants to get Black's d-pawn away from d6. Its removal from that square allows White to advance his e-pawn and lay claim to both d6 and f6.

2.Qe2 b6

3.e5!

White has begun his battle for two advanced posts in the heart of the Black position. He will play Bf4 (adding to his control of d6) or Bg5 (aiming at f6), Nbd2-e4 (hitting f6 and d6), and Rd1 (training more stuff on d6). Notice how, once he creates the weak square, he immediately brings all of his pieces to bear on it. While the weak-square strategy is important, remember this:

Control of a square alone will not necessarily lead to victory. You must also have other advantages that combine to bring the opponent down.

In Diagram 89, White has total control of the wonderful d5 post, and his Bishop is extremely strong on that square. Can't Black's Bishop move to d4 and be just as powerful? The answer, unfortunately for Black, is no. Black's Bishop can get to d4, but it can't work with the rest of his army as nicely as White's does. White is in the middle of attacking the kingside with his pawns and Rooks, which will place themselves behind those advancing pawns, and his Bishop, which aims in that direction, will help White with his attack.

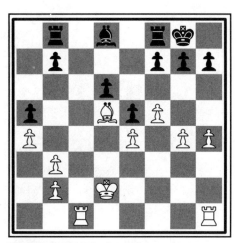

DIAGRAM 89. Black to play.
Karpov–Mecking
Hastings, 1971–72

Black's Bishop will look very picturesque on d4, but it simply can't do anything in relation to the other Black pieces. Remember:

Chess is a team effort. One macho piece cannot win a game by itself!

White's army is playing a team game, and Black's is not. That's why White is going to win.

1...g5

White threatens to grab all the space on the kingside with g4-g5, so Black attempts to block him.

2.fxg6

White does not even consider 2.h5?? because that move totally locks the position up on the side of the board where White wants to play. He is following this strategy:

> *Open lines when you want to attack, and close lines when you are trying to defend.*

2...hxg6

3.Kd3

The immediate 3.h5?? would lose the Exchange to 3...Bg5+.

3...Kg7	**4.h5 Bb6**
5.Rh3 Bc5	**6.Rf1**

Now Black doesn't know whether White will double Rooks on the f-file with 7.Rhf3 or on the h-file with Rfh1.

6...f6

7.hxg6

White opens the h-file. He will now use the combined power of his Rooks and Bishop to play for a direct assault on the Black King.

7...Kxg6	**8.Rfh1 Rbe8**
9.Rh7 Kg5	

Black was afraid he might eventually be checkmated after Rh1-h5, so he goes for a walk with his King. As it turns out, this walk takes him to his doom.

10.Ke2

White's King joins in the hunt! Now 11.Kf3, which takes the f4 square away from the Black King, followed by 12.Rg7 checkmate is the threat.

10...Kf4	**11.Rh3 Bd4**
12.Rg7	

Because 13.Rf3 checkmate is inevitable, Black gives up. As this game demonstrates:

> *A strong piece + a captured square for it to rest on + some other complementary advantage(s) = trouble for your opponent!*

At times, a square can be the focal point of a big fight. One side may want to use it for attacking purposes whereas the other side may want to clog it

DIAGRAM 90. **Black to play.**

up for defensive reasons. Diagram 90 illustrates this type of situation. This position seems to be fairly clear cut: White's pawns are aimed at the kingside (his pawns on d4 and e5 point in that direction and give him more space on that side of the board), while Black's pawns aim at the queenside. Because you should always attack with pawns in positions with closed centers, Black will play for ...c6-c5, which will give him more queenside territory and also open files for his Rooks. White, on the other hand, will play for f4-f5, which adds to his kingside space, rips open lines so that his minor pieces and Rooks can participate, and frees the c1-h6 diagonal for his Bishop.

If Black just wants a race to see who can implement his plan first, then 1...c5 will suffice; but is it worth asking whether Black can instead prevent White's f4-f5 move? Of course it is! You should always know what both you and your opponent can and cannot prevent. In this case, White can't really stop Black from playing ...c6-c5, but Black can prevent White from playing f4-f5. Because the f4-f5 push is so important to White, isn't it worth Black spending a couple moves to stop it?

If Black decides to prevent White's plan, he should try to do it in a beneficial way. For example, 1...f5? is a poor move because 2.exf6 leaves Black with a backward e-pawn on an open file. The move that I like is **1...Nh6!**, which not only prevents f4-f5 but also announces Black's intention of turning f5 into a fine support point for the Knight! After **2.Nf3 Nf5 3.0-0**, Black should play **3...h5!**. This strange-looking move is not intended to start a kingside attack. Black is stopping White from playing g2-g4 and reclaiming the f5 square. Now f4-f5 has been prevented, White's Bishop and Rook are doomed to remain trapped behind the f4-pawn, and Black's Knight has been blessed with a magnificent post. Black has claimed a square that was important to White's plans as a home for his own pieces.

Note that Black will not be satisfied with the control of one square but will mix the fine position of his Knight with his original plans on the queenside. He will continue with ...c5 (opening the c-file, gaining space, and attacking the White center), ...Nc6 (joining the f5-Knight and the c5-pawn in their assault on d4), and ...Qb6, after which all his pieces are striking the d4-pawn in unison. Play through these moves on your own board, and you will see a great example of a whole army working together to achieve one goal. The fact that Black first stopped White's plan makes this whole strategy all the sweeter.

Next, we'll look at a complete game that illustrates the weak-square strategy.

Karpov–Spassky
Leningrad, 1974
9th Match Game

This game shows a full-bodied fight for several squares in both camps. The position that interests us occurs after the following moves:

1.e4 c5	**2.Nf3 e6**
3.d4 cxd4	**4.Nxd4 Nf6**
5.Nc3 d6	**6.Be2 Be7**
7.0-0 0-0	**8.f4 Nc6**
9.Be3 Bd7	**10.Nb3**

Black's next move is designed to force White to give Black access to the b4-square. The price: a permanent weakening of the b5-square.

10...a5?!

11.a4

White stops the enemy a-pawn in its tracks but creates a weakness on b4. The difference between Black's weakness on b5 and White's on b4 is that the b4-square is not a permanent hole. At some later stage of the game, White can move his Knight and reclaim it by c2-c3.

11...Nb4   **12.Bf3 Bc6**

13.Nd4

This Knight can now either take the Bishop on c6 or jump into the lovely hole on b5.

13...g6

14.Rf2

White brings another defender to guard c2, allowing the White Queen to roam and also preparing for Rd2 in a few moves.

14...e5

Black creates a hole on d5, but knows that this hole is no big deal because his pieces all attack that square, thereby preventing White's pieces from dominating it.

15.Nxc6 bxc6

16.fxe5 dxe5

Hasn't White given up his control of b5 and d5 by allowing Black to bring a pawn to c6 (where it guards both these points)? Yes, he has. But White has also created new holes on c4 and c5, as well as pawn weaknesses on a5 and c6. And he has also gained the two Bishops, an advantage that he makes use of later in the game.

17.Qf1!

White grabs the c4-square. Note that taking the d-file with Rd2 would be pointless because it is not clear yet whether the f-file is more important.

17...Qc8

18.h3

Now Black's Knight is kept out of g4. Black will have a difficult time finding useful moves because in this Bishop vs. Knight situation, his Knights don't have any advanced support points. (The Knight on b4 will eventually be chased away.)

18...Nd7

If Black plays 18...Qe6, White will bring his Bishop to c4 by 19.Rc1 (which defends c2 because the immediate Be2 would cut off the f2 defender from the c2 pawn) 19...Rfd8 20.Be2 Rd4 21.b3 followed by Bc4.

19.Bg4 h5

20.Bxd7

White is willing to give up his two-Bishop advantage because he feels that the d7-Knight could eventually play to b6 and fight for c4. When playing for possession of a square, don't hesitate to trade pieces that can challenge you for that post.

20...Qxd7

21.Qc4

The White Queen is very strong here. It attacks c6 and also eyes f7.

21...Bh4	**22.Rd2 Qe7**
23.Raf1! Rfd8	**24.Nb1!**

White prepares to chase the b4-Knight away. With the position as shown in Diagram 91, Black has to come to terms with the fact that the square he put so much effort into controlling was just a temporary possession.

24...Qb7	**25.Kh2 Kg7**
26.c3 Na6	**27.Re2**

White decides that he wants to double Rooks on the f-file so that they can work with his Queen in attacking f7. He avoids the trade of this Rook and now threatens 28.g3 Bf6 29.Ref2 Rd6 30.Bg5!.

27...Rf8

28.Nbd2

All of White's pieces will take part in this battle.

28...Bd8

Black doesn't fall for 28...Qxb2?? 29.Nf3, after which his Queen and his Bishop are both attacked.

DIAGRAM 91. Black to play.

29.Nf3 f6

30.Red2

Now the f-file is blocked off, so White shows renewed interest in the d-file. Note that Black's price for playing ...f7-f6 is to allow the White Queen access to the e6-square.

30...Be7   31.Qe6 Rad8

32.Rxd8 Bxd8

White would have answered 32...Rxd8 with 33.Nxe5! fxe5 34.Rf7+.

33.Rd1 Nb8

The once-proud b4-Knight has been reduced to a pathetic creature on the back rank.

34.Bc5

White has already made use of c4 and e6. Now he jumps into c5 as well.

34...Rh8

35.Rxd8!

Black gives up because 35...Rxd8 36.Be7 will lead to a winning attack on the kingside after 36...Rc8 37.Qxf6+.

Lines of Weak Squares

So far we have looked only at the control of individual squares. However,

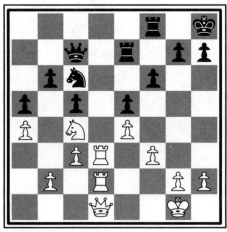

DIAGRAM 92.

sometimes a whole line of squares can become vulnerable to enemy infiltration. For example, in Diagram 92, Black's game is bad no matter whose move it is! Black is doomed because White controls a host of squares, whereas Black controls no advanced posts at all. The White Knight dominates the board on c4 (where it eyes b6 and d6), whereas the Black Knight is kept out of b4 and d4 by the little pawn on c3.

White's Rooks are no less impressive. They can penetrate into the Black position on d5, d6, or d7.

In Diagram 93, we see a whole line of weakened squares along the a1-h8 diagonal. White has wisely played f2-f3 and avoided giving up squares to the Black Bishop, but Black has failed to take the same precautions! White will play **1.Qc3**, and nothing can be done about a decisive penetration into h8.

DIAGRAM 93. White to play.

Steinitz–Blackburne
London, 1876

The final game in this chapter shows what happens in actual play when a line of squares becomes vulnerable. It also shows that players were well aware of strong and weak squares way back in the 1800s!

1.e4 e5	2.Nf3 Nc6
3.Bb5 a6	4.Ba4 Nf6
5.d3 d6	6.c3 Be7
7.h3 0-0	8.Qe2 Ne8

This opening is an old-fashioned way of playing the Ruy López. White's next move prevents Black from playing ...f7-f5, but it creates a hole on f4.

| 9.g4 b5 | 10.Bc2 Bb7 |
| 11.Nbd2 Qd7 | 12.Nf1 |

This White Knight is heading for e3, where it can jump into the temporary hole on f5. I call this hole *temporary* because Black can reclaim control of it with ...g7-g6. However, that advance also has some negative aspects: It weakens the dark squares around Black's King.

12...Nd8

Black knows about weak squares, too! He is heading for e6, where his Knight eyes the hole on f4.

13.Ne3 Ne6

14.Nf5 g6

Black decides that the Knight has to be chased away and is willing to pay the price for doing so. However, now White will try to make use of the holes around the Black King.

15.Nxe7+

This Bishop could have defended the dark squares by playing ...Bf6-g7, so it had to be removed.

15...Qxe7

16.Be3

If Black's Knight ever jumps to f4, White will chop it off with Bxf4. Then the doubled pawn on f4 will be weak, and White will be able to create a full pawn center with d3-d4.

16...N8g7   17.0-0-0 c5

18.d4

White has two Bishops, so he wants to open up the position. He would also like to blast open the a1-h8 diagonal so that he can take advantage of the weak dark squares around the Black King.

18...exd4

19.cxd4 c4?

This bad move gives up control of d4 and allows White's dark-squared Bishop to take up residence there. Black's game slides into the gutter after this error, which just goes to show that you should never give up squares with such reckless abandon!

20.d5 Nc7   21.Qd2 a5

22.Bd4

As Diagram 94 shows, the White Bishop is eating up the holes on f6 and g7. Black tries to block him, but White will not be denied this feast.

22...f6

23.Qh6

Why not make use of this tasty hole?

23...b4

24.g5

White blasts open the a1-h8 diagonal for the Bishop. The holes that Black created earlier with 14...g6 have finally come back to haunt him.

24...f5

25.Bf6

DIAGRAM 94. Black to play.

With 14...g6, Black gave up control of both f6 and h6. Now we see why such a surrender can have serious consequences: White's pieces have turned both these squares into homes!

25...Qf7   **26.exf5 gxf5**

27.g6!!

A move of frightful power. White gives his Knight access to g5 and also opens the g-file for his Rooks. Time and again, we have seen how top players bring all their pieces into a fight. Now it's time to start doing the same thing in your own games.

27...Qxg6

Black will lose material, but 27...Qxf6 28.Qxh7 checkmate and 27...hxg6 28.Ng5 Qxf6 29.Qh7 checkmate are certainly no better.

28.Bxg7 Qxh6+

Black agrees to lose a piece and thereby agrees to lose the game. He has no choice, though, because 28...Qxg7 loses the Queen to 29.Rhg1, after which the Rooks enter the game and wipe Black out.

29.Bxh6

Black could resign here, but he plays on for a few pointless moves before he comes to terms with his imminent defeat and resigns.

29...Rf6	**30.Rhg1+ Rg6**
31.Bxf5 Kf7	**32.Bxg6+ hxg6**
33.Ng5+ Kg8	**34.Rge1**

PROBLEM 20. It's Black's turn to play. A player with a 1300 rating, Black was doing quite well against his 1900-rated opponent. He played **1...Be7** and eventually went down in defeat after a hard battle. What was wrong with this move?

Territorial Domination

O ne of the most important acquisitions in a game of chess is space. Good players never seem to get enough of it. Like Karpov, I am a space addict, and any other positionally inclined Grandmaster is just as convinced as we are about the virtues of territory.

You gain territory through the strategic use of your pawns. In general, all the squares behind your pawns are considered your space unless an enemy pawn can attack them. For example, in Diagram 95, the Xs denote controlled territory. A glance is all you need to know that White has more Xs behind his pawns than Black does, so White has more space in all three sections of the board (queenside, center, and kingside). The X'ed squares in the White camp are all safe landing spots for the White army. The X'ed squares in the Black camp are the only ones Black has for his own pieces. Note that the squares with your pawns on them are not considered your territory, but they become your terri-

tory as soon as you push the pawns. For example, f4 is not technically a White square, but after 1.f4-f5, White can lay claim to an extra unit of space because f4 is now behind the pawn chain.

Possession of extra space is usually an advantage, but as the ancient Romans discovered, you can't just claim a stretch of territory for yourself; you have to control it to prevent it from falling into the hands of the enemy. As a result, collecting more

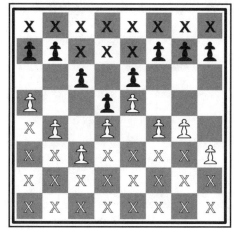

DIAGRAM 95.

space than your opponent is both a boon and a responsibility. The extra territory gives you plenty of room for your pieces and allows you to squeeze the enemy as you systematically increase your spatial advantage. However, advancing borders also need to be defended against foreign infiltration.

The following basic rules apply to a space-gaining strategy:

- Extra space is a long-range advantage. Don't be in a hurry! Take your time and act like a python, slowly squeezing your victim to death in your deadly coils.

- Once you have a significant advantage in space, play to defend your borders, don't let the enemy break free of his bonds, and slowly but surely take morc and more of the board for yourself.

- To maintain your space advantage, avoid trading pieces. You want the enemy pieces to get in the way of each other and suffocate under their own weight. Your opponent, who has less space, will attempt to trade pieces. A small apartment with eight people may be an intolerable living situation; that same apartment with just two people could be quite acceptable.

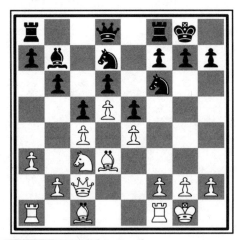

DIAGRAM 96. White to play.
Silman–Formanek
World Open, 1989

Space on the Wings

Let's make no mistake about it: The center is the most important area of the board, and you should play in that sector whenever you can. However, if the center is blocked by pawns, then neither player has a choice: You must both turn your attention to the wings. For example, in Diagram 96 White has more space in the center, but that section of the board is completely locked up by pawns. Though the center will not see any action, his extra space does give White's pieces more freedom of movement. He uses that extra mobility to immediately strive for spatial gains on the wings. The strategy here:

A blocked center means play on the wings.

1.g3

This move prepares for f2-f4. The immediate 1.f4 is bad because 1...exf4 2.Bxf4 Qe7 gives Black a fine square on e5 for his Knights.

1...Ne8

2.f4

White intends to answer 2...exf4 with 3.gxf4, after which White enjoys a considerable territorial advantage on the kingside and use of the half-open g-file. Notice that the White King will be safe when it moves to h1.

2...Qe7   3.f5 f6

4.g4

Nobody can dispute White's edge in kingside territory. His next few moves are designed to increase this advantage and to create an open file so that his Rooks can enter the battle.

4...g5   5.h4 h6

6.Kf2 Nc7   7.Rh1 Rf7

Now White can open the h-file at will with hxg5. Of course, he has no intention of doing so immediately because Black can then challenge that file with ...Rh7. Instead, White will double or even triple on that file and only open it at the moment most favorable to him.

8.Be3

Black is cramped and cannot really do anything but defend, so White takes his time and places his pieces on their best squares.

8...Rh7   9.Rh3 Kg7

10.Rah1 Rah8

Now 11.hxg5 will be met by 11...hxg5, when massive exchanges on the h-file will make Black happy because he is the one with less space. White must remember the following:

If you have more space, don't trade pieces!

11.Ne2

The Knight moves toward g3, where it will always threaten to jump into the hole on h5.

11...Kg8	**12.Ng3 Ne8**
13.b4	

Now White grabs some queenside space as well. Why not lay claim to the whole board?

13...Nf6	**14.Qd2 Bc8**
15.Bc2 Qc7	**16.Bb3 Qe7**
17.Ba4	

White has all the time in the world. Black's lack of space makes him helpless, so White takes care of the needs of each of his pieces. Because this Bishop is bad, White gets it outside of the pawn chain.

17...Bd7	**18.Bc6 Qd8**
19.Rb1 Qc7	**20.b5**

White has a lock on both sides of the board and eventually wins.

On occasion, you may find that your opponent can eventually shake off a spatial disadvantage. The end of a spatial advantage is not necessarily the end of your control, though. If you have played your cards right, you can usually gain new advantages in exchange for the loss of your land. As an example, look at the position in Diagram 97. White has two center pawns (on d4 and e3), whereas Black has only one (on e6). You should use every advantage you possess, so White will advance his e-pawn, gain central space, and force the Black pieces away from their central posts.

DIAGRAM 97. White to play.
Capablanca–Lasker
Havana, 1921

1.Rfd1

This useful move defends d4 (which might get a little loose after e3-e4) and discourages Black from fighting for space with ...c6-c5 or ...e6-e5, either of which only helps to activate the White Rook.

1...Bd7

2.e4 Nb6?

Black clearly has less space than his opponent, so he should have traded a pair of Knights with 2...Nxc3.

3.Bf1 Rc8

Black still hopes to create a bit of queenside space with an eventual ...c6-c5.

4.b4

White puts a stop to ...c5 and gains queenside space.

4...Be8   5.Qb3 Rec7

6.a4

While Black is slithering around on his back two ranks, White quietly maps out more space on the queenside.

6...Ng6   7.a5 Nd7

8.e5!

White grabs more central territory, keeps the Black pieces out of f6, and creates a wonderful home for a White Knight on d6. It is true that 8.e5 gives Black access to d5, but White rightly feels that d6 is simply more important!

8...b6

Black has to break out of this bind or he will lose without a fight.

9.Ne4 Rb8   10.Qc3 Nf4

11.Nd6 Nd5   12.Qa3 f6

This move threatens 13...fxe5 14.dxe5 Nxe5! 15.Nxe8 Nxf3+, so White is forced to make a trade or two and give Black a bit more room to move about in. Unfortunately for Black, he will have new problems to face in the form of his weakened pawns on c6, e6, and f6.

13.Nxe8 Qxe8	14.exf6 gxf6
15.b5 Rbc8	16.bxc6 Rxc6
17.Rxc6 Rxc6	18.axb6 axb6

White has traded in the bulk of his extra space for permanent targets on b6, e6, f6, and h7. The ability to trade one advantage for another is a hallmark of all great players.

19.Re1

The Rook quickly turns its attention to e6.

19...Qc8	20.Nd2 Nf8
21.Ne4	

Because e6 has been well defended, White now focuses on f6.

21...Qd8

22.h4

White wins this game because he has four targets to attack compared with Black's one (the pawn on d4). The fact that the Black King is more vulnerable than its White counterpart also plays a part in the final result. The remaining moves show White slowly making use of all of these factors:

22...Rc7	23.Qb3 Rg7
24.g3 Ra7	25.Bc4 Ra5
26.Nc3 Nxc3	27.Qxc3 Kf7
28.Qe3 Qd6	29.Qe4 Ra4
30.Qb7+ K-g6	31.Qc8 Qb4
32.Rc1 Qe7	33.Bd3+ Kh6
34.Rc7 Ra1+	35.Kh2 Qd6
36.Qxf8+!	

Faced with 36...Qxf8 37.Rxh7 checkmate, Black resigns.

By now, it should be clear that giving up too much space can enable your opponent to get a stranglehold on you. At the first hint of territorial deprivation, you must strike out and try to claim some space of your own.

Here's how I fought back in one of my games. As you can see in Diagram 98, White has more space in the center while I have more queenside space. However, why should I let my opponent have all the fun in the middle? I shouldn't!

1...c5!

This move challenges White in the center and also increases my own control of queenside territory.

2.c3 e5!

I stop White cold in the middle. Now 3.d5, which increases White's territory slightly, is probably the best

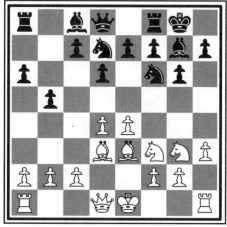

DIAGRAM 98. **Black to play.**
Lobron–Seirawan
Lucerne Olympiad, 1982

move, but it would close the center and stop all of White's play in that sector.

3.dxe5? dxe5

Now the space in the middle is equal, and I still own my extra territory on the queenside. This extra space gives me the superior position.

4.0-0 c4!

Okay, so I'm greedy! I love taking any space my opponent will give me.

5.Bc2 Bb7   6.Qd2 Re8

7.Rad1 Qe7

This very useful move gets my Queen off the uncomfortable d-file and gains control of c5. I will now be able to place my Knight and increase my pressure on e4 and d3.

8.Bh6 Nc5   9.Bxg7 Kxg7

10.Qe3 h6

Before continuing play in the middle and on the queenside, I cover all the squares around my King. Now f5, g5, and h5 are off-limits to White's forces.

11.Rd2 Rad8   12.Rfd1 Rxd2

13.Rxd2 Qc7   14.Nh4

White threatens to sacrifice a piece by playing 15.Nhf5+ gxf5 16.Nxf5+ followed by Qxh6.

14...Kh7

Now Nhf5 will no longer be a check, and I will have time to capture the first intruder and then defend my h-pawn with ...Ng8.

15.Nf3 Ne6

My Knight is eyeing f4, and this move also gives me the option of trading Queens with ...Qc5. I don't mind a Queen exchange because White's only chance for counterplay lies on the kingside. Without his Queen, his chances of attacking my King would be nonexistent.

16.a4 Kg7	**17.Rd1 Qc5**
18.Qxc5 Nxc5	**19.axb5 axb5**
20.Rd6 Ncd7!	

I don't fall for 20...Ncxe4? 21.Nxe4 Bxe4 22.Bxe4 Nxe4 23.Rb6! Rd8 24.Rxb5 Rd1+ 25.Kh2, which leads to equality. By playing 20...Ncd7, I give my e-pawn more support and keep White's Rook out of b6.

21.Kf1 Ra8

My Rook prepares to penetrate the White position along the a-file.

22.Rd1 Ra2

23.Rb1 Nc5

I exerted pressure on e4 (which makes my pieces on b7 and f6 attacking while White's men on c2 and g3 are defending) and b2 (courtesy of my spatial advantage on that wing) and eventually won a long game.

PROBLEM 21. It's White's turn to play. He clearly has more queenside space, but Black is about to map out his own territory with ...f7-f5. Should White try to take over the kingside as well by playing 1.f2-f4?

Using Pawns to Dominate the Center

Possession of a full pawn center can be a potent weapon in the hands of a player who knows how to make use of it. Such a center gains space and takes critical squares away from the enemy pieces. So good players often work to implement this strategy:

Make your center indestructible, and it will choke the life out of your opponent.

Let's look at some examples.

In Diagram 99, White's pawns on d4 and e4 constitute a full pawn center. They take away the e5 and d5 squares from the Black pieces, deprive Black's light-squared Bishop of the use of f5, and block Black's other Bishop on b6. White is not in any hurry to advance these pawns, because as soon as he does so, he will give up control of some square. For example, e4-e5 weakens his control of d5 and f5, and d4-d5 both activates the enemy dark-squared Bishop and gives up control of e5.

White's correct strategy in this position is to make his center unassailable. Then Black's pieces can do nothing but sit around and brood about their own helplessness. White can prepare an advance at his leisure, only pushing the pawns when it does the most good. Moves like Rad1 and Rfe1 are possible, and the more aggressive plan of Nd2 followed by f2-f4 is also extremely strong.

Note that it is Black's move, but the fact that the ball is in his court does not give him any cause to rejoice. What can he do? White's center is as solid as a rock and cannot be injured by Black's impotent army.

DIAGRAM 99. Black to play.

DIAGRAM 100. White to play.
Seirawan–Shirazi
U.S. Championship, 1992

In Diagram 100, I have another type of center. My pawns on c4 and e4 do not qualify as a full pawn center, but they still give me a clear advantage in central space. As a result, Black's pieces are having a lot of trouble finding good homes, whereas their counterparts in my army seem to fall on good posts without any effort at all.

1.Nd5 Bh6

2.f4 e5

Black tries desperately to be active, but all he really achieves is the weakening of both the d5-square and the d6-pawn. Best was 2...Ne5, with a difficult game.

3.Bxg4 Bxg4   4.Be3 Bg7

5.f5!

This strong move gains kingside space and also entombs the dark-squared Bishop on g7.

5...g5

6.a4!

I intend to ultimately break through in the center (I was lusting after that weak pawn on d6!), but I first snatch up some territory on the wings. This greedy strategy makes sense. After all, if I have all the space on the kingside, in the center, and on the queenside, what does that leave Black? Absolutely nothing! Placing my opponent in a state of complete helplessness is something that I love to do whenever I can.

6...Bh5

7.a5

Forward! I want *all* your space.

7...Rf7

Black has nothing to attack and nowhere to go with his pieces, so I can take my time and slowly squeeze him to death.

> **8.b3 Rd7**
>
> **9.Qf2**

I am threatening to capture on a7. If Black plays 9...a6?, he will give me access to the b6-square and will lose the Exchange after 10.Nb6.

> **9...Qb8   10.Nc3 Be8**
>
> **11.Nb5**

The Knight was nice on d5, but here it attacks both a7 and d6.

> **11...b6**

The natural-looking 11...a6 weakens b6 and allows me to jump on that point with 12.Nc3, 13.Na4, and 14.Nb6 (or 13.Nd5 and 14.Nb6).

> **12.axb6 axb6**
>
> **13.Qd2**

I avoid 13.Bxb6? Rxa1 14.Rxa1 Rb7, with a discovered attack on the b5-Knight by the e8-Bishop. Any Knight retreat would then allow ...Rxb3, and the trades could only help Black, who has less space.

> **13...Bf7   14.Qd3 Rxa1**
>
> **15.Rxa1 Bf8**

Black's pieces are cringing on the back rank, but it is not so easy to break through and beat him. I continue to take my time and penetrate his position slowly but very surely, always being careful to avoid giving him any sort of counterplay. My strategy here is:

When your opponent is helpless, keep him that way!

> **16.Qd2 Rb7   17.h4 h6**
>
> **18.Nc3 Be7   19.Ra6**

Notice how I am focusing on those b6 and d6 targets.

> **19...Kg7   20.Qa2 Qc7**
>
> **21.Qa4 d5**

Panic. I threatened to win the b-pawn with Qb5 and Na4, so Black gives up a pawn on his own terms and tries to open up some opportunities for counterplay.

22.Nb5 Qd7   23.cxd5 Be8

24.Na7

The player with more space usually avoids exchanges, but the player with more material usually courts them! In this case, I see a winning endgame, so I welcome all trades.

24...Qxa4   25.bxa4 b5

26.axb5 Bxb5   27.Nxb5 Rxb5

28.d6 Bd8   29.Ra8 Bb6

30.Bxb6 Rxb6   31.d7

At times, both sides will prepare to make a central advance. Timing then becomes critical: Don't let your opponent distract you from your goal. If he succeeds, you will never achieve it! Here's an example.

Faced with the position in Diagram 101, most players will immediately worry about White's threat of Bxd5. However, instead of reacting to a threat, you should first come to terms with the strategic needs of the position. Then and only then can you address its tactical peculiarities. White threatens to capture on d5 with Bxd5. How should Black deal with this threat? Let's first take a quick look at the actual game continuation:

DIAGRAM 101. Black to play.
Abrahamson–Ashe
Los Angeles, 1994

1...c4   2.Qc2 h6

3.Bh4 Nf5   4.Bg3 Nxg3

5.hxg3

Now White threatens 6.Nbxc4.

5...Rb8

6.e4!

And White takes the initiative in the center.

What do you think of these moves? Did both sides play well? Did their respective plans succeed?

The truth is, Black played quite poorly. His plan should be based on the acquisition of central space by ...e7-e5 (a move that also seeks to soften up the a1-h8 diagonal for his dark-squared Bishop, to say nothing of the fact that it creates a half-open e-file for his Rooks). Did this plan come to fruition? Absolutely not! Instead of worrying about that threat of Bxd5, Black should have tried harder to make his dreamed-of ...e7-e5 push a reality. Here's an analysis of the game:

1...c4?!

This move *does* stop the threat of Bxd5, but it also takes some of the pressure off of d4. Don't forget: One of the points of ...e7-e5 is to activate the dark-squared Bishop. Placing pawns on c5 and e5 accomplishes that goal because they directly attack d4. A single pawn on e5, while still nice, doesn't have quite the same effect.

Instead of 1...c4, I would be more inclined to play 1...h6 2.Bh4 Nf5 3.Bg3 Nxg3 4.hxg3 e6, which gives Black two Bishops and a very flexible pawn structure that favors those Bishops. If White initiates 2.Bf4 e5 3.dxe5 instead, Black plays 3...c4 followed by 4...Nxe5. He does not mind this move now because White has already captured on e5, giving up his strong point on d4 and activating Black's dark-squared Bishop.

2.Qc2 h6	**3.Bh4 Nf5**
4.Bg3 Nxg3	**5.hxg3 Rb8?**

Once again Black reacts to a threat (without asking if it is real or imagined, and without insisting on the success of his own plan). This time, though, his passive response will have serious consequences. Black should have played to set up 6...e5! and grabbed the center for himself. Then 7.Nbxc4 e4 8.Nd6 exf3 9.Nxb7 Qc7 wins a piece for Black and 7.dxe5 Nxe5 gives Black the superior position. Remember:

Once you begin to react to enemy threats and, as a consequence, forget about your own dreams, you will find that defeat is waiting just around the corner.

6.e4

With this move (the mirror image of the one Black had so desperately wanted to play), White gains central space and control of the game. After 6...e6 7.e5 (gaining even more central territory), the closed position hurts the Black Bishops. Black's strategy has failed completely! He never got the central space he wanted (via ...e7-e5), and his Bishop pair has gone from a potential advantage to a clear burden.

Defending Against a Pawn Center

Are central pawns really so strong? They were thought to be in the 1800s and the first part of this century. But then a new modernist view insisted that center pawns can also be treated as weaknesses. This view gave birth to a new strategy:

> *If your opponent insists on building a large pawn center, you must aim your pawns and pieces at it and try to chop it down.*

For example, after **1.d4 Nf6 2.c4 g6 3.Nc3 d5 4.cxd5 Nxd5 5.e4 Nxc3 6.bxc3**, White has a full pawn center. Why did Black allow White to claim the center as his own?

Black's moves, known as the *Grünfeld Defense*, are quite popular, so we know there must be a method to Black's madness. Black has allowed White to build up this impressive center because he intends to attack it and show that it is actually a target! To prove his point, Black must take aim at the center and hit it with everything he's got.

6...Bg7

Black eyes the d4-square and prepares to castle. Never forget to put your King in a safe place.

7.Bc4 0-0

8.Ne2 c5

Now Black has three pieces hitting d4.

9.0-0

White avoids 9.d5, because he would then give up some control of the e5-square and open up the a1-h8 diagonal for the Black dark-squared Bishop.

9...Nc6

Black trains more stuff on d4!

10.Be3

White reacts by defending that pawn with everything but the kitchen sink.

162

10...Qc7

Black threatens some discoveries (via ...cxd4) on the undefended c4-Bishop.

11.Rc1

Now 11...cxd4 12.cxd4 leaves the Bishop well defended.

11...Rd8

The battle for d4 never seems to end, does it?

12.h3

Many players prefer to keep loading up on d4 with 12.Qd2 followed by 13.Rfd1. Note that the immediate 12.f4? is a mistake because 12...Bg4 would get rid of a critical defender of d4.

12...b6   13.f4 Na5

14.Bd3 f5!

Now if White plays poorly with 15.e5, Black will turn the once-mighty White center into something that looks more like a leaky roof with ...c4, ...e6, ...Bb7, and ...Bd5, as you can see in Diagram 102.

This picture favors Black because he has succeeded in making the White pawns advance, leaving all the light squares vulnerable to occupation by the Black forces. Remember:

The idea of a pawn center is to deprive the enemy pieces of nice central squares.

Strangely enough, White's pawns are now actually hurting their own army. The e3-Bishop is locked in, the Knight is trapped by the pawns on f4 and d4, and the Rooks are doing absolutely nothing. Now that White is the helpless one (his central space advantage has been rendered useless), Black will take advantage of his queenside space (and queenside majority of pawns) by playing ...Nc6, ...b5, ...a5, and ...b4.

DIAGRAM 102.

163

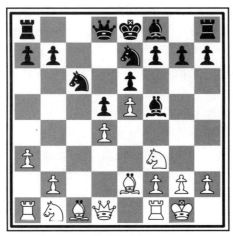

DIAGRAM 103. Black to play.
Yermolinsky–Seirawan
U.S. Championship, 1992

The next example from one of my games shows yet again the importance of attacking a pawn center before it can squeeze you. In Diagram 103, White's pawn on e5 gives him an edge in central space. Instead of bowing to that center, though, I try to prove that it is weak by attacking it at the base.

1...Be4!

I want all my pieces to land on squares that attack d4. My Bishop can chop off White's defending Knight, my e7-Knight is heading for f5, and my Queen can go to b6.

2.Nbd2 Nf5

3.b4

White gains queenside space and prepares to defend d4 with Bb2.

3...a5

I am already battling my opponent's spatial superiority in the center, so I have no intention of letting him grab queenside space as well! I avoid 3...Ncxd4 because this move opens up the center (not a good idea when your King still resides there!) and might lead to 4.Nxd4 Nxd4 5.Nxe4 dxe4 6.Qa4+ Nc6 (6...Qd7?? 7.Qxd7+ Kxd7 8.Rd1 picks up the Knight) 7.Rd1, after which I am in danger of being overrun. For example, 7...Qc7?? 8.b5 Nxe5 9.b6+ Qc6 10.Bb5 results in my Queen heading the list of casualties.

4.bxa5

Now 4.b5? Ncxd4 5.Nxd4 Nxd4 6.Nxe4 dxe4 7.Be3 Bc5 is fine for me because White no longer has a check along the a4-e8 diagonal.

4...Qxa5

I have a good position. My pieces are active, White's d4-pawn is a target, and his a3-pawn is also in need of defense.

5.g4? Nfxd4   6.Nxd4 Nxd4

7.Nxe4 Nxe2+   8.Qxe2 dxe4

9.Qxe4 Bc5!

White's King is now a bit loose, his g-pawn has gone too far, and his other pawns on a3 and e5 are also potential targets. All I have to do is castle, and I can claim an advantage. Playing 9...Bc5 sacrifices a pawn but gives me time to get my monarch to safety. The initiative is now completely mine.

10.Qxb7 0-0   11.Qe4 Qc3

12.Ra2 Qb3!

My threats of ...Qxa2 and ...Ra4 guarantee me at least the return of my sacrificed pawn. The game will eventually be drawn, but White's once-proud space-gaining center is now remembered only by the weakling on e5.

PROBLEM 22. It's White's turn to play. White enjoys more central space than his opponent. Should he grab even more territory with 1.d5?

Attacking the King

You might think it strange to find a section on attacking the King in a book about strategy. However, attacking on any side of the board *is* a strategic undertaking. If the position calls for you to attack your enemy's monarch, then that is the correct strategy for the position. This type of strategic decision is not a matter of personal taste or style. When the board dictates that you should rip the head off the enemy King, then that is what you must do.

Now for a word of warning: If all the conditions for a kingside attack exist and you decide to go for the King's throat, don't assume that you are in a "checkmate-or-die" situation. You might be, but a kingside attack per-se doesn't necessarily demand all or nothing. You have to stay flexible. If your attack nets you a pawn, feel free to trade off and go into a winning endgame with a material advantage. If your attack leaves the enemy with various pawn weaknesses, don't hesitate to change your strategy to a positional "hunt-and-destroy-targets" type of battle. An attack on the King can lead to checkmate, but it can also lead to a host of other advantages that you must be willing to exploit.

One other bit of advice: Watch out for central counterplay. One of the finest rules of chess that should be used religiously by the defender and carefully considered by the attacker is:

The best reaction to an attack on the wing is a counterattack in the center.

Creating the Conditions for a Kingside Attack

Whether or not to launch an attack against the enemy King should not be an emotional decision. It's not a macho display, and it's not a course of action you should undertake just because you *like* to attack. A player charges the enemy King because certain conditions tell him that this is the correct strategy to follow. What are these conditions? The following list shows the four main conditions to look for when deciding on a kingside attack. The list is not complete because lots of small factors can fit together to make the success of an attack more likely, but it does give you a feel for the kind of advantage that can translate to kingside play.

- If you have a space advantage in the vicinity of the enemy King, you will usually play in that sector.

- If several of your pieces are close to the enemy King while his defenders are few or far away (that is, you have superior force), your chances of a Kingside attack succeeding are probably excellent.

- If the pawns surrounding the enemy King have been ripped apart or weakened in any way, you can consider an assault if one of the previous conditions also exist. (If the King is open but you have no pieces on that side of the board, then what are you going to checkmate him with?)

- If you have a substantial lead in development, you must make use of it before your opponent catches up and your development edge fades away. A lead in development is a signal for attack!

One of the most common attacking situations occurs when both Kings have castled on opposite sides. Pushing the pawns in front of your own King can be dangerous because it weakens your King's pawn cover, so it is a normal practice to seek your play on the side of the board where you have *not* castled. In that sector, you can push your pawns to your heart's content in an effort to gain space and open files for your Rooks, without damaging the integrity of your King's protective-pawn safety net.

Not so common is the type of game you get when both sides place their Kings directly in the path of the enemy attack! No subtle plans are called for here! Instead we commonly see a blood-frenzy akin to sharks at feeding time. Each player does everything he can to checkmate the enemy monarch before his own King goes down. Under these circumstances, a fifth condition can be added to the list:

■ When both sides are playing for checkmate, then time, or tempo, becomes more important than material, or force.

Let's look at an example of a dual attack. The position in Diagram 104 is a very popular one on the international circuit and also here in the United States. (It occurs after 1.e4 c5 2.Nf3 d6 3.d4 cxd4 4.Nxd4 Nf6 5.Nc3 g6 6.Be3 Bg7 7.f3 Nc6 8.Qd2 0-0 9.Bc4

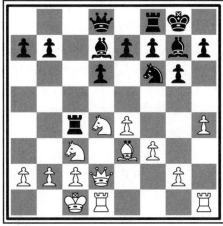

DIAGRAM 104. White to play.
Karpov–Korchnoi
Moscow, 1974

Bd7 10.h4 Rac8 11.Bb3 Ne5 12.0-0-0 Nc4 13.Bxc4 Rxc4.) The Kings reside on opposite sides of the board: White's King is sitting on a half-open c-file; Black's King is not faced with an open file yet, but White will do everything he can to create one.

14.h5!

White sacrifices a pawn to speed up his own attack. It is very important to understand that in this position, time is of the essence. If either side plays passively or wastes a move, the enemy will push his attack through and emerge victorious.

14...Nxh5

Black wins a pawn but allows White to open the h-file (bringing the White Rooks into the attack) without any loss of tempo. This transaction accelerates the White attack but leaves Black with a small material advantage. What good is a material advantage in a situation like this? None at all if it comes down to checkmate, but the extra pawn gives Black two possibilities that he did not have before:

■ He will most likely win any endgame because of that extra unit, so White cannot trade pieces indiscriminately.

169

■ He can sacrifice a pawn to stop the White attack and not incur a material disadvantage.

In this way, the extra pawn acts like ballast in a hot air balloon: He can throw some over the side if the balloon begins to sink.

15.g4

Again White forces Black to react to his move.

15...Nf6

16.Nde2!

In the midst of his attack, White suddenly pulls his Knight back in retreat! Why would he do such a strange thing? The first part of the answer is concerned with defense. White knows that Black will sacrifice the Exchange by ...Rxc3 if the White Queen ever moves away. If the Queen can't recapture on c3, then bxc3 will be forced, leaving the White King rather exposed. So playing 16.Nde2 gives extra support to the c3-Knight and allows the White Queen to move toward the kingside. The second part of the answer is concerned with attack and with what White really wants to do: He longs to play Bh6 and get rid of Black's most important defender. (This Black piece is also a great attacker.) However, the immediate 16.Bh6 takes a White defender away from d4 and walks into 16...Nxe4! 17.Nxe4 Rxd4. So playing 16.Nde2 also prepares for the important Bh6 move.

16...Qa5

This attacking move lost its popularity after this game, and players now favor the defensive 16...Re8, which answers 17.Bh6 with 17...Bh8, retaining the important Bishop.

17.Bh6 Bxh6

18.Qxh6 Rfc8

Black is building up quite a bit of force along the c-file. He might even be contemplating a double Exchange sacrifice via 19...Rxc3 20.Nxc3 Rxc3. White's next move stops this idea in its tracks.

19.Rd3! R4c5

20.g5!

White draws the enemy Rook away from the c-file. This second pawn sacrifice gives White the time he needs to break through with his own attack.

20...Rxg5

21.Rd5!

If White can get rid of that defending Knight on f6, he will checkmate his opponent. The obvious try would be 21.Nd5 (answering 21...Nxd5?? with 22.Qxh7+ Kf8 23.Qh8 checkmate), but then Black would play 21...Rxd5! (keeping the important Knight) 22.Rxd5 Qxa2, with a strong attack. The idea behind 21.Rd5 is to get rid of the g5-Rook so that it can't sacrifice itself on d5. Then the White Knight can jump into d5 and trade itself for that pesky piece on f6.

21...Rxd5

22.Nxd5 Re8

White threatens to win immediately with 23.Nxe7+ followed by 24.Nxc8.

23.N2f4

White is following a strategy that I have repeated throughout this book:

Don't just attack with one or two pieces! Use everything you have.

With 23.N2f4, White brings his last available piece into the attack against Black's King. Notice that 23.Nxf6+ exf6 24.Qxh7+ Kf8 25.Qh8+ Ke7 allows the Black King to run away.

23...Bc6

White threatened 24.Nxf6+ exf6 25.Nd5, which keeps Black's King off e7 and leaves him helpless before the threat of Qxh7+ followed by Qh8 checkmate. After 23...Bc6, however, 24.Nxf6+ exf6 25.Nd5 can calmly be met with 25...Bxd5. (If Black had played 23...Be6—a move based on the same idea as 23...Bc6—White was prepared to play 24.Nxe6 fxe6 25.Nxf6+ exf6 26.Qxh7+ Kf8 27.Qxb7 Qg5+ 28.Kb1 Re7 29.Qb8+ Re8 30.Qxa7 Re7 31.Qb8+ Re8 32. Qxd6, which wins all the Black queenside pawns and gives White the endgame odds that Black so proudly claimed earlier—see the note to 14...Nxh5.)

24.e5!

A real surprise that shows White is going all out for the knockout. Now 24...Nxd5 can still be met with 25.Qxh7+ and 26.Qh8 checkmate. (We'll see how White handles 24...Bxd5 in a minute.) So what does 24.e5 accomplish? And how does White intend to answer 24...dxe5? The point of this third pawn sacrifice is that it closes the 5th rank. After 24...dxe5, the Black Queen no longer eyes g5 and h5, allowing White to play 25.Nxf6+ exf6 26.Nh5! gxh5 27.Rg1+ with checkmate on the next move. If White tries this play without throwing in 24.e5! first, Black can hold on after 24.Nxf6+ exf6 25.Nh5 Qg5+, trading Queens and going into an Exchange-down but tenable endgame with 26.Qxg5 fxg5 27.Nf6+ Kf8 28.Nxe8 Kxe8, hoping for a draw.

24...Bxd5   25.exf6 exf6

26.Qxh7+

The strong-looking 26.Nh5?? actually loses to 26...Re1+.

26...Kf8

27.Qh8+

Black did not wish to see 27...Ke7 28.Nxd5+ Qxd5 29.Re1+, so he gives up.

Castling on opposite sides makes your decision to play for an attack fairly clear-cut. In the Karpov-Korchnoi game, we saw both sides trying to rip open the pawn cover around the enemy King. White took precautions and avoided this fate, but Black went under when his kingside pawns got shredded. The three other conditions to watch for, as I said at the beginning of the chapter, are kingside space, pieces aimed at the enemy King (greater force), and a lead in development. Let's look at examples of each of these factors.

Superior Space on the Kingside

In the position in Diagram 105, Black has more space on the kingside whereas White has territory on the queenside. Because the center is completely blocked (which means that nobody can play there), both sides have to find their play in the sector of the board where they own superior space. Here their respective strategies should be obvious: White will play on the queenside and try to open lines of attack with cxd6, Rc1, and Nb5; Black will play on the kingside and try to open a file so that his Rooks can join in the battle. The only way Black can achieve this goal is by ...g6-g5-g4. He will prepare this advance by playing ...g5, ...h5, ...Rf7, ...Bf8 (both defending and attacking moves—the Rook defends White's entry point on c7 and prepares to go to g7, and the Bishop defends d6 and makes room for the Rook), ...Rg7,

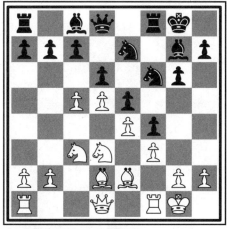

DIAGRAM 105. Black to play.

and finally ...g4. So the battle plans for both sides are clear.

Superior Force on the Kingside

Positionally, I am doing quite well in Diagram 106. My Queen is attacking the weak a3-pawn, and I can attack the pawn on c3 with ...Rac8. Unfortu-

nately, I didn't take my opponent's kingside build-up seriously enough. His Queen, both Rooks, Knight, and Bishop all aim at my King. This gives him a superior force in that area, so all he has to do is find a way to get those pieces to my King.

1.Nxg6!

A pretty move that creates a road into my position. This attack will cost White a piece or two, but few good things in life are free.

1...hxg6

Even worse is 1...fxg6? 2.Rxe6 Qf7 3.Rxe8+, followed by 4.Bxf7+.

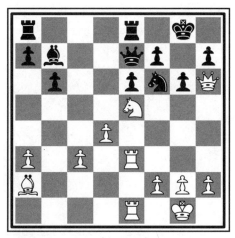

DIAGRAM 106. White to play.
Adams–Seirawan
Wijk aan Zee, 1991

173

2.Rh3 Nh5

I had only one way to stop immediate checkmate.

3.Rxh5!

White opens another road on the g-file to my King.

3...gxh5

4.Re5 f6

I keep the Rook off of g5.

5.Re3 h4

Now I keep the Rook off of g3. I'm hanging on as best I can, but in the long run I won't be able to survive.

6.Qxh4 Kf7

Now White can finish me off with 7.d5! Qxa3 (7...e5 8.d6+ picks up my Queen) 8.dxe6+ Ke7 9.Qh7+ Kd6 10.Qd7+ Kc5 11.Qd4+ Kb5 12.c4+, and I lose my Queen for nothing after 12...Ka4 13.Qd7+ Kb4 14.Qd6+.

A Lead in Development

I have a considerable lead in development in Diagram 107, but Black is a pawn ahead and hopes to capitalize on it after he castles. The situation is

DIAGRAM 107. White to play.
Seirawan–Zarnicki
Buenos Aires, 1993

critical for me. If I don't find a way to break through and wipe Black out, that lost pawn will come back to haunt me. In other words, I *must* attack!

1.Rxd6!

Because I am already a pawn down, losing a bit more wood doesn't bother me. By taking this Bishop, I get rid of Black's guardian of the dark squares, allowing my Knight to come to e5 and, in turn, bringing my g2-Bishop to life.

1...Qxd6

2.Rd1

I don't want to give Black a chance to castle, so I play with nothing but threats to get his attention.

2...Qc7

3.Bf4

I attack the Queen and gain possession of the e5-square.

3...Qb7

4.Ne5

Now all my army is participating in the attack. Black still can't castle; he has to defend against my threat of 5.Bxc6, which wins me loads of material. (At this point, I don't care whether I checkmate the guy. Winning loads of material is good enough.)

4...Bd7

He is ready to castle again. I must react forcefully or my attack will falter.

5.Rxd7!

Grist for the mill! Now c6 falls, and I get all of my material back—with dividends!

5...Nxd7   6.Bxc6 Qa6

7.Nxd7

I pick up a free Knight, which leaves us with near material equality (though I usually prefer the three pieces over the two Rooks because it gives me three attacking units to two). In addition, I threaten to eat the Rook with Bxa8, thereby stopping Black from castling and also threatening to win the Queen with Nxc5+. The game is as good as over.

7...Qc8

8.Ba4

I could play 8.Bxa8 Qxa8 9.Ne5, but then my opponent could castle. In my mind, I saw my light-squared Bishop as being stronger than either of his pathetic Rooks. Why should I trade it for an undeveloped piece when I could retain it and continue to harrass his King?

8...Ke7

Black has no other way to stop my threat of 9.Nxb6+.

9.Qd3

I refuse to give the poor guy any rest. Now I threaten 11.Qd6+ Ke8 12.Nf6, with checkmate! Notice how I use every piece I own.

9...f6   10.Qd6+ Kf7

11.Ne5+!

Black was threatening to get his h8-Rook into the game via ...Rd8, so I sacrifice a piece to destroy the pawn cover around his King and make room for my light-squared Bishop to jump to d7.

11...fxe5

12.Bd7 Qd8

Black would lose after 12...exf4 13.Qxe6+ Kf8 14.Bxc8.

13.Qxe6+ Kf8

14.Bxe5

The spector of Bd6+ is too much to deal with.

14...g6

15.Bf6

And Black gives up. Why did my attack succeed? Though it appeared that I was at a disadvantage because I was down a pawn, my lead in development gave me more fighting units than my opponent. Dynamically, I was *ahead* in material for the short term. Of course, if Black had held me off for a while, I would have been in trouble, but energetic play allowed me to make use of my army's superior development. Always bear this in mind:

A lead in development gives you a dynamic material advantage for a few moves because your developed pieces are taking part in the game while your opponent's undeveloped ones are not. If you have a lead in development, you must use it before it goes away!

PROBLEM 23. It's White's turn to play. Where should White seek his play, what is the reasoning behind this decision, and how should he go about achieving his goal?

Attacking Out of Necessity

Sometimes you will find the tide of battle has turned against you. You might be a pawn down, or you might be positionally busted on the queenside (you have weak pawns, you control less space, your opponent's Rooks are going to penetrate your position, and so on). What do you do? As in boxing, you might look at his chin (alias his King) and assess whether you have any realistic chance for a knockout. Do you have any justification (aside from desperation) for going after his monarch? Do you have more space? Are your pieces aimed at the King's sector of the board? If you have no advantages whatsoever, any attack is probably doomed to fail before you even begin it. However, if you have some advantages on the kingside and things look bleak elsewhere, why not take a chance and become a slugger?

This type of last-chance attack, aside from having some positional justification, earns you psychological points. Your opponent, expecting a safe victory, now faces nasty threats against his King. Will he calmly withstand your onslaught? Or will he panic and, in a state of terror, make a fatal error?

When you attack out of necessity, you are not always desperate, though. Quite often your opponent will have certain advantages in one area while you will have advantages in another. In such a situation, you don't have any choice: You must either use your advantages or lose without a fight. You *must* play wherever your strategic advantages lie!

As an example, look at the position in Diagram 108, which results from 1.d4 Nf6 2.c4 e6 3.Nf3 d5 4.cxd5 exd5 5.Nc3 c6 6.Bg5 Be7 7.Qc2 g6 8.e3 Bf5 9.Bd3 Bxd3 10.Qxd3 Nbd7 11.Bh6 Ng4! 12.Bf4 0-0 13.0-0 Re8 14.h3 Ngf6 15.Ne5 Nb6! 16.Bg5 Ne4 17.Bxe7 Qxe7 18.Qc2 Nd6 19.Na4 Nbc4 20.Nxc4 Nxc4 21.Nc5 Nd6!

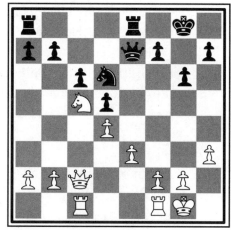

DIAGRAM 108. Black to play.
**Bobotsov–Petrosian
Lugano, 1968**

22.Rac1 (a Queen's Gambit Declined). White tried a minority attack (see Chapter Seven for more on this topic), but Black completely outplayed him. The trade of light-squared Bishops left the c4-square weak, and b2-b4 (the normal way to play a minority attack) would allow Black to jump to c4 via ...Nc4. In addition, the Black Knight on d6 is perfectly placed. It defends b7 and eyes c4, e4, b5, and f5.

The real issue now centers around the players' respective plans. White's play on the queenside has been stopped, and he cannot easily do anything elsewhere. Black's play has not even started, but his pawn chain aims at the kingside, and his pieces can jump to that side with great speed. If Black wants to have any chance of winning this game, he has to play for a kingside attack. He may not conquer the White King, but he will force his opponent to make some sort of positional concessions. (For example, if White eventually has to play f2-f3, his e-pawn will become a target on the open e-file.)

22...Qg5!

The first sign that Black is on the attack. His Queen eyes both e3 and g2.

23.Qd1 h5

Black prepares a pawn storm on the kingside. (The idea behind a pawn storm is to open files for the Rooks. Here Black will eventually play ...g5-g4.) He also keeps the White Queen out of g4.

24.Kh1 Re7   25.Nd3 Ne4

26.Nc5 Nd6

Black is in no hurry because White can't really do anything. However, Black does want to avoid exchanges because every trade reduces his army and thus reduces his attacking potential.

27.Nd3 Qf5   28.Ne5 f6

29.Nf3 Rg7

Black is almost ready to play ...g6-g5-g4.

30.Nh2 Re8

Why not get all your pieces in the game before you attack?

31.Kg1 Ne4

32.Qf3 Qe6

Black definitely does *not* want to trade Queens!

33.Rfd1 g5!

The attack starts. Black sacrifices a pawn to open files to the White King. Notice that Black is not concerned that his own King is a bit exposed because White does not have enough of an army on the kingside to do any harm there.

34.Qxh5

White might as well take the pawn. If he doesn't, Black will play ...g5-g4 and rip open the White King.

34...f5   35.Re1 g4

36.hxg4 fxg4

Black is a pawn down, but all his pieces are superior to their White counterparts. His Rooks enjoy more scope, his Knight is much superior to the old nag on h2, and the White Queen is trapped behind enemy lines and subject to attack by the whole Black army.

37.f3 gxf3

38.Nxf3 Rh7

Black has changed plans. His target was the White King, but now he has decided to hunt down its consort!

39.Qe5 Qc8   40.Qf4 Rf8

41.Qe5 Rf5

White's poor Queen has nowhere to go, and White gives up.

Now here's another example of attacking out of necessity from one of my games. In Diagram 109, Black has two Bishops, but I am not concerned because I have kept the center as closed as possible. I have gone into this position thinking that with the center closed, I will eventually be able to play b2-b4 and get a nice

DIAGRAM 109. **Black to play.**
Seirawan–Lautier
Belgrade, 1991

queenside attack going. Unfortunately, I should have been more concerned about my opponent's play on the other wing.

1...Ne7

This simple little retreat wakes me up! Aside from the fact that Black can someday open the center for his Bishops with ...c7-c5, he is bringing all his pieces to the kingside for an attack.

2.g3

I try to neutralize his dark-squared Bishop and also prepare to bring my own Bishop to the kingside as a defender.

2...g6!

Black intends to play ...h6-h5-h4, ...Kg7, and ...Rh8, which enables his Rooks to join the hunt for my King.

3.Bf3 h5   4.Nf4 Bxf4

5.gxf4

So I have captured his dark-squared Bishop, but my King is now a bit exposed. The interesting thing about this game so far is that Black's play on the kingside has grabbed my attention and stopped me from continuing with my own plans on the opposite wing. He is following this strategy:

Use an attack to get your opponent's attention and make him worry. Often he will stop pursuing his own plans and turn completely to the defense.

5...Nf5

6.Kh1 c5!

By blasting open the center, Black activates the Rook on d8 and the Bishop on e6. I will ultimately be unable to counter his initiative because of the unstable state of my King.

7.dxc5 d4   8.Ne4 Qe7

9.Qe2 Nh4

Black threatens 10...Nxf3 followed by ...Bd5 with a nightmarish pin.

10.Nd6 d3

I can't take this pawn because then the Bishop on f3 would be undefended.

11.Qd1 b6	12.b4 bxc5
13.bxc5 Qc7	14.e4 Bh3

If I play 15.Rg1, then 15...Qxc5 threatens my Knight and my pawn on f2.

15.Qxd3 Bxf1	16.Rxf1 Qxc5
17.e5 Nxf3	18.Qxf3 Rb8

Black's extra Exchange gives him a winning position, which he eventually converts into a victory.

My last example also shows Black on the offensive. In Diagram 110, it isn't hard to see that White is a pawn ahead and has the superior pawn structure. The only advantage Black can boast about is a bit of central space and a significant lead in development. Because development is only a temporary advantage, Black has to attack with all his might and try to convert his developmental lead into something more permanent. Choice is not a factor in this decision; Black must attack or he will lose.

1...Nd4

Pretty self-evident. The Knight takes up a nice central post and gains time by attacking the enemy Queen.

2.Qb1 f5

Now the well-placed White Knight is forced to take a step backward.

3.Nc3 e4

Black's excellent move opens up the h8-a1 diagonal for his dark-squared Bishop, blocks the White Bishop on g2, and gains space in the center.

4.d3

White tries to get rid of that bothersome pawn on e4, but he must be very careful. Any opening of the center will favor the player with better development—Black, in this case.

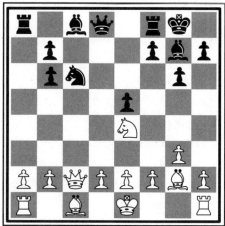

DIAGRAM 110. Black to play.
Tatai–Karpov
Las Palmas, 1977

4...b5

5.Be3

As I said earlier, the player with better development has, in a way, a material advantage because his extra working units give him more useable force. This is why White is so desperately trying to get his pieces out. Other possible moves, such as 5.e3 Nf3+ 6.Bxf3 exf3 7.Nxb5 Qa5+ 8.Nc3 b5, leave Black in charge, and playing 5.a3 b4 6.axb4?? Rxa1 7.Qxa1 Nc2+ simply loses the game.

5...b4	**6.Nd1 Re8**
7.dxe4 fxe4	**8.Bxd4**

The Knight on d4 was too strong and had to be eradicated. Unfortunately, the Black dark-squared Bishop now becomes rather dominant.

8...Qxd4

9.a3

White would like to castle, but he realizes that 9.0-0 Qd2 10.Bxe4 Bh3 11.Bg2 Bxg2 12.Kxg2 Rxe2 13.Qc1 Qd5+ 14.Kg1 Bd4 will completely tie him up.

9...Bg4

10.Qc2 Qd3!

Very nice. Black never gives White a moment's rest.

11.exd3 exd3+

12.Kd2 Re2+

The attack continues even after the Queen has left the board.

13.Kxd3 Rd8+

Every piece that Black owns is taking part in the attack.

14.Kc4

If White plays 14.Bd5 Rxd5+ 15.Kc4 Rxc2+ 16.Kxd5 Bf3+, he leaves Black a piece ahead.

14...Rxc2+	**15.Kxb4 Rcd2**
16.f3	

White has no choice. Any Knight move allows 16...Rxb2+.

16...Bf8+

17.Ka5 Bd7

Black has woven a checkmating net around the White King. Now 18.Bf1 Bc5! takes away all legal squares from the King and creates the unstoppable threat of 19...Ra8+ with checkmate to follow. White resigns.

The obligation to attack can arise anywhere on the board. You might be forced to attack on the queenside or in the center. Just be aware that you have to demand active play, and the way to find out where that play exists is to figure out where your existing advantages lie.

**Sherbakov–M. Gurevich
Helsinki, 1992**

ite's turn to play, . He could try to pe for a draw, but misery is only for se all of White's the Black King, kind of knockout material and po- do not count (you as you want); it's ation! Fortunately decisive blow. See

Faulty Strategies

An old chess saying states, "A poor plan is better than no plan at all." When you play with a poor plan, you are at least trying to improve your position. Perhaps the plan will fail against better play, but you should at least get credit for trying! If you play planlessly, however, you will shuffle your pieces back and forth in an aimless fashion, waiting for your opponent to either put you out of your misery or make a game-losing blunder.

Which brings to mind another chess saying: "If you don't know what to do, let your opponent come up with an idea. It's bound to be wrong!" Though this bit of chess wisdom is obviously offered tongue in cheek, and though it contrasts sharply with the first bit of wisdom, it nevertheless holds a grain of truth. The fact is that chess is a near-perfect game played by far-from-perfect people. Errors of some kind are seen in virtually every game, and all victories are due to the loser's mistakes and the winner's ability to take advantage of them—how he punishes his opponent for creating those weak pawns, giving him more space, and so on.

All this doesn't mean that you should quietly wait for mistakes to occur. If you do nothing, *you* are making mistakes, and your position will be so bad that you won't be able to take advantage of the opponent's errors. No, you must play with a clear plan in mind at all times. But you must also be alert for your enemy's inevitable moment of suicidal blindness, which will allow you to drive the advantages that you have so carefully cultivated through the heart of his position.

The form your enemy's mistake will take cannot be predicted. It might be a blunder that loses copious quantities of material; it might be a subtle strategic error that allows your plan to triumph over his; it might be a poor piece of calculation; or it might be a weak move brought on by psychological collapse. Your opponent will make these mistakes, you will make these mistakes, and I will make these mistakes. Remember yet a third chess saying and you will be able to get through these mistakes with a smile on your face:

The winner is the player who makes the next-to-last mistake.

Good luck.

Misunderstanding the Position

Chess advantages are useful only if they help you in the particular situation in which you find yourself on the board. For example, your ability to use a pawn majority to create a passed pawn is most useful in an endgame. As a result, if you possess a healthy majority, you should usually steer the game into a simplified type of position where your majority will carry some weight. It does you no good to rave about the wonders of your pawn majority if your opponent can swoop in with his whole army and behead your King. Always remember:

An "advantage" that is inappropriate to the position is no advantage at all.

Any gain you make is useful only if you can create a position where its virtues can be demonstrated. In other words, once you gain a Bishop vs. a Knight, a Knight vs. a Bishop, a passed pawn, more space, or anything else, you must make the position on the board conform to the needs of the advantage you have created. If you notice that you can gain a Bishop vs. a Knight but that the resulting position will be closed, you may very well want to think twice before engineering this situation. If you notice that you can create a superior pawn formation but at the cost of giving your opponent more space, you may want to think long and hard about which advantage is more useful at the present time. You must be able to prove to yourself that the advantage you gain gives your plans and possessions superiority over your opponent's plans and possessions.

Attacking Prematurely

The desire to reward yourself with a premature attack is one way to lose track of what is really happening in a position. For example, the position in Diagram 111 is about equal, but for some reason White decides that he has a right to checkmate Black on the kingside. Why? Evidently, White thinks the position favors him, and he wants to press home his illusory advantage.

DIAGRAM 111. White to play.
Cardoso–Benko
Potoroz, 1958

1.g4?

By starting a pawn storm in this way, White weakens his own King and ignores the central situation. If he had control of the center or if the center were closed, then such a wing attack might be justified, but here Black can strike in the middle with ...e5 and ...d5. To make matters worse, the White Bishop on c4 is undefended. A saner alternative for White would have been either 1.Bd3 or 1.Be2.

1...d5!

Black remembers the rule:

The best reaction to an attack on the wing is a counterattack in the center.

If Black can get away with this counterattack, White's whole strategy will be an obvious failure because all the play will be concentrated in the middle. This response will make White's g2-g4 move look rather out of place, to say the least!

2.Bd3

If White plays 2.exd5, Black has 2...Nb4 (with a discovered attack on c4) 3.Be2 Nbxd5.

2...dxe4

Black must open up the center. He can't allow White to close it by playing e4-e5.

3.Nxe4 Nd5

4.Bd2 a5

The threat of ...a5-a4 torments White on the queenside, and the wide-open center keeps his attention fixed in that area also. White can't even consider a kingside attack now.

5.c3 Rd8   6.g5 a4

7.Nc1 Qb6+

Black, who is threatening the White King and the pawn on b2, and also threatening moves like ...Ne3, went on to win the game. Notice whose King is more vulnerable in this final position.

Getting Hung Up on Development

Another way to lose track of what is happening in a position is to get so involved in simple development that you fail to take the dynamics of a particular situation into account. I am as guilty of this type of one-track playing as anyone, as this next game illustrates.

Granda Zuñiga–Seirawan

Buenos Aires, 1993

In this game, I lose my sense of danger early on and continue to develop my pieces in a routine fashion, unaware of the surprise that awaits me.

DIAGRAM 112. White to play.

1.Nf3 Nf6	**2.c4 c5**
3.Nc3 e6	**4.g3 b6**
5.Bg2 Bb7	**6.0-0 Nc6**
7.e4 e5	**8.d3 g6**

I think everything is fine after playing this move. I know I am behind in development but, as Diagram 112 shows, the center is closed, and I don't anticipate any problem. However, my opponent is about to bring me back to the real world.

9.Nxe5!!

I cannot believe what I am seeing! This shock could have been prevented, of course, by 8...d6, but the possibility of his giving up a piece so early in the game never even entered my mind. Now White can push my pieces back and take advantage of his lead in development, which I had thought was without value just moments ago. To make matters even worse, I have to adjust to a defensive mind-set. Unfortunately, I still refuse to believe that I have made an error of judgment and, instead of implementing some sort of damage control, I play as if my opponent's sacrifice is unsound.

9...Nxe5	**10.f4 Nc6**
11.e5 Ng8	**12.f5**

White has a very strong attack, and his lead in development becomes more and more menacing as the position opens up.

12...Nh6?

Overconfident, I lose touch with reality. A much more challenging defense would have been 12...Rb8! (which defends my Bishop and frees my Knight from the pin along the h1-a8 diagonal) 13.e6 dxe6 14.fxe6 f5 15.Rxf5 Qd4+ 16.Rf2, leaving a sharp, unclear position.

13.Ne4!

Oops. Now I can't keep him out of f6 because 13...Be7 just hangs my h6-Knight to 14.Bxh6, whereas 13...Bg7 allows 14.Nd6+.

13...Nxf5	**14.Nf6+ Ke7**
15.Nd5+ Ke8	**16.Nf6+ Ke7**
17.g4	

White's powerful attack eventually breaks through and leads to my demise.

Playing Complacently

One of the most common mistakes a player can make is to play mindlessly along, repeating known ideas used before in similar situations. The player thinks he is playing by the book but, because one or two details are askew, the position is different and should be evaluated differently.

Seirawan–Karpov

Haninge, 1990

In this game, we see no less a player than the careful Karpov fall into this type of mental trap.

1.c4 e5	**2.g3 g6**
3.d4 d6	**4.dxe5 dxe5**
5.Qxd8+ Kxd8	**6.Nc3 c6?**

As you can see in Diagram 113, Black's sixth move gives his King the c7-square and takes d5 away from the White Knight. I suspect that Karpov thought he had entered a line that usually begins with 1.d4 d6 2.c4 e5 3.dxe5 dxe5 4.Qxd8+ Kxd8 5.Nc3 c6, which leads to a satisfactory position for Black. In fact, I have successfully played Black with this line of play several times. However, the fact that I have played g3 and Black has played ...g6 favors me, because the White Bishop can now go to h3, whereas ...g6 does not help Black at all. In fact, it actually weakens f6 and the a1-h8 diagonal. So a Black move that is excellent in the position that results from a line starting with 1.d4 is now a mistake, but my opponent doesn't notice this subtle fact until it is too late. Why does he make this error? Because he isn't thinking yet! He is just playing on instinct and relying on his knowledge of a similar position—knowledge that proves erroneous in the present situation!

7.f4!

I have a slight lead in development, and the Black King is in the center. I go out of my way to blast open lines of attack so that I can take advantage of these factors.

7...Be6

Black places his Bishop on a nice square. Playing 7...Nd7 would make it very hard to develop this piece in the future, and 7...exf4? 8.Bxf4 Be6

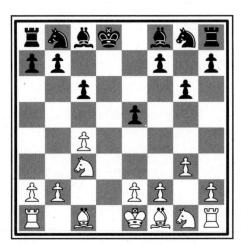

DIAGRAM 113.

9.0-0-0+ Nd7 10.Nf3 would leave the Black King without a safe haven.

8.Nf3

I have no interest in 8.fxe5 because 8...Nd7 would leave me tied to the defense of that miserable e-pawn for the rest of the game. Instead, I choose to develop rapidly and generate chances for an attack.

8...Bxc4

Black hopes that I will accept a simple trade with 9.Nxe5 Be6, after which he has everything under control.

9.Bh3!

Now I threaten 10.Nxe5 because 10...Be6 would lose to 11.Bxe6 followed by 12.Nf7+. Black doesn't want to accelerate my development with 9...exf4 10.Bxf4, so he tries to block off my Bishop on h3.

9...f5

10.b3!!

I don't want to waste my time taking back that pawn on e5. Instead, I prepare to place my Bishop on b2, where it will create real threats along the a1-h8 diagonal.

10...Bb4   **11.Bb2 Bd5**

12.e4!

Since making his mistake on move 6, Black has not had a moment's rest. With 12.e4, I continue my strategy of ripping open the center. Now 12...Bxe4 13.0-0-0+ followed by 14.Nxe4 would be very strong for me.

12...fxe4

13.0-0-0!

I seem to live for development, but this temporary piece sacrifice works because of the poor placement of the Black King and the vulnerability of the Black Rook on h8.

13...Bxc3!

Black stops me from taking on d5.

14.Bxc3 exf3   **15.Bxe5 Nd7**

16.Bxh8

I win the Exchange and use my material edge to win the game.

Overlooking Tactical Factors

So far we have witnessed errors that result from overconfidence, the mindless adherence to simple development, and the unthinking usage of basic themes that may not be appropriate to the current position on the board. All errors of these types involve a touch of laziness; the perpetrator of the error does not take the time to really come to grips with the position. Laziness is the cornerstone of most mistakes. If you make an error because the position is too difficult to really figure out, then you have nothing to be ashamed of. However, if your mistake is due to a lack of thought, you must swallow your excuses and find a way to increase your level of concentration.

Another type of mistake is tactical. You make a move that may be right positionally but that fails to take into consideration the tactical peculiarities of the exact situation. Let's look at an example of this type of error.

In Diagram 114, Black understandably wants to close off the queenside because I have more space there, but he doesn't take into account the unprotected state of his Rook on a8.

1...a5?

2.b5 Nd8

DIAGRAM 114. **Black to play.**
Seirawan–Van Wely
Wijk aan Zee, 1992

That Rook on a8 is being eyed by my Bishop on g2, but so many pieces and pawns are in the way that Black feels safe from any surprise attack. If Black explored the danger on the h1-a8 diagonal more thoroughly, he would see what is coming and avoid 1...a5. However, that tinge of laziness, that blind sense of security, once again brings a player to his knees.

3.exf5!

I get rid of that first obstacle on the long diagonal.

3...Bxf5

Also losing is 3...Nxf5? 4.g4! hxg4 5.fxg4 Nh6 6.Bxh6 Bxh6 7.g5 Bg7 8.Nxb6!, when the Rook on a8 gets eaten just as it does in the game.

4.g4! hxg4

5.fxg4

There goes another obstacle on that diagonal. Suddenly, my g2-Bishop is completely open.

5...Nxg4

6.Nxb6

The last piece moves out of the Bishop's way.

6...cxb6   7.Bxa8 Qc8

8.Bf3

I have again used my material advantage to obtain a victory.

PROBLEM 25. It's White turn to play. He has played a very aggressive game (the opening moves were 1.d4 d6 2.Nc3 g6 3.h4 Bg7 4.h5 Nc6 5.Nf3 e5 6.h6 Bf6 7.d5 Nb8 8.e4 Be7 9.Bb5+ Nd7) and now continues in the same vein with 10.g4. Is this attacking move justified?

**Arencibia–Seirawan
Manila, 1990**

Basing a Decision on Emotion Rather Than Reason

Chess is a game of the intellect first and a creative endeavor second. These two attributes combine to help players create beautiful works of art that last for centuries. Anger, fear, and overconfidence are common emotions that may help you in the odd game but that ultimately lead to defeat because they cloud the intellectual and creative processes. These emotions are as dangerous in chess as they are in life. If you dislike your opponent, don't let anger make you play too aggressively. If you are afraid of your opponent, don't be a chicken and play for a draw. If you are confident you can win, don't allow your sense of danger to desert you.

We are all emotional beings, but when emotion tells you which move to play, you should do a reality check. Are you in danger of spinning out of control? If you find that your mind is taking a break and you have lost your concentration, get up and walk around (if you have sufficient time on your clock), take a few deep breaths, jump up and down—do anything that will put your mind back at the helm. Having said that, I recognize that there are times when nothing will put your emotions on hold. If your wife has just left you or your lawyer tells you that your financial empire has turned to dust, a pleasant game of chess may ease your pain a bit, but don't expect to play at your full potential.

Diagram 115 comes from a game where emotions were out in force. Black was the higher rated player and wanted to win very badly. Unfortunately, he had no way to accomplish his goal from this position. His unobtainable desire led to an emotional reaction. Black set a trap. He played **1...Kf6??**, hoping to win the pawn endgame after **2.Nf4** (his idea is Nxd5, xb6, xc4, xa5—quite a series of captures!) **2...Bxf4 3.Kxf4 h4**. However, this "trap" should have been Black's downfall. After 4.e4 dxe4 5.Kxe4, the protected passed pawn should have allowed White to march over, win the h-pawn, and then win the game.

DIAGRAM 115. Black to play.

It turned out that White was incapacitated by stark terror (most players are afraid of higher rated opponents). Believing that Black's trap was real, he retreated the Knight to f2! Black eventually won this game because of his fearful opponent's major blunder. This game is evidence of the saying:

Terror is a self-fulfilling prophecy.

In this game, we saw overconfidence sowing the seeds of defeat and fear germinating the seeds and eventually harvesting the loss. Overconfidence (which sometimes manifests itself as *wishful thinking*) is obviously less incapacitating than terror, but overconfidence is nevertheless an emotional reaction that will lead to defeat against a good opponent. Remember:

Overconfidence leads you away from the realities of the position to the world of wishful thinking.

The next game is an example of overconfidence at work. In Diagram 116, White has more space in the center and on the queenside. Other than ...Nf4, Black has no counterplay whatsoever. White should be playing to expand his queenside territorial edge with b4, Be3, and c4-c5. (If White is worried about strange sacrifices on the kingside, such as ...Bxh3 or ...Nf4 followed by ...Nxg2, he could first play Re1 followed by Bf1 and then roll Black up with that c4-c5 idea.) Instead, White gets emotionally bent out of shape, experiences feelings of grandeur, and decides that he has every right to

blast his opponent off the board. His reasoning goes something like this: "Since I have the advantage on the queenside and in the center, why not take over on the kingside also?"

1.f4?

Horrible. With one move, White creates a backward pawn on e4 and gives Black use of the e5-square, activity on the e-file for the Black Rook, and two Bishops. (By losing his dark-squared Bishop, White can easily become weak on that color.) Why hand all these nice tidbits to your

DIAGRAM 116. White to play.
Tartakower–Emanuel Lasker
New York, 1924

opponent? Why give him counterplay where none existed? If you want to prove that your game is superior, you must use the advantages your position gives you. Don't allow some strange macho quirk in your personality (or a simple bad mood) to push aside common sense and create self-inflicted wounds.

1...exf4   2.Bxf4 Nxf4
3.Rxf4

White had more space, but he has allowed several exchanges to take place. By now, you should know that trading benefits the side with less space.

3...Be7!

Black wants to gain two advantages: He wants to get his Knight to e5, and he wants to make use of his dark-squared Bishop (a piece White no longer possesses) by placing it on an active post like g5. Because these two advantages are more or less static (and therefore permanent—see the distinction between static and dynamic advantages discussed in Chapter One), Black first bolsters any potential weak points in his camp and reorganizes his Knight and Bishop so that they can get to their appointed squares.

4.Raf1

Playing 4.Nf3 Nh5 would embarrass the Rook on f4.

4...Rf8

Black defends f7 and gives the e8-square to the light-squared Bishop.

5.Qd3 Be8

Now d7 is available for the Knight.

6.Qg3

White threatens 7.Rxf6 Bxf6 8.Rxf6.

6...Qd8

Black not only stops White's threat but also backs up the e7-Bishop so that it can safely go to g5 after the Knight moves out of the way.

7.Nd1 Nd7

The liberated Bishop is heading for the promised land on e5.

8.Ne3 Bg5

White must have a sinking feeling in the pit of his stomach at this point. He had a great position a few moves earlier, and now as a result of his unreasonable desire to attack the Black King, Black has acquired several advantages.

9.Rg4

No better is 9.Rf5 Bh4, when 10.Qf3 or 10.Qg4 are met with 10...Ne5, and 10.Qf4 g6 leaves the Rook hanging out to dry.

9...f6　　　　10.Qf2 h5

11.Rg3

White is now in full retreat. He has been completely outplayed by his legendary opponent.

11...h4!

12.Rg4 Bh5

Black won the Exchange and eventually won the game.

It's not necessary to study countless individual positions to conclude that emotion has a negative impact on any chess game. Learn to monitor your feelings during a game, and if you sense fear, depression, insecurity, or overconfidence setting in, be aware that your susceptibility to a lack of reason is increased. Take precautions: Write down your move before you play it and ask if it conforms to the demands of the position. Is it too timid? Too bold? Is it part of your plan? Does the intended move strengthen your advantages? Remember: You are playing your opponent and the board, not an unreasonable mind that has turned against you.

PROBLEM 26. Black is a class C player facing an Expert. It is his move. He sees that 1...Qxc2 is possible, with a threat of checkmate on f2, but White is a far stronger player and has powerful replies such as 2.Qxa8+, 2.Qxf7+, or 2.Bxf7+ at his disposal. What should Black do?

The Great Masters of Strategy

I n chess, as in life, each player has a style that is distinct and personal. Some styles are attacking, some defensive, and some positional or strategic. A modern Grandmaster is expected to play well in all situations, but he usually excels in only one of these styles of play. In boxing, the public always loves a slugger, and the chess public is subject to the same sort of discrimination. They love the wild attacker and the beautiful combinations that he produces. However, it is the Grandmaster with the positional style who demonstrates the deepest understanding of chess.

In this chapter, we will spend a little time with the six greatest exponents of strategy. Each of these men has given something to the game that has enriched future generations of players.

Wilhelm Steinitz

Born in Prague in 1836, Wilhelm Steinitz moved to Vienna as a young man, became enchanted with chess, and by 1862 was playing professional chess in England. Playing with the attacking style of his contemporaries, the young London-based Steinitz was quickly recognized as one of the finest players in the world.

In 1873, Steinitz's style suddenly turned positional. He became interested in pawn structure, piece placement, and all the other aspects of positional play that produce static advantages. You might think that such a major change in philosophy would have damaged his game, but the result was just the opposite. Instead of being merely one of the world's best players, he became a force unto himself—a player far ahead of his time.

As he honed his newfound skills, Steinitz created a new school of chess thought that only the world's elite players could understand. He pioneered the idea that you must first create some sort of positional superiority before you can successfully attack. He also became a master of defense and repelled attacks that would have caused other players to run screaming in fear. One of his greatest gifts to the chess world was his *Accumulation Theory*, which states that a game can and should be won by the accumulation of small advantages.

In 1883, after 20 years in England, Steinitz emigrated to the United States and eventually became an American citizen. Now recognized as unofficial World Champion, Steinitz played the first official world title match in 1886 against Zukertort. He won this battle with ten wins, five losses, and five draws.

In January 1892, James G. Cunningham wrote about Steinitz in the *British Chess Magazine*:

> He is a man of great physical vigour, and possesses a well-preserved constitution. Everything about him denoted power rather than grace, strength rather than beauty. His stature was short but [his] form massive, his chest broad, his bearing sturdy. His features were rugged in outline, and his face the face of a man of action rather than a man of thought...with bright tawny looks, round face, a crushed-up nose...broad forehead, deep-set eyes, and a rough shaggy beard of bright tawny hue, the whole balanced squarely on a thick neck, that again on a short massive body.

Cunningham's words paint a portrait of a man in his prime, which makes Steinitz's collapse a few years later all the more remarkable. In 1894, at the age of 58, Steinitz lost the title that was so dear to him to an unheralded

25-year-old German Master named Emanuel Lasker. Shocked by this reversal, Steinitz's physical and mental health took a turn for the worse. When he challenged Lasker to a return match a few years later, he was horribly crushed. Once likeable and proud, Steinitz became cranky and irrational in his final years. He died in poverty in 1900.

I feel it fitting to end this biography of the man now known as the *father of modern chess* with the excellent tribute paid to him by Emanuel Lasker in his *Manual of Chess*:

> ...the greatest landmark in the history of chess is reached: William Steinitz announces the principles of strategy, the result of inspired thought and imagination...I who vanquished him must see to it that his great achievement, his theories, should find justice, and I must avenge the wrongs he suffered.

Lasker–Steinitz
World Championship Match, 1894
17th Match Game

1.e4 e5	2.Nf3 Nc6
3.Bc4 Bc5	4.d3 Nf6
5.Nc3	

Lasker was never a master of opening theory, which explains the tame line he chooses here.

5...d6

6.Be3 Bb6

Black does not want to play 6...Bxe3, a move that strengthens White's center and gives him a half-open f-file for his Rooks.

7.Qd2 Na5	8.Bb5+ c6
9.Ba4 Bxe3	

Black is forced to play this move anyway because b2-b4 might well have embarrassed his Knight. Instead of lamenting his loss of choice in the matter, Steinitz plays to double other pawns as well. By so doing, he hopes to achieve a superior pawn structure and, as a result, a superior endgame.

10.fxe3 b5

11.Bb3 Qb6

Black eyes the potential pawn weakness on e3.

12.0-0

White is probably quite satisfied with his position. His control of d4 and f4, plus the possibility of attack down the half-open f-file, are trumps that he must enjoy holding.

12...Ng4

Black attacks the e3-pawn, but the goal of this obvious assault is not to win that pawn. The real point of Black's play is to continue with ...f7-f6 and kill off any potential White may have had on the f-file. So the attacking 12...Ng4 is actually a defensive move!

13.Rae1 f6	**14.h3 Nh6**
15.Ne2 Nxb3	**16.axb3 0-0**

Steinitz has created a very firm position, whereas White's position is inflexible because of his double pawns. Black now plans to hold everything together on the kingside and in the center while striking out on the queenside with ...a7-a5 and then a4.

17.Ng3 a5

18.d4

Lasker must be a bit frustrated here because this advance hardly threatens the rock-hard pawn on e5. In fact, as you can see in Diagram 117, playing 18.d4 does more harm than good because it takes away all pawn protection from the e4-pawn.

Why does Lasker make such a concession? Because he sees that the center is dead and the queenside is in Black's hands. This leaves him

DIAGRAM 117.

only the kingside, but Steinitz's defensive preparations have made it all but impossible to break through over there.

18...Nf7   19.Qf2 Ra7

20.Rd1 a4

White's doubled pawns on the queenside are not really weak, so Black offers to get rid of them if White is willing to open lines over there. Naturally, White refuses this offer because it makes no sense to open files that only the enemy can use.

21.b4 Qc7   22.Ne1 c5

23.Qd2 Be6

Now White can open the d-file if he wishes to, but he cannot use it to penetrate the Black position because d4, d5, d6, d7, and d8 are all covered by Black pieces.

24.d5 Bd7

More long-range advantages for Steinitz: The center is dead, the kingside is safe, the queenside is Black's, and White's center pawns all rest on light-colored squares, making them potential targets for the Bishop later in the game.

25.Ra1 cxb4

Now that everything is safe, Black switches to the queenside attack that he has been preparing for so diligently.

26.Qxb4 Rc8   27.Qd2 Qc4

28.Rf2 Ng5

White is now dreaming only of survival. At the moment, his pawns on c2 and e4 are being pressured.

29.Qd3 Rac7   30.h4 Nf7

31.Qxc4 Rxc4   32.Rd2 g6

Now the White Knight cannot jump to f5.

33.Kf2 Nd8

The Black Knight heads for the battleground on the queenside.

34.b3 R4c7   35.Rdd1 Nb7

36.Rdb1 Kf7

Black is in no hurry, so he takes a moment off to protect his pawn on f6 and bring his King a bit closer to the center.

37.Ke2 Ra8   38.Kd2 Na5

39.Kd3 h5   40.Ra2 Raa7

Black threatens to win a pawn with 41...axb3 42.cxb3 Nxb3! 43.Rxa7 Nc5+ and 44...Rxa7.

41.b4 Nc4

New advantages for Black to crow about: The c4-square has fallen into his hands, and his a-pawn is now passed.

42.Nf3 Ra8

43.Nd2 Nb6

The White Knight on d2 has no future because of its lack of support points, so Black refuses to exchange it.

44.Rf1 Rac8   45.Nb1 Ke7

46.c3 Nc4   47.Raf2 Na3!

Black is trying to undermine the defense of c3. Now 48.Nxa3? loses to 48...Rxc3+ followed by 49...Rxa3.

48.Ne2 Nxb1

49.Rxb1 Bg4

Once again Black threatens to get rid of the defender of c3, this time with 50...Bxe2+.

50.Rc1 Rc4

51.Rc2 f5

White resigns. He is surrounded and does not wish to experience any more punishment. The e4-pawn is hanging, 52.exf5 loses to 52...Bxf5+, and 52.Ng3 also fails to 52...fxe4+ 53.Kd2 (even worse is 53.Nxe4 Bf5) 53...Bd7 54.Rc1 Be8 55.Ne2 Bf7, after which Black also picks up the d5-pawn.

Akiba Rubinstein

The youngest of 12 children, Akiba Rubinstein was born in 1882 in the Polish border town of Stawiski. His parents wanted him to be a rabbi, but after he learned the game of chess at the relatively late age of 16, his thoughts were on nothing else. After several years of skill development, Rubinstein exploded onto the international scene and was one of the world's dominant players from 1905 to 1911. In 1912, he won tournament after tournament (five in all), and the year was dubbed the *Rubinstein Year*. Everyone demanded a match between Rubinstein and Lasker, clearly the only player who was close to Rubinstein in strength. Sadly, this match never took place. The beginning of deep psychological problems that eventually turned into full-fledged mental illness, the appearance of the Cuban chess genius Capablanca, and the advent of World War I all combined to dash his championship hopes.

Though he remained one of the world's strongest players until about 1921, his pathological shyness and the erosion of his confidence led to a gradual disintegration of his powers. He finally retired from chess in 1932 and spent his final years until his death in 1961 with his family in Belgium.

Rubinstein's style formed a bridge between the styles of Steinitz and the players of today. A mastery of openings, a deep understanding of the consequences of different types of pawn structures, and a skill in the endgame that has never been surpassed were all part of his repertoire. Most notable, however, was his ability to connect the openings he played with the kinds of endgames that could be reached from them. This incredibly deep planning is commonly seen in modern champions, but it was virtually unheard of in Rubinstein's day.

Today, Rubinstein's games are carefully studied by all the finest players. His moves and concepts still seem fresh, his handling of the endgame is still remarkable, and his opening ideas are still all the rage.

Rubinstein–Tarrasch
Teplitz–Schoenau, 1922

1.d4 d5	2.c4 e6
3.Nc3 c5	4.cxd5 exd5
5.Nf3 Nc6	6.g3

Black's opening was eventually named after Tarrasch, who insisted that the isolated d-pawn that results from this opening will be a source of strength rather than weakness. The 6.g3 move is an invention of Rubinstein's and is now considered to be the main line. Here, we are seeing a game between the two originators of this line: Tarrasch playing his beloved opening, and Rubinstein trying to demonstrate its shortcomings with his own 6.g3.

6...Nf6	7.Bg2 Be7
8.0-0 0-0	9.a3

Not a bad move. Nowadays 9.Bg5 is the most common way for White to handle this position.

DIAGRAM 118.

9...Be6	10.dxc5 Bxc5
11.b4 Be7	12.Bb2

White is training his sights on the d4-square, following the rule that you should always try to control the square directly in front of the isolated pawn.

12...Ne4?

A natural move, but one that is shown to be bad in a surprising way.

13.b5!

The position is now as shown in Diagram 118.

Rubinstein's truly remarkable 13th move shows that he was never afraid to step out of the boundaries of convention. In Diagram 118, he seems to be forcing the Black Knight to a5, where it can pounce on the hole on c4. Rubinstein has seen that this Knight will actually be vulnerable on a5 and that the c4-square will never be of any real consequence. On top of all that, the Knight's absence from c6 allows White's own Knight to take up residence on d4.

13...Na5

14.Nxe4

The first point: The isolated d-pawn is brought back in connection with its kingside brothers, but it turns out to be far more vulnerable on e4 than it ever was on d5!

14...dxe4

15.Nd4 Qd5

White threatened both 16.Bxe4 and 16.Nxe6. Black didn't like 15...Bd5 16.Nf5 because the dual threats of 17.Qxd5! Qxd7 18.Nxe7+ and 17.Bxg7 were impossible to meet. Also bad was 15...Nc4 16.Nxe6 Qxd1 17.Raxd1 Nxb2 18.Rd7.

16.Qc2

Now White threatens to chop off the e4-pawn.

16...f5

17.Qc3!

The real point of White's 13th move is finally revealed. White threatens both 18.Qxa5 and a Knight move (18.Nxe6 or 18.Nxf5) with a resultant discovered attack on g7.

17...Nc4

The only way to resist because 17...Bf6 loses quickly to 18.Qxa5 Bxd4 19.Rad1 Bb6 20.Qc3.

18.Nxf5! Bf6

Again Black has no choice because 18...Bxf5 allows White to end the game abruptly with 19.Qxg7 checkmate.

19.Qxf6?

A rare example of Rubinstein laziness. Seeing a winning endgame, he doesn't bother to look for something even better: 19.Ne7+! Kh8 20.Nxd5 Bxc3 21.Nxc3 Nxb2 22.Bxe4.

19...gxf6   20.Ne7+ Kf7

21.Nxd5 Bxd5

White would meet 21...Nxb2 with 22.Nc7 followed by Nxe6 and Bxe4.

22.Rfd1 Ke6   23.Bc3 Rfd8

24.Rd4 f5   25.g4!

Rubinstein's great endgame technique will make things look easy, though in fact the opposite-colored Bishops create great difficulties for him. Playing 25.g4 undermines the e4-pawn and increases the scope of the g2-Bishop.

25...Nd6

Black defends e4 and threatens the pawn on b5. Has Rubinstein missed something?

26.Rad1

No, he has calculated everything out to a win. This threat to the d5-Bishop forces Black's hand.

26...Nxb5

If Black played 26...Bb3, Rubinstein had a pretty checkmating attack prepared: 27.gxf5+ Kxf5 28.Rxd6 Bxd1 29.Bh3+ Kf4 30.e3+ Kf3 31.Rf6+ Ke2 32.Bf1 checkmate (analysis by Hans Kmoch).

27.gxf5+ Kf7

Playing 27...Kxf5 allows White to capture the Bishop with check.

28.Rxd5 Rxd5   29.Rxd5 Nxc3

30.Rc5 Nxe2+   31.Kf1 Nf4

32.Bxe4

White is still only one pawn ahead, but now his Bishop has reached a very active square, and his Rook will find happiness on the 7th rank.

32...Rd8

33.Rc7+ Kf6

Black threatens 34...Rd1 checkmate.

34.Ke1 Re8		**35.f3 Nd5**
36.Rxb7			

The two extra pawns guarantee White a relatively easy victory.

36...Nc3	**37.Rb4 Nd5**
38.Ra4! Re7	**39.Kf2 Nb6**
40.Ra5	

Black's momentary activity is at an end, and now White's Bishop and Rook are superior to their Black counterparts.

40...Rc7	**41.Kg3 Nd7**
42.Ra6+ Kg7	**43.Kf4**

During the last few moves, White has taken his time and improved the placement of his Rook and King while forcing the enemy pieces into passive positions.

43...Nb6	**44.h4 Rf7**
45.Kg5 h6+	**46.Kf4 Kf8**
47.a4	

The poor Black Knight will not even be allowed the b6-square.

47...Rc7	**48.a5 Nc4**
49.f6 Rd7	**50.Rc6**

White gives up the a-pawn but places the Knight on the rim and out of play. He now has a pawn, Rook, Bishop, and King vs. Black's King and Rook. It's clear that the Black army will be outnumbered.

50...Nxa5	**51.Rc8+ Kf7**
52.Ke5 Nb7	**53.Bf5**

Black resigns. If he moves his Rook to safety (for instance, 53...Rd1), then 54.Rc7+ picks up the Knight.

José Raúl Capablanca

Born in Cuba in 1888, José Raúl Capablanca learned how to play the game at the age of four and beat Juan Corzo, the Champion of Cuba, in 1901. He attended Columbia University in 1906 but spent little time studying; instead, he played hundreds of chess games against New York's finest players at the Manhattan Chess Club. It was there that he met Lasker and Alekhinc. The great Alekhine commented that he had never seen another player who possessed such a "flabbergasting quickness of chess comprehension."

Quitting school so that he could play chess full-time, Capablanca played a match with the very experienced U.S. Champion Frank Marshall and crushed him by eight wins to one. Because of this victory, the unknown Capablanca was allowed to play in the mighty San Sebastian tournament of 1911. Many people were upset that the untested youngster was seeded into this elite group, but he shut everyone up when he won the event outright. Accepted as one of the best two or three players in the world, Capablanca challenged Lasker to a title match but the World Champion's conditions were so numerous that the two sides were unable to agree on mutually acceptable terms.

In 1913, Capablanca managed to get a post in the Cuban Foreign Office; he had no specific duties but was expected to act as a kind of goodwill ambassador. Always in the public spotlight, the good-looking, well-dressed young man made an impression wherever he went. With all his financial needs taken care of by the Cuban government, the always courteous and charming Capablanca continued playing chess and appeared to have the world on a string. After coming in second to Lasker in St. Petersburg 1914, he raised the level of his game so high that he lost only once in the next ten years! His successes included numerous tournament victories and a World Championship match victory over an aging Lasker in 1921.

Considered an invincible chess machine, he stunned the chess world when he lost the title to Alekhine in 1927. No longer in his prime, Capablanca was beaten by age, laziness (he didn't take his opponent very seriously), and the ascent of a new kind of player. Alexander Alekhine's incredible preparation and relentless energy made hard work and dedication an integral part of the game. These were traits that Capablanca had failed to nurture, so he fell by the wayside and was never granted a rematch. He died in 1942.

Capablanca was the first great technical player, and he developed liquidation to a fine art. Possessing flawless positional judgment and legendary endgame skill, the great Cuban would avoid messy complications, retain subtle strategic elements that could later be used to ensure him some kind of advantage, and steer the game into positions of crystal clarity. Loved, feared, and even worshipped by his fellow Grandmasters, Capablanca was considered the most naturally talented player anyone had ever seen. Alekhine, who was surprised by his own victory over the Cuban, said that "the world would never see the like of such a genius again." And World Champion Max Euwe put things into perspective when he wrote (in 1975), "I honestly feel very humble when I study Capablanca's games."

Capablanca–Alekhine
St. Petersburg, 1914

1.d4 d5	2.c4 c6
3. e3 Nf6	4.Nf3 e6
5.Nbd2 Nbd7	

The best answer to White's rather humble developing scheme is 5...c5, taking advantage of the fact that White's Knight (which can no longer go to c3) can't put pressure on d5.

6.Bd3 Be7   7.0-0 0-0

8.Qc2 dxc4?

Again, 8...c5 was indicated. The move 8...dxc4 just brings the White Knight to a strong central post.

9.Nxc4 c5   10.Nce5 cxd4

11.exd4 Nb6

Black is hoping to make use of White's isolated d-pawn, but in this situation, the pawn's space-gaining qualities are a considerable advantage whereas its potential weakness is hardly noticeable.

12.Ng5

White threatens 13.Bxh7+ Kh8 14.Ngxf7+ Rxf7 15.Nxf7 checkmate. Of course, Capablanca knows that Black will see this threat, but the only way to stop it is to play ...g6, a move that weakens the dark squares around the Black King.

12...g6   13.Ngf3 Kg7

14.Bg5 Nbd5   15.Rc1 Bd7

16.Qd2 Ng8

Black's move keeps White's dark-squared Bishop out of h6.

17.Bxe7 Qxe7

18.Be4!

White is trying to clarify the position by taking on d5 and leaving Black with a bad Bishop vs. a good Knight.

18...Bb5?

The young Alekhine falls in with his opponent's plans. He would have done better to play 18...Ngf6 19.Bxd5 Nxd5 20.Ng4 f6 21.Qh6+ Kh8, which produces a defensible position.

19.Rfe1 Qd6

20.Bxd5 exd5

Playing 20...Qxd5 is not possible because of 21.Rc5.

21.Qa5!

The position is now as shown in Diagram 119. Capablanca is aware that his Knights are superior to the enemy Bishop (which is striking at nothing), so he prepares a transition into an endgame by 22.Qc7!, a move that allows the Rook to enter the 7th rank.

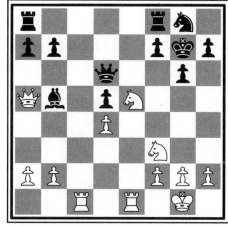

DIAGRAM 119.

> **21...a6**   **22.Qc7! Qxc7**
> **23.Rxc7 h6**

Black must accept the loss of a pawn because 23...Rb8 loses to 24.Ng5 with the double threat of 25.Ngxf7 and 25.Ne6+, winning the f8-Rook.

> **24.Rxb7**

Nothing exciting has happened, but Black is completely lost. This quiet way of pushing the enemy into the abyss is typical of Capablanca's style.

> **24...Rac8**   **25.b3 Rc2**
> **26.a4 Be2**   **27.Nh4!**

A crushing blow! Now 28.Nhxg6 is threatened, and 27...g5 loses the Bishop (at the very least) to 28.Nf5+ followed by 29.Ng3.

> **27...h5**   **28.Nhxg6 Re8**
> **29.Rxf7+**

It is surprising that Alekhine does not resign here.

> **29...Kh6**   **30.f4 a5**
> **31.Nh4**

White threatens 32.Nf5 checkmate.

> **31...Rxe5**   **32.fxe5 Kg5**
> **33.g3 Kg4**   **34.Rg7+ Kh3**
> **35.Ng2**

Nothing can be done to stop 36.Nf4 checkmate, so Alekhine gives up.

Simple looking, wasn't it? That's why Capablanca was known as an unbeatable chess machine. He made other players look like children!

Aaron Nimzovich

Born in Russia in 1886, Aaron Nimzovich was the rebel of the chess world. While most players were learning the doctrines of Steinitz and Tarrasch, the acknowledged high priests of chess, Nimzovich was preaching a whole new set of ideas. *Prophylaxis* and *Over-protection* were two of his most important concepts, and soon his chess philosophy was labeled as *Hypermodernism*.

Though many players laughed at Nimzovich's outlandish theories, no one could ignore him. How can you ignore one of the world's top five players? He was never given a chance to play for the World Championship, and his tournament achievements (he had *many* fine results) have been largely forgotten. He died in 1935, but his ideas live on in his classic books *My System* and *Chess Praxis*, which have served to instruct later generations in Nimzovich's own brand of chess strategy.

Today, all top players make use of the ideas of Steinitz and Nimzovich. These two men can be classed as the greatest chess thinkers in the game's history.

Yates–Nimzovich
London, 1927

    1.e4 c5

    2.Nf3 Nf6

This unusual version of the Sicilian Defense has been named the *Nimzovich Variation* (just one of many openings named after this great man). Like the Alekhine Defense (1.e4 Nf6 2.e5 Nd5), the Nimzovich Variation of the Sicilian Defense dares White to advance his pawns and attack the Knight. Black's idea is that these advanced pawns will turn out to be targets.

3.e5

White, of course, wants to prove that his advanced e-pawn is a tower of strength.

3...Nd5

4.Bc4

Only 4.Nc3! can cause Black any worries because 4...Nxc3 5.dxc3 gives White more space and the chance to develop his pieces rapidly, whereas 4...e6 5.Nxd5 exd5 6.d4 tries to take advantage of the doubled Black d-pawns.

4...Nb6	**5.Be2 Nc6**
6.c3 d5	**7.d4 cxd4**
8.cxd4 Bf5	

Black wants to play ...e7-e6, so he must first get his Bishop outside the pawn chain.

9.0-0 e6	**10.Nc3 Be7**
11.Ne1	

To quote Nimzovich himself, "If the attack planned by this move, namely f4 with g4 and f5, should really prove possible to carry out, this would be a proof of the incorrectness of 8...Bf5, and that would be an absurdity." Nimzovich, who always felt that you should strengthen your center if possible, recommended 11.Be3 0-0 12.Rc1 followed by a3, b4, and Nd2-b3-c5 with the establishment of an outpost on c5.

Yates was a fine attacking player but here his desire to start aggressive action gets the best of him, and he makes the obvious strategic error of placing his Knight on the back rank before his development is complete. The Knight's absence from f3 weakens his control of d4, and Nimzovich takes immediate advantage of this fact.

11...Nd7!

Now 12.f4 cannot be played because 12...Nxd4! 13.Qxd4?? Bc5 pins the Queen to its King. Also good for Black is 12.Be3 Ndxe5! 13.dxe5 d4 14.Bd2 dxc3 15.Bxc3 Qc7.

12.Bg4 Bg6	
13.f4	

Yates initiates a tactical operation but fails to take into account the positional consequences.

13...Nxd4!

The Knight is still taboo because of 14...Bc5.

14.Nxd5!

The point of Yates's line of play. He sees that 14...exd5 15.Qxd4 Bc5 now fails to 16.Bxd7+. Nimzovich, however, has seen much deeper into the position. Instead of being satisfied with little tactical tricks, he has come to understand that the critical d5- and f5-squares will fall into his hands. He is also well aware that control of these squares will give him control of the game.

14...Nc6

15.Nxe7 Qb6+

A nice zwischenzug that prevents the enemy dark-squared Bishop from developing on e3.

16.Kh1 Nxe7

This Knight now eyes both d5 and f5.

17.Qa4?

White should have fought for control of some central squares by playing 17.Qe2.

DIAGRAM 120.

17...h5	**18.Bh3 Bf5**
19.Qa3 Qb5	

Black attacks the Rook on f1 and makes way for his other Knight to jump into b6.

20.Kg1 Nb6

21.Qf3 Nbd5

The difference in positions is beginning to become clear, as you can see in Diagram 120. Black's pieces on d5 and f5 enjoy the support of a pawn, whereas the mirror-image squares on f4 and d4 are not suitable for the same kind of occupation by White's forces.

22.b3 Qb6+

23.Rf2 Rc8

A natural and tempting move that Nimzovich criticized harshly. Since he has no intention of castling kingside, he felt that this move broke his army into two separate groups (one on the kingside and another on the queen-side). With hindsight, he liked 23...0-0-0! much better because after ...Kb8 followed by ...g6, ...Rd7, and ..Rc8, he would have achieved full centralization with his whole army working in unison. Nimzovich also pointed out that the tactical 23...Bg4! might have been the best move of all because after 24.Bxg4 hxg4 25.Qxg4 Rxh2 26.Qxg7 0-0-0 27.Kxh2 Qxf1 28.Nd3 Qe2, Black is winning. Good or not, 23... 0-0-0! is the move you should pay attention to here, because the thinking associated with it fits better with Nimzovich's ideals and, as a result, is much more instructive.

24.Bd2 Rh6   25.Rd1 Bxh3

26.Qxh3 Nf5

Black's Knights make a magnificent impression.

27.Qd3 Rg6

28.Nf3 Rg4

Black's pieces are split between the two sides, but they are so well placed that it doesn't really make a difference. It is almost as if they are converging on the sides in a sort of pincher effect.

29.h3 Rg3

30.a4 Nh4

The pins are starting to drive White crazy. Now 31...Nxf3+ is a winning threat.

31.Kf1 Rc6   32.a5 Qd8

33.Kg1 Nf5   34.Kh2

So White has managed to push back the first wave of Black's attack. However, Black's pieces are so much better than their White counterparts that he nonetheless maintains a static advantage.

34...a6 35.Qb1 Qe7

36.Nd4?

Seeing that 36...Nxd4 loses the Exchange after 37.Kxg3, the aggressive Yates lashes out. Unfortunately, this erroneous move hastens his defeat because tactics usually work for the side with all the positional trumps. In this case, of course, the side with all the trumps is Black.

36...Qh4!

Black threatens 37...Rxh3+ 38.gxh3 Qxf2+. Yates panics and goes down quickly.

37.Be1 Nxf4

38.Rxf4

Playing 38.Nxf5 fails because 38...Rxg2+ 39.Rxg2 Qxh3+ followed by ...Qxg2 checkmate.

38...Rxh3+ 39.gxh3 Qxf4+

40.Kg2 Ne3+

After White resigned, Nimzovich was awarded a special prize of £10 for the best played game in the tournament. No wonder chess players often starved to death!

Tigran Petrosian

Born in 1929 in Tbilisi, Tigran Petrosian learned the complexities of positional play from Nimzovich's books. As a result, he became the greatest master of prophylaxis the world has ever seen. In his prime, his ability to anticipate any plan his opponent came up with, plus his wonderful endgame technique, tactical alertness, and inexhaustible patience made him nearly unbeatable.

Never a player to win a lot of games, Petrosian didn't come in first in many tournaments. In match play, however, his skills made him stand out over all other players. After a two-month struggle in 1963, he snatched the World Championship from Botvinnik by winning five games, losing two, and drawing fifteen. He then defended his title successfully against Spassky, this time winning four games, losing three, and drawing seventeen. He lost his second match to Spassky in 1969 and succumbed to cancer in 1984.

Petrosian enjoyed slowly improving the position of his pieces. He also loved closed positions where he could quietly fight for the control of key squares. This cautious style made him one of the least popular of all World Champions, and his genius was rarely appreciated by players below master strength. A great pity, because his games are models of depth and subtlety and will reward anyone who takes the time to study them.

Petrosian–Taimanov
U.S.S.R. Championship, 1955

1.d4 d5	2.c4 e6
3.Nf3 Nf6	4.Nc3 c6
5.e3 Nbd7	6.Bd3 Bb4

This Semi-Slav Defense has become very popular in recent times, though 6...dxc4 7.Bxc4 b5 (a line created by Rubinstein) is the way most people handle the position nowadays.

7.0-0 0-0

8.Qc2 Bd6

Black's ...Bb4-d6 turns out to be a waste of time. Petrosian doesn't immediately try to refute his opponent, though; he just sort of flows over Taimanov like an ancient but irresistible glacier.

9.b3 dxc4	10.bxc4 e5
11.Bb2 Re8	12.Ne4 Nxe4
13.Bxe4 h6?	

White's greater space gives him a clear advantage, but this move quickly loses control of the light squares and leads to a complete disaster. A better line of play is 13...g6 14.Bd3 Qe7 15.c5 Bc7 16.Bc4!, which leaves White in a better position. But Black can still put up a fight.

14.Rad1 exd4

15.Bh7+!

This surprise forces the Black King onto the uncomfortable a1-h8 diagonal. As you can see in Diagram 121, the immediate 15.Rxd4 would have been met by 15...Nf6.

15...Kh8

16.Rxd4

Now 16...Nf6 would be answered by 17.Rfd1 Nxh7 18.Rxd6 Qe7 19.Rxh6.

16...Bc5

White also comes out on top after 16...Qe7 17.Re4 Qf8 18.Rh4 Ne5 19.Ng5! f5 20.Bg6 Nxg6 21.Rxh6+ Kg8 22.Rxg6 (analysis by O'Kelly).

17.Rf4 Qe7   18.Re4! Qf8

19.Rh4

White threatens to take advantage of the pin on the a1-h8 diagonal by playing Rxh6.

19...f6

This move takes care of all the problems along the a1-h8 diagonal, but now

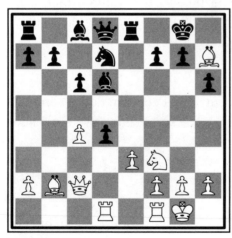

DIAGRAM 121.

Black has a terminal case of light-squared leukemia.

20.Bg6

Such complete control of all these juicy squares must have made Petrosian a very happy man.

20...Re7

21.Rh5

White makes room for the Knight to come to h4, where it can take part in the light-square orgy.

21...Bd6   22.Rd1 Be5

23.Ba3 c5

Now d5 (another light square!) becomes available to the White pieces. Petrosian's game is so crushing, though, that he doesn't need it.

24.Nh4

A humiliated Taimanov saw that he had no defense against the threat of 25.Bh7 and 26. Ng6+ and gave up.

I can personally attest to the way other Grandmasters deferred to Petrosian. During tournament analysis sessions players all speak at once, but whenever Petrosian said anything, everyone would shut up and listen. It's also interesting to note that when a young Karpov lost to Petrosian, he looked up at his great opponent and asked, "Please, can you tell me where I went wrong?"

Anatoly Karpov

Anatoly Karpov was born in 1951 in Zlatoust, a small town in the Ural Mountains, where he was taught chess, like Capablanca, when he was just four years of age. A small man with protruding eyes, Karpov gives the impression that he has a frail mental and physical constitution. This is an illusion, however. Within that fragile frame is a mind of incredible determination and resolve.

In 1975, Karpov won the World Championship from Bobby Fischer by a forfeit. Embarrassed that he had acquired the title in this fashion, he played in almost every strong tournament, trying desperately to prove that he deserved the champion's mantle. By winning just about every event he played in (and he participated in more tournaments than any champion before or after him), he accumulated the finest tournament record in history. He once said: "To be champion requires more than simply being a strong player; one has to be a strong human being as well." This comment speaks volumes about this great player.

Karpov eventually lost the World Championship in 1985 to Garry Kasparov after holding it for 10 years. He regained it in 1993 when Kasparov was stripped of the title by the FIDE. Once again he was World Champion, and once again he had acquired it by forfeit! Though no longer in his prime, he showed that he still deserves the title by winning the super tournament at Linares in 1994. By scoring 2½ points more than second-place Kasparov, Karpov once again demonstrated his incredible knowledge of the game and his amazing mental toughness.

Possessing a unique positional style, Karpov always seems to have his pieces well defended and makes use of a space advantage better than anyone else in history. This great champion's philosophy is best described by Karpov himself:

> Let us say that a game may be continued in two ways: one of them is a beautiful tactical blow that gives rise to variations that don't yield to precise calculation; the other is clear positional pressure that leads to an endgame with microscopic chances of victory...I would choose the latter without thinking twice. If the opponent insists on sharp play I don't object; but in such cases I get less satisfaction, even if I win, than from a game conducted according to all the rules of strategy with its ruthless logic.

Karpov–Spassky
Leningrad, 1974
11th Match Game

1.d4 Nf6	2.c4 e6
3.Nf3 d5	4.Nc3 Be7
5.Bg5 h6	6.Bh4 0-0
7.e3 b6	8.Be2 Bb7
9.Bxf6 Bxf6	10.cxd5 exd5
11.0-0 Qd6	

A well-known line of the Tartakower Variation of the Queen's Gambit Declined has been reached. Black will try to play ...c7-c5 and activate his dark-squared Bishop and queenside pawns. This move may lead to some pawn weaknesses, but Black is willing to take on these potential liabilities in exchange for active piece play.

12.Rac1 a6

13.a3

Karpov has prevented Black's plan because 13...c5? would turn out very badly after 14.dxc5 bxc5 15.Ne4! followed by 16.Nxc5. This and his following move demonstrate his mastery of prophylaxis.

13...Nd7

14.b4

As well as preventing ...c5, this move also gains space on the queenside.

14...b5

Because ...c5 has been prevented, Black changes plans and creates a strong support point on c4 for his Knight. It's true that ...b5 creates a backward pawn on c7, but once the Knight gets to c4, it will block the c-file and make any attack on c7 quite unlikely.

15.Ne1

A logical move that heads for c5. However, this move turns out to be the only mistake Karpov commits in this game. By playing 15.Nd2! followed by Nb3 and possibly Na5, he would have prevented the freeing advance ...a6-a5.

15...c6

16.Nd3 Nb6?

The move 16...a5! was correct, with equal chances. Spassky never recovers from this one slip.

17.a4 Bd8   **18.Nc5 Bc8**

19.a5

This is an important advance. Now White's a-pawn will not be vulnerable to the Black Knight on c4, whereas Black's a-pawn will be in need of constant defense because it is under the hungry eye of the c5-horse.

19...Bc7

Creating a tiny threat of ...Qxh2 checkmate.

20.g3 Nc4

21.e4!

The queenside is closed, so Karpov hastens to create active play in the center.

21...Bh3   **22.Re1 dxe4**

23.N3xe4 Qg6   **24.Bh5!**

White kicks Black around and refuses to be sucked into 24.Bxc4? bxc4 25.Rxc4 f5! followed by 26...f4, with a strong attack for Black.

24...Qh7

25.Qf3

The pawn on c6 has suddenly turned into a target. White also threatens to trap the enemy light-squared Bishop with g3-g4.

25...f5?

Black stops the threat but creates too many weaknesses in the center. Weakening, aggressive moves like this one cannot succeed when played from a state of positional inferiority.

26.Nc3

DIAGRAM 122.

Suddenly Black is positionally bankrupt. White threatens Qxc6, and Ne6 or Re6 can also be played at any moment. Black has no choice but to win the White Bishop and hope he can survive the storm.

26...g6   **27.Qxc6 gxh5**

28.Nd5

As Diagram 122 shows, Black is up a piece, but his King is open and the White army dominates the center. Black can't handle White's threats of Qxc7, Nxc7, Re7, and Re6.

28...f4

A desperate bid for counterplay.

29.Re7 Qf5

Playing 29...Rf7 fails to 30.Qxa8+.

30.Rxc7

Black would like to continue his attack with ...fxg3, but Ne7+ would pick up the Black Queen.

30...Rae8

31.Qxh6

Now Black must do something about Qg7 checkmate.

31...Rf7	**32.Rxf7 Kxf7**

33.Qxf4

White's material advantage makes the win a certainty.

33...Re2	**34.Qc7+ Kf8**

35.Nf4

Black gives up. Like Capablanca, Karpov makes his victories look remarkably easy.

Other Great Strategists

A final word of explanation, and perhaps apology, is needed. Though it is obvious that great players like Lasker, Alekhine, Tal, and Kasparov were excluded from this list because we are looking at positional, not tactical geniuses, the absence of Botvinnik and Fischer may upset a few fans. In fact, both these World Champions were nearly accorded a place in this chapter and were excluded only at the last moment.

Mikhail Botvinnik was a brilliant strategic player, but I feel that science played an even greater role in his games. The depth of his preparation (encompassing mental, physical, and theoretical aspects of chess) was unparalleled, and he seems to belong in a slightly different category: He was the first great scientific player.

Bobby Fischer could also have made this list of strategic geniuses, but once again, I saw him heading a category of his own: Perfect opening play brought about by intense preparation (Alekhine was the first great opening theorist and Fischer followed in his footsteps), an intense will to win (reminiscent of Emanuel Lasker), incredibly simple and lucid middlegame skills (watching him, you had to wonder whether Capablanca had been reborn), and superior endgame powers (a combination of Rubinstein and Capablanca).

Solutions to Problems

PROBLEM 1: In the actual game, Black blindly holds on to his Queen with 9...Qg6?? and pays the price after 10.Rd8+ Kf7 11.Bc4+ Be6 12.Nxe5 checkmate. Instead of exhibiting such suicidal greed, Black should catch up in development with **9...Bxc3+** (This move is not really necessary, but it never hurts to weaken the enemy pawn structure.) Then after 10.bxc3 Nf6! 11.Rxd6 cxd6, White has run out of threats, and Black is still ahead by a bundle with an extra Rook.

PROBLEM 2: White should trade Queens, of course! The ugly looking 1.Qd2!, heading for g5 or h6, proves to be more than Black can handle. In response to 1...Bf5, White decides that everything is under control and grabs a bit more food with **2.Rxa6** before making the trade. After 2...Rxa6 3.bxa6 Ra8 4.Qg5+ Qxg5 5.Bxg5 Rxa6 6.gxf3 gxf3 7.Nxf3, White wins in a few more moves.

PROBLEM 3: Playing **1...h3** would force White to resign. All of Black's pieces are protected, the h-pawn is running for a touchdown, and White's vain hope for a stalemate will never materialize because Black has been careful to give White's King the c2 square to run to.

Playing 1...Kc3?? is another matter. At first glance it looks very good because checkmate is threatened on d2 and 2.Rc1+ Qxc1+! 3.Kxc1 h3 makes a Queen of the pawn. Unfortunately, Black has not left the White King any squares to move to, and White can take advantage of this oversight by playing 2.Rb3+!, after which 2...Kxb3 leads to a draw by stalemate, whereas 2...Kd4 3.Rxe3 Kxe3 4.Ke1 h3 5.Kf1 is a dead, drawn, King and pawn endgame.

PROBLEM 4: No. Playing 1...Rxa2 allows Black to play 2.Nh2 followed by 3.Ng4+, when the White Knight suddenly enters the game with great effect.

In the game, Fischer stops this possibility with a nice Exchange sacrifice that led to a winning endgame: 1...Rxh5! 2.Rxh5 Rf2+ 3.Kg3 Rxf1 4.Rh8 Kxe4 (White's pawns start to fall like flies) 5.Ra3 Rg1+ 6.Kh2 Rc1 7.Rxa4 Rc2+ 8.Kh1 c5 9.Ra3 Kxf5. Black manages to win the game on the strength of his connected passed pawns on the kingside.

This Exchange sacrifice is an advanced idea, and I didn't expect most of you to notice it. You can be proud of yourself if you noticed that the usual moves would allow the White Knight to become dangerous. Start to develop an eye for enemy counterplay, and your results will rapidly improve.

PROBLEM 5: The two squares that Black might be able to claim are c5 and b4. Once you see the goal, the actual route is rather easy to find: **1...Nb7** followed by 2...Nc5 (attacking the b3-pawn). If the Knight then wants to go to b4 (though c5 is better because the Knight can attack something from that post), it can jump to a6 and then on to b4.

PROBLEM 6: The White Bishop on d3 is clearly bad because its center pawns sit on its color and block it. The White Bishop on d2 is good, as is the Black Bishop on d7. The Black Bishop on d4 is bad but active because it has managed to take up a threatening position outside the pawn chain.

PROBLEM 7: Playing 1.d3 is all right, but it does nothing for the White Rooks. Playing **1.d4!** is much more dynamic. After 1...exd4 2.Nxd4, White has made a gain in space. He has also created a half-open d-file that can be used by his Rooks. If Black does not take on d4, then White can take on e5 whenever he wants and create a fully open d-file.

PROBLEM 8: Actually, White is winning easily despite the negative material count. After **1.Ree7**, White creates the dreaded doubled Rooks on the 7th rank. These hungry pigs will eat everything they can get their snouts on while they simultaneously torment the Black King. Here's the play: 1...f6 2.Rxg7 h5 3.Rh7 (threatening 4.Rh8 checkmate) 3...Kg8 (3...Ke8 4.Rc7 Kd8 5.Rcg7 leads to checkmate) 4.Rdg7+ Kf8 5.g4! hxg4 6.h5. Then nothing can be done to prevent 7.h6 followed by 8.Rhh8 checkmate.

PROBLEM 9: Some players might think that Black's King is better off because it still has the right to castle, but castling would just place the King out of the game. On the other hand, White's King is very comfortable on c2. Nothing can attack it; it defends b2 and the three penetration points on the d-file (d3, d2, and d1); and it is ready to rush toward the enemy when a few more pieces are exchanged. If you preferred the White monarch's position, you are beginning to get a good feel for when a King is safe in the center and when it is not.

PROBLEM 10: If you voted for 1...0-0, you made the wrong choice. What would the Black King do on g8? Nothing whatsoever. At the moment, the White Bishop is more active than its Black counterpart. Black should get his King involved in the game and play **1...Ke7!** followed by 2...Be6 (after the trade, Black's King would be better placed than White's), which results in a very comfortable position.

PROBLEM 11: I am happy if you said that this early Queen move is bad. However, there is actually more to the move than a simple "good" or "bad" label indicates. The Queen is well placed on d4 if nothing can attack it. Is that the case? White is not worried about 4...e5 because that move weakens the d5-square and leaves Black with a backward d-pawn. More bothersome is 4...Nc6, but then White could play 5.Bb5, pinning the annoying Knight. After 5...Bd7 6.Bxc6 Bxc6, the White Queen gets to stay on its perch but at a price: Black now has the two Bishops. This new situation leads to different strategies and fresh problems for both sides. All in all, 4.Qxd4 is playable but certainly nothing for Black to fear.

PROBLEM 12: If you thought that Black should advance his pawn to d5, you have not yet grasped what I have been saying about Bishop vs. Knight strategies. The horrible 1...d5?? doesn't lose material, but I have adorned it with two question marks to denote a blunder of the worst sort. Why would I judge this little pawn advance so harshly? Because it instantly loses the battle of Bishop vs. Knight. With one move, Black closes the center (which favors the Knight), blocks his Bishop by placing a pawn on a white square (which also favors the Knight), and hands the e5-square over to the enemy so that it can become a permanent home for the enemy horse.

Playing a move that does all these terrible things is obviously positional suicide. Much more sensible is **1...d6!**. This innocent-looking move turns out to be very useful. Now the c5 and e5 squares are inaccessible to the White pieces, the a8-h1 diagonal remains open, and the enemy horse has no advanced squares to jump to. After 1...d6, the Black Bishop, blasting away on its fine diagonal, is clearly superior to the White Knight.

PROBLEM 13: No! Playing 1...Nxc2?? would be a positional blunder of incredible proportions because you would be trading off a dominant Knight for a truly pathetic Bishop. After 2.Rxc2, White would suddenly be able to make use of the d-file by playing 3.Rd2 and 4.Rd5+, which is impossible as long as the Knight remains on the wonderful d4-square. In the actual game, Petrosian played **1...Rg5** and tortured his helpless opponent for a long, long time. Black eventually won when he found a way to break into the White position.

PROBLEM 14: Black should play **1...g5!** without a second thought. White's problem is that all his pawns are fixed on light-colored squares, making them vulnerable to attacks by the enemy Bishop. With 1...g5!, Black also fixes the g4 and h3 pawns on light squares and simultaneously places his own kingside pawns on black squares. Don't forget to use your pawns to restrict the movement of the enemy! After 1...g5! 2.Bd3 h6 3.Be2 (3.Bf5 Bg2 picks up the h3-pawn) 3...Be4! (and not 3...Bg2 4.Kf2 Bxh3?? 5.Kg3, after which the Bishop is trapped) 4.a3 a5! (fixing the b3-pawn on a vulnerable square and threatening to win it with ...Bc2) 5.Kd2 (letting the Black King in, but 5.Bd1 loses the h-pawn after 5...Bg2 6.Kf2 Bxh3 7.Kg3 Bf1 and the Bishop escapes, whereas 5.Bf1 hangs b3 after 5...Bc2) 5...Kf4 followed by ...Kg3 with material gain.

PROBLEM 15: Playing 1.f4 is tempting. It forces the Knight back and fixes White's kingside pawns on light-colored squares. However, this pawn advance is really a poor move. The reasoning behind this assessment takes into account the ability of the Black Rooks to penetrate the White position. At the moment they can't. The e1, e2, e3, and e4 squares are all well defended. After 1.f4?, though, the picture changes. Now e3 is vulnerable and will be used as a home for the Black Rooks. Black might also be able to bring his Knight to that square by ...Nh7...Nf6, ...Ng4, and ...Ne3. The moral? Watch out for pawn moves that tempt you with promises of attack but leave gaping holes in their wake!

PROBLEM 16: White can win immediately by breaking the blockade on b7 with **1.Bd5!**, which leaves Black with no good defense. Remember, if you have a passed pawn, break the enemy's blockade and ram that pawn down his throat!

PROBLEM 17: Black has the advantage. White's pawn majority on the queenside is doubled, and is thus devalued because it cannot produce a passed pawn. Play might proceed like this: 1.a4? (White should play **1.Rc3** and hang on for dear life) 1...Rd3, and now neither 2.a5+ Kb7 or 2.axb5 axb5 brings White any benefit at all.

PROBLEM 18: Both sides possess three pawn islands in this well-known theoretical position. Black's pawns on a7 and d5 are potentially weak, and White's pawns on f3, f2, and h2 are nothing to boast about. Though many books about openings claim a slight advantage for White, I have always felt confident with the Black side. My centralized King can take part in the battle, and my d-pawn also happens to be a passed, and therefore dynamic, pawn. In my game with Ivanov, White played 1.0-0 and after 1...Ke6 2.Re1+ Kf5 3.Be3 Be7 4.Rad1 Rhd8 5.Rd4 g5! (stopping checks on f4) 6.Red1 Ke6 7.Re1 Kf5 8.Red1 Ke6, the chances were completely even.

PROBLEM 19: If you noticed that there is a Bishop vs. Knight battle going on, pat yourself on the back and buy yourself something decadent. I wanted White to play g2-g3, which places another pawn on a black square and hurts his dark-squared Bishop by not allowing it to get outside the pawn chain via a Be3-f2-h4 maneuver. After 2.g3, I immediately gained space on the queen-side and prepared a minority attack with 2...b5!. Later I was able to play ...Rb8, ...b5-b4, and ...bxc3, a series of moves that left White with attackable weaknesses on the queenside. I eventually attacked and surrounded these targets, which proved to be enough for the victory.

PROBLEM 20: Black's Knights are both sitting on excellent posts. His c5-Knight is safe enough because if White plays b4, he will weaken the c4 square (which Black could make use of with ...Nd7-b6-c4), and if he plays Bxc5, Black can respond with ...Bxc5 (when the Bishop is very strong on the a7-g1 diagonal). What Black doesn't appreciate is that his other Knight is not yet permanently situated. He should make sure that f5 would remain in his control by playing **1...h5!**. By playing 1...Be7 instead, he allows 2.g4!, after which 2...Nh6 3.h3 produces a very different picture. His once-proud Knight on f5 is now a useless old nag that cannot get back into the game. The moral: When you control an important square, make sure it remains in your hands!

PROBLEM 21: White should continue to play in his own sector with Nb3, Rc1, and eventually c4-c5, opening lines that will allow White to penetrate into the Black position. A move like 1.f4? is poor because, aside from not following his own queenside plans, White pays too great a price for kingside space. After 1.f4? exf4, White has opened up the a1-h8 diagonal for the Black Bishop (which was a bad Bishop until it was granted this new lease on life), given himself a backward pawn on the half-open e-file, and created a wonderful resting place for a Black Knight on e5. Don't create space if doing so will give your opponent a host of other advantages!

PROBLEM 22: No. 1.d5? is a very poor move. You want to *control* squares with your center, not give them up! Playing 1.d5 gives up the c5-square for no reason at all and takes away the option of opening the center at some favorable moment with dxe5 (which could be prepared for by playing Ba3, Qc2, Nc4, and so on).

PROBLEM 23: The center is locked by pawns, so White must turn his attention to the queenside and the kingside. Because Black possesses the most space on the queenside, only one side of the board is available for White to consider. Does he have any advantages on the kingside? Yes. He has more space (his pawns on e5 and h4 give him much more territory there) and more force (all of his pieces aim in that direction). To cap things off, Black has very few defenders on the kingside, and the closed center stops

Black from seeking a counterattack in the middle. White can go after Black in several ways. One method is 1.Rh3 followed by 2.Rg3. However, the most forceful by far is a sacrifice known as the *Classic Bishop Sacrifice*, which goes like this:

1.Bxh7+

By giving up a piece, White destroys the pawn cover around the Black King and also brings the poor monarch out for a walk.

1...Kxh7

2.Ng5+

White's Queen and Knight can now join in the attack with gain of time.

2...Kg8

The choices are limited: 2...Kh6? gives up the Queen after 3.Nxe6+, and the only other possibility, 2...Kg6?, loses in the same fashion after 3.h5+ Kh6 4. Nxe6+.

3.Qh5

White threatens checkmate on h7. This Classic Bishop Sacrifice does not usually work if Black can stop this checkmate with ...Nf6 (here, White would be answered with the simple exf6) or ...Bf5. (If the Knight on d7 and the pawn on e6 were gone, Black could play ...Bf5 and be safe. Of course, that's a lot of ifs!)

3...Re8	**4.Qxf7+ Kh8**
5.Qh5+ Kg8	**6.Qh7+ Kf8**
7.Qh8+ Ke7	**8.Qxg7 checkmate**

PROBLEM 24: Because his dark-squared Bishop and his Knight both hit g7, and because his Queen can join in that fight, the punch has to land there. Here's the blow-by-blow:

1.Bxg7!

White sheds the kingside pawn shield.

1...Bxg7

2.Qg5

Now g7 falls, and the game is suddenly over. What good did Black's extra pawn do him? None whatsoever! White's attack on the kingside proved to be the winning one, but if he had not taken advantage of it right away he surely would have lost.

2...Kf8

3.Rxe6!

Black was hoping to run his King to a safer place after 3.Qxg7+ Ke7. After 3.Rxe6! the pawn position around the Black King is completely tossed aside.

3...Qe5

Desperation, but 3...fxe6 4.Qxg7+ Ke8 5.Bxh7 leaves Black unable to cope with the threat of 6.Bg6+.

4.Rxe5 Bxe5 5.Re1 Re8

6.Qh6+ Ke7 7.f4

At the end, White doesn't care about checkmating the Black King anymore. He just wants to win all of Black's pieces. His army in tatters, Black resigns.

It doesn't matter whether or not you saw 1.Bxg7. It *does* matter whether or not you recognized that White had to do something on the kingside.

PROBLEM 25: Playing 10.g4 has no real purpose and, aside from weakening the g-pawn, ultimately leads to the loss of the f4-square. White's King is still in the middle, and he has not yet completed his development, so what gives him the right to attack? A sane series of moves is 10.Be3 Ngf6 11.Nd2, which gives extra support to e4 and keeps the enemy Knight out of g4. But because White has been attacking earlier, he is stuck in that mind-set and throws himself on his sword.

10.g4? Ngf6

11.Nh4?!

What can this Knight do here? Coming forward is not necessarily good!

11...a6

12.Bd3 Nc5

The Knight comes to a good square and uncovers an attack on g4 by the Bishop on c8.

13.g5 Nh5

The Knight heads for f4, and the e7-Bishop attacks g5. Who is *really* doing the attacking here?

14.Rg1 Nf4	15.Bxf4 exf4
16.Nf3 0-0	17.Be2 f6
18.Nd4	

White understandably didn't like the look of 18.gxf6 Bxf6, when Black has the two Bishops and control of the e5-square. His move is an attempt to win material, but it fails to a tactical sequence that I had foreseen several moves earlier.

18...fxg5

19.b4

The point of 18.Nd4. If my Knight retreats to d7, then 20.Ne6 wins material.

19...Bf6!

White's dark-square weaknesses begin to show. Now 20.bxc5 dxc5 does nothing for White because his d4-Knight can't move (because of ...Bxc3).

20.Qd2 Be5!

I'm still playing on those same weaknesses. The tempting 21.bxc5 now fails to 21...Qf6 22.Rd1 dxc5, whereas 22.0-0-0 fails to 22...f3, which threatens the Bishop on e2, and ...Bf4, which wins the Queen.

| 21.Rd1 Qf6 | 22.Bg4 Bxg4 |
| 23.Rxg4 Nd7 | 24.Nde2 f3 |

White did not want to suffer through 25.Nd4 Bf4 26.Qd3 Ne5, which forks the Queen and the Rook on g4, so he resigned.

The tactics all worked for Black because White's groundless attacking play caused him to make some positional concessions (like the bothersome dark-squared Bishop) that gave Black more firepower in the fight that ensued.

PROBLEM 26: When facing someone rated several hundred points higher than yourself, you have a tendency to think that this omnipotent opponent sees everything. Such an attitude, of course, dooms you to certain defeat. Everyone is human, and everyone makes very bad mistakes. You should try to play the same way against everyone, no matter whether they are a beginner or the World Champion.

In this position, Black is a pawn down, so if he can't find something soon, he will most likely lose. He could defend by playing 1...Qe8??, but then 2.Bxf7+ Qxf7 3.Qxa8+ would win easily for White. Another defense is 1...Rf8, but White would have a definite advantage after 2.b3. I can see many players losing to their higher rated opponents after these continuations and chalking it up to statistics. However, they could grab a moment of glory with the risky-looking **1...Qxc2!**, because 2.Qxa8+ Kh7 leaves White powerless to prevent 3.Kg1 Qxf2+ 4.Kh1 Qxg2 checkmate. The other replies to 1...Qxc2! are no better for White: 2.Bxf7+ Kh7 is easy for Black, whereas 2.Qxf7+ Kh8 also spells the end.

I suspect that Black might have seen 1...Qxc2 if White had been rated much lower than Black and if Black had been in the position of having to look for a way to win. I also suspect that the rating difference would then have given Black the confidence to find the solution! Time and time again, the silly little numbers that appear after a name incite bravery or fear in players, no matter what their type of mental makeup. Play the board, not the rating, and you will see your results take a big turn for the better!

Glossary

Active: A preference for aggressive or tactical types of play, in relation to an opponent's style. Otherwise, an aggressive move or position.

Advantage: A net superiority of position, usually based on force, time, space, or pawn structure.

Algebraic notation: Sometimes referred to as *chess notation* or simply *notation*. A way of denoting chess moves. There are probably as many ways of writing chess moves as there are languages. However, algebraic notation has become the international standard.

Essentially, each square on the chessboard is given a letter and a number. The files are assigned the letters a, b, c, d, e, f, g, and h, from left to right from White's perspective. The ranks are assigned the numbers 1, 2, 3, 4, 5, 6, 7, and 8, from bottom to top from White's perspective. Thus, the bottom left corner is square a1 and the top right corner is square h8.

When a piece travels from one square to another, algebraic notation enables you to identify the piece and the square to which it is moving. For example, if the Rook moves from square a1 to square a8, you write Ra8. For pawn moves, you write only the square to which the pawn moves; for example, e4. Castling kingside is written O-O, and castling queenside is written O-O-O.

Analysis: The calculation of a series of moves based on a particular position. In tournament play, you are not allowed to move the pieces during analysis but must make all calculations in your head. When the game is over, opponents commonly analyze the game they have just played, moving the pieces about in an effort to discover what the best moves would have been.

Annotation: Written comments about a position or a game. The comments can take the form of narrative, chess notation, or a combination of both.

Attack: To start an aggressive action in a particular area of the board, or to threaten to capture a piece or pawn.

Battery: Doubling Rooks on a file or a Queen and a Bishop on a diagonal.

Berserker: A playing style characterized by frenzied attacks with one or two pieces. Named after ancient Scandinavian warriors who worked themselves up into battle frenzies and then charged their opponents with little regard for strategy or personal danger.

Bishop pair: Two Bishops vs. a Bishop and a Knight or two Knights. Two Bishops work well together because they can control diagonals of both colors. *See also* Opposite-colored Bishops.

Blockade: To stop an enemy pawn by placing a piece (ideally a Knight) directly in front of it. Popularized by Aaron Nimzovich.

Blunder: A terrible move that loses material or involves decisive positional or tactical concessions.

Breakthrough: A penetration of the enemy position.

Calculation of variations: The working out of chains of moves without physically moving the pieces.

Castle: Moving a King and Rook simultaneously. Castling is the only move in which a player can deploy two pieces in one move. Castling allows a player to move his King out of the center (the main theater of action in the opening) to the flank, where it can be protected by pawns. Additionally, castling develops a Rook.

When White castles kingside, he moves his King from e1 to g1 and his h1-Rook to f1. When Black castles kingside, he moves his King from e8 to g8 and his h8-Rook to f8. When White castles queenside, he moves his King from e1 to c1 and his a1-Rook to d1. And when Black castles queenside, he moves his King from e8 to c8 and his a8-Rook to d8.

Center: The area of the board encompassed by the rectangle c3-c6-f6-f3. Squares e4, d4, e5, and d5 are the most important part of the center. The e- and d-files are the *center files*.

Checkmate: An attack against the enemy King from which the King cannot escape. When a player checkmates his opponent's King, he wins the game.

Classical: A style of play that focuses on the creation of a full pawn center. Classical principles tend to be rather dogmatic and inflexible. The philosophy of the classical players was eventually challenged by the so-called "hypermoderns." *See also* Hypermodern.

Clearance sacrifice: A move that sacrifices an obstructing piece to make way for a strong move.

Closed game: A position that is obstructed by blocking chains of pawns. Such a position tends to favor Knights over Bishops, because the pawns block the diagonals.

Combination: A sacrifice combined with a forced series of moves, which exploits the peculiarities of the position in the hope of attaining a certain goal.

Connected passed pawns: Two or more passed pawns of the same color on adjacent files. *See also* Passed pawn.

Control: To completely dominate an area of the board. Dominating a file or a square, or simply having the initiative, can constitute control.

Counterplay: When the player who has been on the defensive starts his own aggressive action.

Cramp: The lack of mobility that is usually the result of a disadvantage in space.

Critical position: An important point in the game, where victory or defeat hangs in the balance.

Decoy: A tactic that lures an opponent's piece to a particular square.

Defense: A move or series of moves designed to thwart an enemy attack. Also used in the names of many openings initiated by Black. Examples are the French Defense and the Caro–Kann Defense.

Deflection: A tactic that involves chasing the opponent's main defending piece away from the critical area so that the defense falls apart.

Development: The process of moving pieces from their starting positions to new posts, from which they control a greater number of squares and have greater mobility.

Discovered attack: An ambush. A Queen, Rook, or Bishop lies in wait so that it can attack when another piece or pawn moves out of its way.

Discovered check: A discovered attack that involves checking your opponent's King.

Double attack: An attack against two pieces or pawns at the same time.

Double check: The most powerful type of discovered attack, which checks the King with two pieces. The King is forced to move, and the enemy army is thus frozen for at least one move.

Doubled pawns: Two pawns of the same color lined up on a file. This doubling can come about only as the result of a capture.

Draw: A tied game. A draw can result from a stalemate, from a three-time repetition of position, or by agreement between the players. *See also* Stalemate; Three-time repetition of position.

Elo rating: The system by which players are rated. Devised by Professor Arpad Elo (1903–1993) of Milwaukee and adopted by FIDE in 1970. A beginner might have a 900 rating, the average club player 1600, a state champion 2300, and the World Champion 2800.

En passant: A French term that means *in passing*. When a pawn advances two squares (which it can do only if it has not moved before) and passes an enemy pawn on an adjacent file that has advanced to its 5th rank, it can be captured by the enemy pawn as if it had moved only one square. The capture is optional and must be made at the first opportunity; otherwise, the right to capture that particular pawn under those particular circumstances is lost.

Endgame: The third and final phase of a chess game. An endgame arises when few pieces remain on the board. The clearest signal that the endgame is about to begin is when Queens are exchanged.

Equality: A situation in which neither side has an advantage or the players' advantages balance out.

Exchange: The trading of pieces, usually pieces of equal value.

Exchange, The: *Winning the Exchange* means you have won a Rook (5 points) for a Bishop or a Knight (3 points).

Fianchetto: An Italian term that means *on the flank* and applies only to Bishops. A fianchetto (pronouced *fyan-KET-to*) involves placing a White Bishop on g2 or b2 or a Black Bishop on g7 or b7.

FIDE: The acronym for *Fédération Internationale des Échecs*, the international chess federation.

File: A vertical column of eight squares. Designated in algebraic notation as the a-file, b-file, and so on. *See also* Half-open file; Open file.

Flank: The a-, b-, and c-files on the queenside, and the f-, g-, and h-files on the kingside.

Force: Material. An advantage in force arises when one player has more material than his opponent or when he outmans his opponent in a certain area of the board.

Forced: A move or series of moves that must be played to avoid disaster.

Fork: A tactical maneuver in which a piece or pawn attacks two enemy pieces or pawns at the same time.

Gambit: The voluntary sacrifice of at least a pawn in the opening, with the idea of gaining a compensating advantage (usually time, which permits development).

General principles: The fundamental rules of chess, devised to enable less advanced players to react logically to different positions. Also used more often than you would think by Grandmasters!

Grande combination: A combination that involves many moves and features many types of tactics.

Grandmaster: A title awarded by FIDE to players who meet an established set of performance standards, including a high Elo rating. It is the highest title (other than World Champion) attainable in chess. Lesser titles include International Master and FIDE Master, which is the lowest title awarded for international play. Once earned, a Grandmaster title cannot be taken away. *See also* Elo rating; Master.

Half-open file: A file that contains none of one player's pawns but one or more of his opponent's.

Hang: To be unprotected and exposed to capture.

Hole: A square that cannot be defended by a pawn. Such a square makes an excellent home for a piece because the piece cannot be chased away by hostile pawns. Also known as an *outpost*.

Hypermodern: A school of thought that arose in reaction to the classical theories of chess. The hypermoderns insisted that putting a pawn in the center in the opening made it a target. The heroes of this movement were Richard Réti and Aaron Nimzovich, both of whom expounded the idea of controlling the center from the flanks. Like the ideas of the classicists, those of the hypermoderns can be carried to extremes. Nowadays, both views are seen as correct. A distillation of the two philosophies is needed to cope successfully with any particular situation. *See also* Classical.

Initiative: When you are able to make threats to which your opponent must react, you are said to *possess the initiative.*

Interpose: To place a piece or a pawn between an enemy attacking piece and the attacked piece.

Intuition: Finding the right move or strategy by "feel" rather than by calculation.

Kingside: The half of the board made up of the e, f, g, and h files. Kingside pieces are the King, the Bishop next to it, the Knight next to the Bishop, and the Rook next to the Knight. *See also* Queenside.

Luft: A German term that means *air.* In chess, it means *to give the King breathing room.* It describes a pawn move made in front of the King of the same color to avoid Back Rank Mate possibilities.

Major pieces: Queens and Rooks. Also called *heavy pieces.*

Master: In the U.S., a player with a rating of 2200 or more. If a player's rating drops below 2200, the title is rescinded. *See also* Grandmaster.

Mate: Short for *checkmate.*

Material: All the pieces and pawns. A *material advantage* is when a player has more pieces on the board than his opponent or has pieces of greater value. *See also* Point count.

Middlegame: The phase between the opening and the endgame.

Minor pieces: The Bishops and Knights.

Mobility: Freedom of movement for the pieces.

Occupation: A Rook or Queen that controls a file or rank is said to *occupy* that file or rank. A piece is said to *occupy* the square it is sitting on.

Open: Short for *open game* or *open file*. Also refers to a type of tournament in which any strength of player can participate. Though a player often ends up with opponents who are stronger or weaker than himself, the prizes are usually structured around different rating groups, with prizes for the top scorers in each group. Such open tournaments are extremely popular in the United States. *See also* Open file; Open game.

Open file: A vertical column of eight squares that is free of pawns. Rooks reach their maximum potential when placed on open files or open ranks.

Open game: A position characterized by many open ranks, files, or diagonals, and few center pawns. A lead in development becomes very important in positions of this type.

Opening: The start of a game, incorporating the first dozen or so moves. The basic goals of an opening are to develop pieces as quickly as possible; control as much of the center as possible; and castle early and get the King to safety, while at the same time bringing the Rooks toward the center and placing them on potentially open files.

Openings: Established sequences of moves that lead to the goals outlined under Opening. These sequences of moves are often named after the player who invented them or after the place where they were first played. Some openings, such as the *King's Gambit* and the *English*, have been analyzed to great lengths in chess literature.

Opposite-colored Bishops: Also *Bishops of opposite color*. When players have one Bishop each and the Bishops are on different-colored squares. Opposite-colored Bishops can never come into direct contact.

Overextension: When space is gained too fast. By rushing his pawns forward and trying to control a lot of territory, a player can leave weaknesses in his camp or can weaken the advanced pawns themselves. He is then said to have *overextended* his position.

Overworked piece: A piece that is required to singlehandedly defend too many other pieces.

Passed pawn: A pawn whose advance to the 8th rank cannot be prevented by any enemy pawn and whose promotion to a piece is therefore a serious threat. *See also* Promotion; Underpromotion.

Pawn structure: Also referred to as the *pawn skeleton*. All aspects of the pawn setup.

Perpetual check: When one player places his opponent in check, forcing a reply, followed by another check and another forced reply, followed by another check that repeats the first position. Because such a game could be played forever, after the position repeats itself, the game is declared a draw. *See also* Three-time repetition of position.

Perpetual pursuit: Similar to a perpetual check, except that the pursued piece is a Bishop, Knight, Rook, or Queen, instead of the King.

Petite combination: A combination that involves only a few moves.

Pig: Slang for *Rook*. Rooks doubled on the 7th rank are commonly referred to as *pigs on the 7th*.

Pin: When one player attacks a piece that his opponent cannot move without losing a different piece of greater value. When the piece of greater value is the King, this tactic is called an *absolute pin*; when the piece is not the King, the tactic is called a *relative pin*.

Plan: A short- or long-range goal on which a player bases his moves.

Point count: A system that gives the pieces the following numeric values: King—priceless; Queen—9 points; Rook—5 points; Bishop—3 points; Knight—3 points; and pawn—1 point. Some manuals give a King's point count as $3\frac{1}{2}$.

Positional: A move or style of play based on long-range considerations. The slow buildup of small advantages is said to be positional.

Prepared variation: In professional chess, it is common practice to analyze book openings in the hope of finding a new move or plan. When a player makes such a discovery, he will often save this prepared variation for use against a special opponent.

Promotion: Also called *queening*. When a pawn reaches the 8th rank, it can be promoted to a Bishop, Knight, Rook, or (most commonly) Queen of the same color. *See also* Underpromotion.

Protected passed pawn: A passed pawn that is under the protection of another pawn. *See also* Passed pawn.

Queenside: The half of the board that includes the d-, c-, b-, and a-files. The queenside pieces are the Queen, the Bishop next to it, the Knight next to the Bishop, and the Rook next to the Knight. *See also* Kingside.

Quiet move: An unassuming move that is not a capture, a check, or a direct threat. A quiet move often occurs at the end of a maneuver or combination that drives the point home.

Rank: A horizontal row of eight squares. Designated in algebraic notation as the 1 (1st) rank, the 2 (2nd) rank, and so on.

Rating: A number that measures a player's relative strength. The higher the number, the stronger the player. *See also* Elo rating.

Resign: When a player realizes that he is going to lose and graciously gives up the game without waiting for a checkmate. When resigning, a player can simply say, "I resign," or he can tip over his King in a gesture of helplessness. When you first start playing chess, I recommend that you never resign. Always play until the end.

Romantic: The Romantic (or Macho) era of chess from the early- to mid-1800s, when sacrifice and attack were considered the only manly ways to play. If a sacrifice was offered, it was considered a disgraceful show of cowardice to refuse the capture. Today, a player who has a proclivity for bold attacks and sacrifices, often throwing caution to the wind, is called a *romantic.*

Royal fork: A fork that attacks the King and Queen.

Sacrifice: The voluntary offer of material for compensation in space, time, pawn structure, or even force. (A sacrifice can lead to a force advantage in a particular part of the board.) Unlike a combination, a sacrifice is not always a calculable commodity and often entails an element of uncertainty.

Simplify: To trade pieces to quiet down the position, to eliminate the opponent's attacking potential, or to clarify the situation.

Skewer: A threat against a valuable piece that forces that piece to move, allowing the capture of a less valuable piece behind it.

Smothered checkmate: When a King is completely surrounded by its own pieces (or is at the edge of the board) and receives an unanswerable check from the enemy, he is said to be a victim of *smothered checkmate*. A smothered checkmate is most often carried out by a Knight.

Space: The territory controlled by each player.

Space count: A numerical system used to determine who controls more space, in which 1 point is allocated to each square on one player's side of the board that is controlled by a piece or pawn belonging to the other player.

Speculative move: Made without calculating the consequences to the extent normally required. Sometimes full calculation is not possible, so a player must rely on intuition, from which a speculative plan might arise. Often used in reference to a sacrifice. For example, *White plays a speculative sacrifice*.

Stalemate: In the English language, a stalemate refers to a standoff between opposing forces. In chess terminology, a stalemate occurs when one player is so bottled up that any legal move he makes will expose his King to immediate capture. A stalemate results in a draw (a tied game).

Strategy: The reasoning behind a move, plan, or idea.

Study: Theoretical positions, or *compositions*, that highlight unusual tactical themes.

Style: A player's way of playing chess, which reflects his personality and preferences. The types of move a player chooses are usually indicative of the player as a person. Typically, in a game between players of opposing styles (for example, an attacker vs. a quiet positional player), the winner will be the one who successfully imposes his style on the other.

Tactics: Maneuvers that take advantage of short-term opportunities. A position with many traps and combinations is considered to be *tactical* in nature.

Tempo: One move, as a unit of time; the plural is *tempi*. If a piece can reach a useful square in one move but takes two moves to get there, it has *lost a tempo*. For example, after 1.e4 e5 2.d4 exd4 3.Qxd4 Nc6, Black gains a tempo and White loses one because the White Queen is attacked and White must move his Queen a second time to get it to safety.

Theory: Well-known opening, middlegame, and endgame positions that are documented in books.

Three-time repetition of position: Occurs when the players have been moving back and forth, repeating the same position. Often happens when a player, behind in material and facing eventual loss, sacrifices for a perpetual check (*see* Perpetual check). A three-time repetition of position results in a draw (a tied game).

Time: In this book, in addition to the common use of the word ("Black does not have time to stop all of White's threats"), time is a measure of development. Also refers to *thinking time*, as measured on a chess clock. *See also* Time control; Tempo.

Time control: The amount of time in which each player must play a specified number of moves. In international competitions, the typical time control is 40 moves in 2 hours for each player. After each player has made 40 moves, each is given an additional amount of time (usually 1 hour for 20 moves). If a player uses up his time, but has not yet made the mandatory number of moves, he loses the game by forfeit, no matter what the position on the board.

Time pressure: One of the most exciting moments in a tournament chess game. When one or both players have used up most of the time on their clocks but still have several moves to make before they reach the mandatory total of 40 or 45, they start to make moves with increasing rapidity, sometimes slamming down the pieces in frenzied panic. Terrible blunders are typical in this phase. Some players get into time pressure in almost every game and are known as *time-pressure addicts*.

Transposition: Reaching an identical opening position by a different order of moves. For example, the French Defense is usually reached by 1.e4 e6 2.d4 d5, but 1.d4 e6 2.e4 d5 *transposes* into the same position.

Trap: A way of surreptitiously luring the opponent into making a mistake.

Underpromotion: Promotion of a pawn to any piece other than a Queen.

Variation: One line of analysis in any phase of the game. It could be a line of play other than the ones used in the game. The term *variation* is frequently applied to one line of an opening; for example, the Wilkes–Barre Variation (named after the city in Pennsylvania) of the Two Knights' Defense. Variations can become as well analyzed as their parent openings. Entire books have been written on some well-known variations.

Weakness: Any pawn or square that is readily attackable and therefore hard to defend.

Zugzwang: A German term that means *compulsion to move*. It refers to a situation in which a player would prefer to do nothing because any move leads to a deterioration of his position, but he moves something because it is illegal to pass.

Zwischenzug: A German term that means *in-between move*. A surprising move that, when inserted in an apparently logical sequence (for example, a check that interrupts a series of exchanges), changes the result of that sequence.

Index

A

Accumulation Theory, 200
activating
  bad Bishops, 51
  pieces with sacrifice, 105,
    107
active, 237
  Bishops, 51
  vs. inactive pieces, 30
advancing pawns, 105
  drawbacks, 112
advantages
  appropriate vs. inappropri-
    ate, 186
  definition, 5, 237
  favoring Bishops, 83
  material (force), 2, 5, 7
    in endgames, 169
    endgames with, 20
    on kingside, as signal
      for King attack, 173
    rules for, 12
    strategies, 8
    throwing away, 14
    trading with, 15, 20, 26
  pawn structure, 5
  piece mobility, 5
  reality of, 6
  safe King, 5
  space (territory), 5, 149
    in center, 87
    on kingside, as signal
      for King attack, 172
  static vs. dynamic, 5
  time vs. material, 17
Alekhine, Alexander, 60,
  115, 210–211, 225
Alekhine Defense, 214

Alekhine's Gun, 61
algebraic chess notation,
  237, 241
analysis, 237
annotation, 237
attacking
  pawn chains, 81, 120
  weak pawns, 128
attacks, 238
  discovered, 240
  double, 240
  King, 167
    and castling, 168
    conditions for, 167
    and lead in develop-
      ment, 168–169
    of necessity, 177
    with Queen, 76
  minority, 130, 132, 178
  one-piece, 77
  premature, 187

B

Back Rank Mate, 59, 119,
  243
backward pawns, 33
bad Bishops, 50
  activating, 51
  example, 62
  trading, 53, 55
ballast, 10, 170
Bishops, 48
  active, 51
  advantages that favor, 83
  bad, 50
    activating, 51
    examples, 62

Bishops, bad, *continued*
  trading, 53, 55
  and closed diagonals, 42,
    50
  and control of squares, 48
  in endgames with passed
    pawns, 83
  fianchettoed, 241
    example, 136
  getting outside pawn
    chain, 52, 55
  good, 49
    example, 62
  inactive, 42
  vs. Knights, 38, 41, 53, 79
    strategies, 79
  moving pawns out of way
    of, 52
  and open diagonals, 46, 49
  and open positions, 79
  opposite-colored, 245
  pair of, 238
  and wrong-colored Rook-
    pawn draw, 48
blockaders, 42
blockades, x, 238
blocking
  passed pawns with
    Knights, 109
  with pawns, 100
blunders, 238
board
  closing section of, 32
  opening up, 7
book, 238
Botvinnik Formation, 87
Botvinnik, Mikhail, 58, 219,
  225

breakthrough, 238
Browne, Walter, 136

C

calculation, 4, 238
Capablanca, José Raúl, 117,
    205, 210
capturing
    en passant, rule, 241
    squares, 136
Caro-Kann Defense, 240
castling
    and King attacks, 168
    kingside, 238
    for King's safety, exam-
        ple, 23
    purpose of, 238
    queenside, 238
    rule, 238
center, 239
    closed, attacking with
        pawns, 140
    dominating with pawns,
        157
    open, and Kings, 67
    pawns, weak, 162
cheap shots, 20
check
    discovered, 240
    double, 240
    perpetual, 245, 249
        example of avoiding, 21
checkmate, 239
    smothered, 248
chess
    advantages. *See* advan-
        tages
    as art, ix, 29
    notation, 237
    as sport, ix, 29
    as team effort, 138
    as tool, 1
    as warfare, 13

Classical, 239
closed
    centers, attacking with
        pawns, 140
    diagonals, and Bishops, 50
    games, 239
    lines, for defense, 139
    positions, and Knights,
        42, 79, 87
closing
    lines to pieces, 17
    section of board, 32
color, control, 90
combination, 239
complacency, effect of, 189
connected passed
        pawns, 239
control
    of 7th rank, 58
    color, 90
    of space, 44, 149
    of squares, 39, 44, 136,
        141
        by Bishops, 48
        with pawns, 100
        by Queens, 72
counterplay, x, 25, 239
    in response to King
        attack, 167
    trading to restrict, 128
cramping positions, 239
critical position, 240
critical thinking, 3
    examples, 21, 26

D

decisions, based on
        emotions, 193
defending, in the opening
    Caro-Kann Defense, 240
    French Defense, 240, 250
    Two Knights' Defense, 250

defenses, definition, 240,
    243
deficit, material
    in endgame, 7
    and lead in development,
        16
    in middlegame, 7
development, 8
    definition, 8, 240
    getting hung up on, 188
    importance of, 8, 15
    lead in
        and King attacks, 169
        and material deficit, 16
        as signal for King
            attack, 168, 174
        and Rooks, 57
        sacrificing for, 21
diagonals
    closed, and Bishops,
        42, 50
    open, and Bishops, 46, 49
discovered
    attack, 240
    check, 240
double
    attack, 240
        examples, 11, 28, 50
    check, 240
doubled
    pawns, example, 130
doubling, 59
    example, 66
draws
    definition, 240
    by perpetual check, ex-
        ample of avoiding, 21
    stalemate, 248
    three-time repetition of
        position, 249
    wrong-colored Rook-
        pawn, 48
Dutch Defense, 43

E

Elo, Arpad, 241
Elo rating, 241
emotions
    as basis for decisions, 193
    precautions against, 197
endgames
    definition, 241
    and Kings, 68
    Kings in, 84
    material advantage in, 8,
        20, 169
    material deficit in, 7
    with passed pawns,
        Bishops in, 83
    and pawn majorities, 117
en passant, rule, 241
equality, 241
Euwe, Max, 4, 211
Evans, Larry, 4
Exchange, The, 31, 106, 241
exchanging, 241. *See also*
        trading

F

fear, effect of, 194
Fédération International des
        Échecs (FIDE), 1,
        222, 241
fianchettoed Bishops, 241
    example, 136
files, 241
    half-open, 242
    open, 244
        importance of, 62
        and Rooks, 44, 58
Fischer, Bobby, 28, 33, 54,
        62, 75, 122, 137,
        221, 226
five R's, 2
flanks, 241
flexibility, importance of, 167

force, x, 8
    advantage in, 5
    See also material
forced, 242
forfeiting, 247
forks, example, 11, 21, 57,
        106
French Defense, 240, 250

G

gambits, 242
games
    closed, 239
    open, 244
good Bishops, 49
    example, 62
Grandmaster (GM), 242
Grünfeld Defense, 162

H

half-open files, 242
hanging, 242
holes, 136, 242
Hooper, David, 4
hypermodern, 243
Hypermodernism, 214

I

inattention, the effect of,
        26–27
initiative, 239, 243
international chess federa-
        tion. *See* Fédération
        International des
        Échecs
International Master (IM),
        242
interposition, 243
intuition, 243

isolated pawns. *See* pawn is-
        lands; pawns, isolated

K

Karpov, Anatoly, 9, 86, 136,
        190, 221
Kasparov, Garry, 222, 225
King, 64
    attacks, 167
        and castling, 168
        conditions for, 167
        and lead in develop-
            ment, 168–169
        of necessity, 177
    avoiding open centers, 67
    in endgames, 68, 84
    making use of, 65
    pawn protection around,
        17
    safe, 5, 10, 65, 76
        castling for, 23
        example, 32
    threats to, 26
kingside, 243
Knights, 37
    on 1st rank, 133
    on 1st and 2nd ranks, 38
    on 3rd rank, 40
    on 4th rank, 40
    on 5th rank, 41
    on 6th rank, 41
    vs. Bishops, 38, 41, 53, 79
    as blockaders, 109
    and closed positions, 42,
        79, 87
    and pawns
        locked, 42
        passed, 42
    strategies, 86
    and support points, 38, 82,
        86, 136

L

Larsen, Jorgen, 70
Lasker, Emanuel, 99, 201, 205, 210, 225
laziness, effect of, 192, 208
lead in development
    and material deficit, 16
    as signal for King attack, 174
lines, opening and closing, 17
locked pawns, and Knights, 42
luft, x, 243

M

major pieces, 243
majorities
    pawn, 111, 114
        in endgames, 117
        relative importance of, 115
        trading to enhance, 117
Marshall, Frank, 117, 210
Master, 243
mate, 243
material, x, 8, 244
    advantage, 2, 5, 7, 237
        in endgame, 8, 20, 169
        on kingside, as signal for King attack, 173
        rules for, 12
        and sacrifices, 10
        strategies, 8
        throwing away, 14
        vs. time advantage, 17
        trading with, 15, 20, 26
    deficit, and lead in development, 16
    definition, 244
    making good use of, 8
    point count system, definition, 246

middlegame, 244
    material deficit in, 7
minor pieces, 244
minority attacks, 132, 178
    strategy, 130
mistakes, 185
mobility, 244
    of pieces, 5
moves
    quiet, 247
    speculative, 248

N

Nimzovich, Aaron, 58, 214, 238
notation, 237

O

occupying squares, 244
odds
    Queen, 14
    Queen-Knight, 16
open
    centers, and Kings, 67
    diagonals, and Bishops, 46, 49
    files, 244
        importance of, 62
        and Rooks, 44, 58
    games, 243
    lines, for attack, 139
    positions, 244
        and Bishops, 79
opening
    board, 7
    creating open files for Rooks in, 61
    definition, 244
    gambits, 242
    lines for pieces, 17
    moves, 244
openings
    Alekhine Defense, 214

openings, *continued*
    Botvinnik Formation, 87
    Caro-Kann Defense, 240
    Dutch Defense, 43
    French Defense, 240, 250
    Grünfeld Defense, 162
    Petroff Defense, 62
    Queen's Gambit
        Declined, 62, 178
        Tartakower Variation, 223
    Ruy López, 145
    Scotch Opening, 73
    Semi-Slav Defense, 219
    Sicilian Defense, 62
        Nimzovich Variation, 214
    Tarrasch Opening, 206
    Two Knights' Defense, 250
opposite-colored Bishops, 245
overconfidence, effect of, 27, 189, 195
overextending, 245
Over-protection, 214
owning, squares, 137

P

passed pawns, *See* pawns, passed
pawn
    center, defending against, 162
    chains
        attacking, 81, 120
        example, 51
        getting Bishops outside, 52, 55
    islands, 120
        avoiding, 121
        creating for opponent, 122–123
        weakness of, 120

pawn, *continued*
  majorities, 111, 114
    in endgames, 117
    relative importance of,
      115
    trading to enhance, 117
  protection around King, 17
  sacrifices, 105, 179
    vacating squares with,
      108
  storm, 178, 187
  strategies, 99
  structure, x, 5, 99
    as protection, 22
pawns
  advancing, 105
    drawbacks, 112
  backward, 33
  blocking with, 100
  capturing en passant,
    241
  and closed centers, 140
  connected passed, 239
  dominating center with,
    157
  doubled
    definition, 240
    example, 130
  hanging, 242
  isolated, 120 (*see also*
    pawn islands)
  locked, and Knights, 42
  moving out of way of
    Bishops, 52
  passed, 26, 114
    blocking with Knights,
      109
    definition, 245
    and Knights, 42
  placement of, 99
  promoting, 26, 109, 246
  protected passed, 246
  restraining opponent
    with, 103

pawns, *continued*
  restricting opponent with,
    101
  and space (territory), 149
  stopping, 238
  underpromoting, 250
  weak, 127
    examples, 35
perpetual checks. *See*
    check, perpetual
Petroff Defense, 62
Petrosian, Tigran, 31, 43, 81,
    218
Philidor, André, 99
philosophies
  Classical, 239
  Hypermodernism, 243
piece, mobility, 5
pieces
  and control of squares, 44
  major, 243
  minor, 79, 244
  opening lines for, 17
  using all, 13, 63
  value of, viii–ix, 79
  where they go, 37
pigs on 7th, 63, 246
pins, example, 11, 60–61, 246
placement of pawns, 99
plans, 246
players, psychological state
    of, 7, 26–27, 177, 194
playing
  for cheap shot, 20
  styles, 248
    positional, 246
    romantic, 247
point count system, 246
points, 246
  support for Knights, 38,
    82, 86, 136
Portisch, Lajos, 34
positional chess, x, 4
positions
  assessing, 160

positions, *continued*
  closed, 239
  cramping, 239
  open, 244
  simplifying, 247
postmortem. *See* analysis
Potter, William, 14
premature attacks, 187
prepared variations, 246
preventing, opponent's
    moves, 140
principles of chess, x, 8, 242
promoting pawns, 26, 109, 246
prophylaxis, 214, 218, 223
protected passed pawns, 246
protecting
  King, 17
  Queen, 72
psychology, state of players,
    7, 26–27, 177, 194

Q
Queen, 72
  and control of squares, 72
  in King attacks, 76
  protecting, 72
  risking, 75
  trading, example, 156
Queen odds, 14
queening. *See* pawns, pro-
    moting
Queen-Knight odds, 16
Queen's Gambit Declined,
    62, 178
  Tartakower Variation , 223
queenside, 246

R
R's, five, 2
rabioso, 72
ranks, 247
  1st and 2nd, Knights on,
    38, 133

ranks, *continued*
  3rd, Knights on, 40
  4th, Knights on, 40
  5th, Knights on, 41
  6th, Knights on, 41
  7th, Rooks on, 25, 58, 116
rating, 247
  system, 241
resigning, how to, 247
restraining, opponent with
    pawns, 103
restricting
  counterplay by trading,
    128
  opponent with pawns, 101
romantic, 247
Rook-pawns, wrong-colored
    draw, 48
Rooks, 57
  on 7th rank, 25, 116
    doubled, 63
  connecting, 74
  and development, 57
  and open files, 44, 58
Rubinstein, Akiba, 69, 205
Rubinstein Year, 205
rules
  of chess, ix
  for material advantage, 12
Ruy López Opening, 145

S

sacrifices
  definition, 247
  for development, 21
  with material advantage,
    10
  to open lines, 17
  pawn, 105, 179
    vacating square with,
      108

safety, of King, 5, 10, 65, 76
  castling for, 23
  example, 32
science of chess, ix
Scotch Opening, 73
Seirawan method, 8
Semi-Slav Defense, 219
Short, Nigel, 94
Sicilian Defense, 62
  Nimzovich Variation, 214
simplifying. *See* trading
smothered mate, 248
space, x, 149
  advantage, 5, 149, 237
    avoiding trading with,
      150, 151
    in center, 87
    on kingside, as signal
      for King attack, 172
  control of, 44, 149
  count system, 248
  dangers of giving up, 154
  definition, 248
  on wings, 150
Spassky, Boris, 31, 70, 219,
    223
sport of chess. *See* chess
squares
  capturing, 136
  controlling, 39, 44, 136,
    141
    with Bishops, 48
    with Queen, 72
    with pawns, 100
  creating, 136
  lines of, 144
  occupying, 244
  owning, 137
  weak, 135
    caused by pawn
      advance, 113
stalemate, 248

Steinitz, Wilhelm, 145, 199,
    214
storm, pawn, 187
strategies
  Bishops against Knights,
    79
  built around targets, 12
  closing lines for defense,
    139
  defense against pawn
    center, 162
  faulty, 185
  King attacks, 167
  Knights against Bishops,
    86
  material advantage, 8
  minority attack, 130
  opening lines for attack,
    139
  pawn
    domination in center,
      157
    island, 120
    promotion, 109, 114
    sacrifices, 105
    weak, 127
  psychological, 180
  space, 150
  squares, weak, 135, 141
  targets, 127
  trading with material
    advantage, 20
  using pawns to block and
    restrict, 100
  weak
    pawn, 127
    squares, 135, 141
strategy, 3, 248
  vs. calculation, 4
  definition, 4
  importance of, 1
  masters of, 199
  vs. tactics, x, 4

structure, pawn, 5, 99
style. *See* playing styles
support points for Knights,
        38, 82, 86, 136

T

tactics, ix, 26
    definition, 248
    overlooking possibilities
        for, 192
Tal, Mikhail, 225
targets, 45
    creating, 104, 127
    ideal, 13
    pawn center, 162
    role in strategy, 12
Tarrasch Opening, 206
team effort, 138
    example, 171
tempi, 249
tempo, 249
territory, 149. *See also* space
terror, effect of, 194
theory, 249
three-time repetition of
        position, 249
throwing away, material
        advantage, 14
tied games. *See* draws

time, x, 8
    advantage vs. material
        advantage, 17
    controls, 249
    definition, 249
    limits, 249
    loss of, 249
    pressure, 249
trading, 241
    avoiding, 59, 110, 178
        to maintain space ad-
            vantage, 150
        with space advantage,
            151
    bad Bishops, 53, 55
    to enhance pawn majority,
        117
    inactive pieces for active
        ones, 30
    with material advantage,
        8, 15, 20, 26
    Queen, example, 156
    to restrict counterplay,
        128
    to weaken opponent, 29
transposing, 250
traps, 250
tripling, example, 61
Two Knghts' Defense, 250

V

vacating squares with
        sacrifice, 108
value of pieces, ix, 8, 79
variations
    calculating, 238
    definition, 250
    prepared, 246

W

weak
    pawns, 127
        examples, 35
    points, 127
    squares, 135
        caused by pawn
            advance, 113
        creating, 136
        lines of, 144
weaknesses, 250
    exploiting, 127
Whyld, Kenneth, 4
World Champions, rating, 240

Z

zugzwang, 61, 250
zwischenzug, 250
    example, 216

Yasser Seirawan

International Grandmaster Yasser Seirawan is considered the top U.S. contender for the chess World Champion title. The only American contender for the world title since Bobby Fischer retired in 1975, Seirawan has earned numerous titles, including 1979 World Junior Champion, three-time U.S. Champion, 1989 Western Hemisphere Champion, and five-time member of the U.S. Olympic chess teams. In tournament play, he has defeated both Garry Kasparov and Anatoly Karpov, the two top ranking players in the world. He is the only American to have played in the World Cup cycle.

Born in Damascus, Syria, in 1960, Seirawan moved to Seattle at the age of seven. His chess career was launched at the age of twelve, when he began to play in (and win) local and regional tournaments. Seirawan lives in Seattle, Washington, where he is the editor of *Inside Chess* magazine. Readers are invited to write to: Inside Chess, P.O. Box 19457, Seattle, WA 98102, for a complimentary copy.

Jeremy Silman

International Master Jeremy Silman is a world-class chess teacher, writer, and player who has won the American Open (1992), the National Open (1990), and the U.S. Open (1982). He has been champion of the Pacific Northwest, champion of Washington State, and champion of Northern California. A prolific chess writer, he has authored 28 books and dozens of magazine articles, which have been published all over the world.

For the last three years, Silman has been the coach of the United States delegation to the World Junior Championship, taking his team to Brazil, Germany, and Slovakia. He currently resides in Beverly Hills, California.

The manuscript for this book was prepared and submitted to Microsoft Press in electronic form. Text files were processed and formatted using Microsoft Word. Pages were composed by Online Press Inc., using Ventura Publisher for Windows, with text in Century Old Style and display type in Optima Bold.

Principal word processor: Christina B. Dudley
Principal proofreaders: Polly Fox Urban and Christina B. Dudley
Principal typographer: Bill Teel
Interior text designers: Darcie S. Furlan and Kim Eggleston
Principal illustrator: Jeanne Reinelt
Cover designer: Gregory E. Hickman
Cover photography by: Christopher Conrad
Cover color separator: Color Control

Printed on recycled paper stock.

Register Today!

Return this
Winning Chess Strategies
registration card today

Microsoft®Press
mspress.microsoft.com

OWNER REGISTRATION CARD   0-7356-0604-8

WINNING CHESS STRATEGIES

FIRST NAME   MIDDLE INITIAL   LAST NAME

INSTITUTION OR COMPANY NAME

ADDRESS

CITY   STATE   ZIP

                                                  (   )
E-MAIL ADDRESS   PHONE NUMBER

U.S. and Canada addresses only. Fill in information above and mail postage-free.
Please mail only the bottom half of this page.

**For information about Microsoft Press®
products, visit our Web site at
mspress.microsoft.com**

Microsoft®_Press_

|||| |||

NO POSTAGE
NECESSARY
IF MAILED
IN THE
UNITED STATES

BUSINESS REPLY MAIL
FIRST-CLASS MAIL   PERMIT NO. 108   REDMOND WA

POSTAGE WILL BE PAID BY ADDRESSEE

MICROSOFT PRESS
PO BOX 97017
REDMOND, WA 98073-9830